THE BEST TEST PREPARATION FOR THE

CLEP

COLLEGE-LEVEL EXAMINATION PROGRAM

PRINCIPLES OF MARKETING

James E. Finch, Ph.D.
Chairperson, Department of Marketing
University of Wisconsin, LaCrosse, WI

James R. Ogden, Ph.D.
Chairperson, Department of Marketing
Kutztown University, Kutztown, PA

Denise T. Ogden, M.B.A.
Manager of Customer Instructional Services
Dun & Bradstreet, Bethlehem, PA

Research & Education Association
61 Ethel Road West
Piscataway, New Jersey 08854

The Best Test Preparation for the
CLEP PRINCIPLES OF MARKETING

Printed in the United States of America

Library of Congress Catalog Card Number 98-66572

International Standard Book Number 0-87891-904-X

Research & Education Association
61 Ethel Road West
Piscataway, New Jersey 08854

REA supports the effort to conserve and
protect environmental resources by
printing on recycled papers.

About Research & Education Association

Research & Education Association (REA) is an organization of educators, scientists, and engineers specializing in various academic fields. Founded in 1959 with the purpose of disseminating the most recently developed scientific information to groups in industry, government, high schools, and universities, REA has since become a successful and highly respected publisher of study aids, test preps, handbooks, and reference works.

REA's Test Preparation series includes study guides for all academic levels in almost all disciplines. Research & Education Association publishes test preps for students who have not yet completed high school, as well as high school students preparing to enter college. Students from countries around the world seeking to attend college in the United States will find the assistance they need in REA's publications. For college students seeking advanced degrees, REA publishes test preps for many major graduate school admission examinations in a wide variety of disciplines, including engineering, law, and medicine. Students at every level, in every field, with every ambition can find what they are looking for among REA's publications.

Unlike most test preparation books—which present only a few practice tests that bear little resemblance to the actual exams—REA's series presents tests that accurately depict the official exams in both degree of difficulty and types of questions. REA's practice tests are always based upon the most recently administered exams, and include every type of question that can be expected on the actual exams.

REA's publications and educational materials are highly regarded and continually receive an unprecedented amount of praise from professionals, instructors, librarians, parents, and students. Our authors are as diverse as the subjects and fields represented in the books we publish. They are well-known in their respective fields and serve on the faculties of prestigious universities throughout the United States.

Acknowledgments

In addition to our authors, we would like to thank Dr. Max Fogiel, President, for his overall guidance which has brought this publication to its completion; Larry B. Kling, Quality Control Manager of Books in Print, for his editorial direction; Erin Yotko, Editorial Assistant, for her editorial contributions; and Marty Perzan for typesetting the book.

TABLE OF CONTENTS

CONTENTS

INDEPENDENT STUDY SCHEDULE

CLEP PRINCIPLES OF MARKETING
INDEPENDENT STUDY SCHEDULE

Our study schedule allows for thorough preparation for the CLEP Principles of Marketing. While it is designed for six weeks, it can be collapsed into a three-week course by condensing each two-week period into one. Be sure to set aside enough time—at least two hours per day—to study. But whichever study schedule works best for you, the more time you spend studying, the more prepared—not to mention relaxed—you will be on exam day.

It is important for you to discover the time and place for studying that works best for you. Some students may set aside a certain number of hours every morning to study, while others may choose to study at night before going to sleep. Other students may study during the day, perhaps while waiting in line, or they may find other unusual times and places to do their studying. Only you will be able know when and where your studying is most effective. Keep in mind that the most important factor is consistency. Use your time wisely. Work out a study routine and stick to it!

Week	Activity
Week 1	Read and study Chapter 1, which will introduce you to the CLEP Principles of Marketing.
Week 2	Take Test 1 to determine your strengths and weaknesses. Score each section by using the score chart found in Chapter 1. You can then determine the areas in which you need to strengthen your skills.
Week 3	Carefully read and study the Principles of Marketing Review included in this book.
Week 4	Take Test 2, and after scoring your exam, review carefully all incorrect answer explanations. If there are any types of questions or particular subjects that seem difficult to you, review those subjects by studying again the appropriate section of the Principles of Marketing Review.

Week 5	Take Test 3, and after scoring your exam, review carefully all incorrect answer explanations. If there are any types of questions or particular subjects that seem difficult to you, review those subjects by studying again the appropriate section of the Principles of Marketing Review.
Week 6	Study any areas you consider to be your weaknesses by using the Principles of Marketing Review and any other study resources you have on hand. You may want to retake the practices tests using the extra answer sheets provided in the back of the book.

CHAPTER 1
ABOUT THE CLEP
PRINCIPLES OF
MARKETING

Chapter 1

ABOUT THE CLEP PRINCIPLES OF MARKETING

This chapter is divided into 10 sections:

1. **About this Book**
2. **About the Exam**
3. **How to Use this Book**
4. **Format of the CLEP Principles of Marketing**
5. **About Our Course Review**
6. **Scoring the CLEP Principles of Marketing**
7. **Raw Score Conversion Chart**
8. **Studying for the CLEP Principles of Marketing**
9. **Test-Taking Tips**
10. **The Day of the Exam**

By thoroughly reading this introduction, you will learn who should take the CLEP Principles of Marketing exam, how the exam is designed, how to register, how the exam is scored, hints on taking the exam, how to study for the exam, and how to use this book for optimum success.

ABOUT THIS BOOK

This book provides you with an accurate and complete representation of the CLEP Principles of Marketing exam. In it you will find a complete review of introductory marketing, as well as tips and strategies for test-taking. Three practice tests are provided, all based on the current format of the official CLEP Principles of Marketing. Our practice tests last 90 minutes apiece and contain every type of question that you may expect to see on the actual exam. Following each test is an answer key with detailed explanations designed to help you more completely grasp the test material.

ABOUT THE EXAM

Who Takes the CLEP Principles of Marketing and What is it Used for?

CLEP (College-Level Examination Program) examinations are usually taken by people who have acquired knowledge outside the classroom and wish to bypass certain college courses and earn college credit. The CLEP Program is designed to reward students for learning—no matter where or how that knowledge was acquired. The CLEP is the most widely accepted credit-by-examination program in the United States.

Although most CLEP examinees are adults returning to college, many graduating high school seniors, enrolled college students, and international students also take the exams to earn college credit or to demonstrate their ability to perform at the college level. There are no prerequisites, such as age or educational status, for taking CLEP examinations. However, you must meet any specific requirements of the particular institution from which you wish to receive CLEP credit.

There are two categories of CLEP examinations:

1. **CLEP General Examinations**, which are five separate tests that cover material usually taken as requirements during the first two years of college. CLEP General Examinations are available for English Composition (with or without essay), Humanities, Mathematics, Natural Sciences, and Social Sciences and History.

2. **CLEP Subject Examinations**, which include material usually covered in an undergraduate course with a similar title. The CLEP Principles of Marketing is one of 29 subject examinations.

Who Administers the Exam?

The CLEP is developed by the College Board, administered by the Educational Testing Service (ETS), and involves the assistance of educators throughout the United States. The test development process is designed and implemented to ensure that the content and difficulty level of the test are appropriate.

When and Where Is the Exam Given?

The CLEP Principles of Marketing is administered each month throughout the year at more than 1,200 test centers in the United States and can be arranged for candidates abroad on request. To find out the test center nearest you and to register for the exam, you must obtain the free booklets *CLEP Colleges* and *CLEP Information for Candidates and Registration Form*, which are available at most colleges where CLEP credit is granted, or contacting:

CLEP
P.O. Box 6600
Princeton, NJ 08541-6600
Phone: (609) 771-7865
E-mail: *clep@ets.org*
Website: *http://www.ets.org*

HOW TO USE THIS BOOK

What Do I Study First?

Read over the course review and the suggestions for test-taking, take the first practice test to determine your area(s) of weakness, and then go back and focus your study on those specific problems. Studying the reviews thoroughly will reinforce the basic skills you will need to do well on the exam. Make sure to take the practice tests to become familiar with the format and procedures involved with taking the actual exam.

To best utilize your study time, follow our Independent Study Schedule located in the front of this book. The schedule is based on a six-week program, but can be condensed to three weeks if necessary by collapsing each two-week period into one.

When Should I Start Studying?

It is never too early to start studying for the CLEP Principles of Marketing. The earlier you begin, the more time you will have to sharpen your skills. Do not procrastinate! Cramming is *not* an effective way to study, since it does not allow you the time needed to learn the test material. The sooner you learn the format of the exam, the more time you will have to familiarize yourself with it.

FORMAT OF THE CLEP PRINCIPLES OF MARKETING

The CLEP Principles of Marketing covers material that is usually taught in an introductory course in marketing. This type of course is commonly known as Basic Marketing, Introduction to Marketing, Fundamentals of Marketing, or Marketing Principles. Such a course—and thus, the exam itself—covers the role of marketing in society and within a firm, understanding consumer and organizational markets, marketing strategy planning, marketing institutions, the marketing mix, as well as topics like international marketing, ethics, marketing research, services, and not-for-profit marketing. The examinee is also expected to have a basic knowledge of the economic, demographic, social/cultural, political/legal and technological trends that are central to marketing.

There are about 100 multiple-choice questions, each with five possible answer choices, to be answered in two separately timed 45-minute sections.

The approximate breakdown of topics is as follows:

5-8%   The role of marketing in society, including the historical development of marketing in the United States, marketing in different economic systems, and basic marketing functions.

7-11%   The role of marketing within a firm, the concept of marketing, planning and organization, and the marketing environment (the economic, demographic, technological, cultural, political, and legal environments).

15-20% Industrial and consumer markets, including the demographic and behavioral dimensions, measuring and forecasting demand, and marketing segmentation, targeting, and positioning.

40-50%   The marketing mix, including product planning
and management, pricing policies and methods,
channels of distribution, advertising and sales
promotion, and sales management.

8-10%   Marketing institutions, including aspects of
wholesale structure and retail markets and the
role of intermediaries.

11-14%   Miscellaneous topics such as international marketing,
marketing research and information, marketing
of services, ethics, and non-profit marketing.

ABOUT OUR COURSE REVIEW

This book begins with a comprehensive review of marketing principles which is designed to give you an idea of what type of information can be found on the exam. The review covers all major theories and terms of introductory marketing. It is divided into nine major sections:

1. *The Marketing Environment*

2. *Target Markets*

3. *Product Planning and Management*

4. *Distribution Systems*

5. *Wholesaling and Retailing*

6. *Promotional Strategy*

7. *Pricing Policies and Strategies*

8. *Marketing Evaluation and Control*

9. *Marketing Applications in Special Fields*

By studying this review in conjunction with the Independent Study Schedule located in the front of this book, you will be better able to determine your strengths and weaknesses in the subject of marketing and develop a strong base of knowledge to attack the CLEP Principles of Marketing examination with successful results.

SCORING THE CLEP PRINCIPLES OF MARKETING

How Do I Score My Practice Tests?

The CLEP Principles of Marketing is scored on a scale of 20 to 80. To score your practice tests, count up the number of correct answers and enter it on the scoring worksheet below. Next, total your incorrect answers, multiply this number by .25 and enter the number in the scoring worksheet. Subtract the two numbers—this will yield your total raw score. Finally, convert your raw score to a scaled score using the conversion chart on the next page.

(Note: The conversion chart is only an estimation of your scaled score. Since scaled scores vary from one form of a test to another, your score on the actual exam may be higher or lower than what appears on the chart.)

SCORING WORKSHEET

Raw Score: _____ – (1/4 x _____) = _____

                          # correct   *# incorrect*

Scaled Score: _____

When Will I Receive My Score Report and What Will it Look Like?

Your score report will arrive about three weeks after you take the test. Your scores are reported only to you, unless you ask to have them sent elsewhere. If you want your scores reported to a college or other institution, you must fill in the correct code number on your answer sheet at the time you take the examination. Since your scores are kept on file for 20 years, you may also request transcripts from Educational Testing Service at a later date.

RAW SCORE CONVERSION CHART

Raw Score	Scaled Score	Course Grade	Raw Score	Scaled Score	Course Grade
100	80	A	48	50	C
99	80	A	47	50	C
98	79	A	46	50	C
97	78	A	45	50	C
96	78	A	44	49	D
95	77	A	43	49	D
94	76	A	42	48	D
93	76	A	41	48	D
92	75	A	40	47	D
91	74	A	39	47	D
90	74	A	38	46	D
89	73	A	37	46	D
88	72	A	36	45	D
87	72	A	35	45	D
86	71	A	34	44	D
85	70	A	33	44	D
84	70	A	32	43	D
83	69	A	31	42	D
82	68	A	30	41	F
81	68	A	29	41	F
80	67	A	28	41	F
79	66	A	27	41	F
78	66	A	26	40	F
77	65	A	25	39	F
76	64	A	24	39	F
75	64	A	23	38	F
74	63	A	22	38	F
73	62	A	21	37	F
72	61	A	20	37	F
71	61	A	19	36	F
70	61	A	18	36	F
69	60	B	17	35	F
68	60	B	16	35	F
67	60	B	15	34	F
66	60	B	14	34	F
65	60	B	13	33	F
64	60	B	12	33	F
63	60	B	11	32	F
62	59	B	10	32	F
61	58	B	9	31	F
60	57	B	8	31	F
59	56	B	7	30	F
58	55	B	6	29	F
57	55	B	5	28	F
56	55	B	4	26	F
55	55	B	3	24	F
54	55	B	2	23	F
53	54	C	1	22	F
52	53	C	0	21	F
51	52	C	−1	20	F
50	51	C	−2 and below	20	F
49	50	C			

Although colleges and universities often use their own standards for granting credit, the American Council on Education (ACE) usually recommends a minimum scaled score of 50. This score is believed to be the score an individual would have received if he or she had taken the class and attained a C average.

STUDYING FOR THE CLEP PRINCIPLES OF MARKETING

It is very important for you to choose the time and place for studying that works best for you. Some students set aside a certain number of hours every morning, while others may choose to study at night before going to sleep. Other students may study during the day, while waiting on a line, or even while eating lunch. Only you can determine when and where your study time will be most effective. But be consistent and use your time wisely. Work out a study routine and stick to it!

When you take the practice tests, try to make your testing conditions as much like the actual test as possible. Turn your television and radio off, and sit down at a quiet table free from distraction. Make sure to time yourself. Start off by setting a timer for the time that is allotted for each section, and be sure to reset the timer for the appropriate amount of time when you start a new section.

As you complete each practice test, score your test and thoroughly review the explanations for the questions you answered incorrectly; but do not review too much at once. Concentrate on one problem area at a time by reviewing the question and explanation, and by studying our review until you are confident that you completely understand the material.

Keep track of your scores and mark them on the Scoring Worksheet. By doing so, you will be able to gauge your progress and discover general weaknesses in particular sections. You should carefully study the reviews that cover your areas of difficulty, as this will build your skills in those areas.

TEST-TAKING TIPS

Although you may not be familiar with standardized tests like the CLEP Principles of Marketing, there are many ways to acquaint yourself with this type of examination and help alleviate your test-taking anxieties. Listed below are ways to help you become accustomed to the CLEP, some of which may be applied to other standardized tests as well.

Become comfortable with the format of the exam. When you are practicing, simulate the conditions under which you will be taking the actual test. Stay calm and pace yourself. After simulating the test only a couple of times, you will boost your chances of doing well, and you will be able to sit down for the actual exam with much more confidence.

Read all of the possible answers. Just because you think you have found the correct response, do not automatically assume that it is the *best* answer. Read through each choice to be sure that you are not making a mistake by jumping to conclusions.

Use the process of elimination. Go through each answer to a given question and eliminate as many of the answer choices as possible. By eliminating just two answer choices, you give yourself a better chance of getting the item correct, since there will be only three choices left from which to make your guess.

Work quickly and steadily. You will have only 45 minutes to work on 50 questions in each section, so work quickly and steadily to avoid focusing on any one question too long. Taking the practice tests in this book will help you learn to budget your time.

Learn the directions and format for each section of the test. Familiarizing yourself with the directions and format of the exam will save you valuable time on the day of the actual test.

Be sure that the answer oval you are marking corresponds to the number of the question in the test booklet. Since the exam is graded by machine, marking one wrong answer can throw off your answer key and your score. Be extremely careful when filling in your answer sheet.

Work on the easier questions first. The questions for each section of the CLEP Principles of Marketing are not arranged in any particular order of difficulty; however, if you find yourself working too long on one question, make a mark next to it in your test booklet and continue. After you have answered all of the questions that you can, go back to the ones you have skipped.

Eliminating wrong answers. Sometimes a CLEP Principles of Marketing question will have one or two answer choices that are a little odd. These answers will be obviously wrong for one of several reasons: they may be impossible given the conditions of the problem, they may violate mathematical rules or principles, or they may be illogical. Being able to spot wrong answers before you finish a problem gives you an advantage because you will be able to make a more educated guess from the remaining choices if you are unable fully to solve the problem.

Working from answer choices. One of the ways you can use a multiple-choice format to your advantage is to work backwards from the answer choices to solve the problem. This is not a strategy you can use all the time, but it can be helpful if you can just plug the choices into a given formula or equation. The answer choices can often narrow the scope of responses. You may be able to make an educated guess based on eliminating choices that you know do not fit into the problem.

THE DAY OF THE EXAM

Before the Exam

On the day of the examination, you should wake up early (after a decent night's rest, it is hoped) and have a good breakfast. Make sure to dress comfortably, so that you are not distracted by being too hot or too cold while taking the examination. Plan to arrive at the test center early. This will allow you to collect your thoughts and relax before the test, and will also spare you the anxiety that comes with being late. As an added incentive to make sure you arrive early, keep in mind that NO ONE WILL BE ALLOWED INTO THE TEST SESSION AFTER THE TEST HAS BEGUN.

Before you leave for the test center, make sure that you have your admission form and another form of identification, which must contain a recent photograph, your name, and signature (i.e., driver's license, student identification card, or current alien registration card). You will not be admitted to the test center without proper identification.

YOU MUST ALSO BRING SEVERAL SHARPENED NO. 2 PENCILS WITH ERASERS, AS NONE WILL BE PROVIDED AT THE TEST CENTER.

You can wear a watch to the test center, but it must be silent so as not to disturb other test-takers. No dictionaries, textbooks, notebooks, briefcases, or packages are permitted; drinking, smoking, and eating are prohibited.

During the Exam

Once you enter the test center, follow all of the rules and instructions given by the test supervisor. If you do not, you risk being dismissed from the examination and having your scores canceled.

When all of the test materials have been passed out, the test supervisor will give you directions for filling out your answer sheet. You must fill out this sheet carefully since this information will be printed on your score report. Fill in your name exactly as it appears on your identification documents and admission ticket, unless otherwise instructed.

After the Exam

Once your test materials have been collected, you will be dismissed. Then, go home and relax—you deserve it!

CHAPTER 2
PRINCIPLES OF MARKETING
REVIEW

Chapter 2

PRINCIPLES OF MARKETING REVIEW

The following Principles of Marketing review is divided into nine sections, as follows:

1: **The Marketing Environment**

2: **Target Markets**

3: **Product Planning and Management**

4: **Distribution Systems**

5: **Wholesaling and Retailing**

6: **Promotional Strategy**

7: **Pricing Policies and Strategies**

8: **Marketing Evaluation and Control**

9: **Marketing Applications in Special Fields**

By thoroughly studying this course review, you will be well-prepared for the material on the CLEP Principles of Marketing exam.

1 THE MARKETING ENVIRONMENT

MARKETING AND MARKETS

Marketing is the process of planning and executing the development, pricing, promotion, and distribution of goods and services to achieve organizational goals. Marketing directs the flow of products within an economy from producer to consumer by anticipating and satisfying the wants and needs of the market through the exchange process.

A **Market** is made up of all the people or organizations who want or need a product and have the willingness and ability to buy.

Products may be goods, services, ideas, places, or persons.

THE MARKETING CONCEPT

The **Marketing Concept** is a customer-oriented business philosophy which stresses customer satisfaction as the key to achieving organizational goals. This philosophy maintains that all of the organization's efforts should be focused on identifying and satisfying the wants and needs of the customer.

MARKETING FUNCTIONS AND PROCESSES

There are six primary **Marketing Functions**:

1. Environmental Analysis

2. Consumer Analysis

3. Product Planning

4. Price Planning

5. Promotion Planning

6. Physical Distribution (Place) Planning

Environmental analysis and consumer analysis are market research functions which provide the means to evaluate market potential and identify target markets. Product, Price, Promotion, and Physical Distribution planning are known as the marketing mix variables.

The **Marketing Mix** is the combination of four variables which comprise an organization's marketing program: product, price, promotion, and physical distribution. The manner in which these factors are combined reflects the planned strategy of the organization. Unlike environmental forces, these factors are under the control of the organization. These are often referred to as the "four Ps."

Market Segmentation is the process of dividing the total market into distinct submarkets or groups based on similarities in their wants, needs, behaviors, or other characteristics.

Market Segments are groups of customers who are similar to each other in a meaningful way and who will respond to a firm's marketing mix similarly.

A **Target Market** is one particular group of potential customers that the organization seeks to satisfy with a product. It is the market at which the firm directs a marketing mix. Different marketing mixes are developed for each target market to satisfy their specific wants and needs. Target markets may be comprised of market segments or a mass market characterized by a "typical customer."

Product Differentiation exists when a product or brand is perceived as different from its competitors on any tangible or intangible characteristic. The term also refers to the strategy in which one firm promotes the features of its product over the features of competitive products in the same market.

Product Positioning refers to the decisions involved in shaping the product's image in the customer's mind. These images are defined relative to competing products. *Consumer perceptions* (not actual differences between products) are the critical issue.

The **Marketing Plan** is the organization's statement of marketing strategy and the specification of the activities required to carry out the strategy. Marketing plans identify target markets and provide general guidelines for developing the marketing mix. Additional information in the plan may include environmental analysis, market research plans, cost estimates, and sales forecasts.

The process of developing a marketing plan begins with an assessment of the situation confronting the firm. This **situation analysis** identifies the company's relative strengths and weaknesses, as well as the opportunities and threats posed by their **marketing environment**. Based on this information, marketing objectives for specific products and markets are established. The development of the marketing mix reflects the objectives set for each product/market combination.

Marketing Objectives specify the goals of the firm in both quantitative (e.g., sales, profit, market share) and qualitative (e.g., market leadership, corporate image) terms. They reflect the role of marketing in achieving company-wide objectives. To be useful, marketing objectives must be specific, measurable, and indicate the time period for which they are in effect. These goals are, in turn, translated into more detailed goals for marketing mix variables.

ENVIRONMENTAL ANALYSIS

The **Marketing Environment** is composed of two types of factors: those that the organization can control and those that they cannot control. The success of the firm in achieving its goals depends on the ability to understand the impact of uncontrollable factors, and the effective management of controllable factors in response.

External forces which impact all firms within an industry are termed **Macroenvironmental Factors**. These uncontrollable forces are

1. Demographics or Demography,

2. Economic Conditions,

3. Competition,

4. Social and Cultural Factors,

5. Political and Legal Factors (Government), and

6. Technological Factors.

Microenvironmental Factors are external forces which impact each specific company uniquely. Although these forces are largely uncontrollable, the firm can influence these factors to a significant degree. The microenvironmental factors are

1. Suppliers,

2. Marketing Intermediaries, and

3. The Target Market.

The factors over which the firm has direct control are internal resources and decision variables. Changes in the composition of the marketing mix and choice of target markets are the primary means by which the firm can respond to the uncontrollable factors in their environment.

MARKETING STRATEGY AND PLANNING

A firm's **Marketing Strategy** defines the way in which the marketing mix is used to satisfy the needs of the target market and achieve organizational goals. The Product/Market Opportunity Matrix and Boston Consulting Group Matrix provide guidelines to assess the relative value of products and product opportunities.

The **Product/Market Opportunity Matrix** specifies the four fundamental alternative marketing strategies available to the firm. The four types of opportunities identified by the matrix are a function of product and market factors.

	Present Markets	**New Markets**
Present Products	Market Penetration	Market Development
New Products	Product Development	Diversification

1. **MARKET PENETRATION STRATEGY** attempts to increase sales of the firm's existing products to its current markets.

2. **MARKET DEVELOPMENT STRATEGY** attempts to increase sales by introducing existing products to new markets.

3. **PRODUCT DEVELOPMENT STRATEGY** entails offering new products to the firm's current markets.

4. **DIVERSIFICATION STRATEGY** aims new products at new markets.

The **Boston Consulting Group Matrix** is a framework which classifies each product or product line within a firm's "product portfolio." The matrix identifies product categories as a function of their market shares relative to immediate competitors and growth rates for the industry.

RELATIVE MARKET SHARE

		HIGH	**LOW**
INDUSTRY GROWTH RATE	HIGH	STAR	PROBLEM CHILD
	LOW	CASH COW	DOG

1. **STARS** generate large profits, but also consume substantial resources to finance their continued growth.

2. A **PROBLEM CHILD** (sometimes called a "question mark") does not provide great profits, but still requires high levels of investment to maintain or increase market share.

3. **CASH COWS** generate large profits and require relatively little investment to maintain their market share in slow growth industries.

4. **DOGS** are characterized by low profitability and little opportunity for sales growth.

A **Differential Advantage** is made up of the unique qualities of a product which encourage customer purchase and loyalty. It provides customers with substantive reasons to *prefer* one product over another. By contrast, product differentiation simply refers to consumers' ability to perceive differences between competing products.

Marketing Myopia is a term which is used to characterize short-sighted marketing strategy. It refers to the tendency of some marketing managers to focus narrowly on the products they sell rather than the customers they serve. Consequently, they lose sight of customer preferences as these wants and needs change over time.

2 TARGET MARKETS

MARKET CHARACTERISTICS

To achieve the greatest benefit and competitive advantage from target marketing, it is essential that the characteristics used to identify each market be **measurable**. The characteristics used to specify target markets can be demographic or behavioral in nature.

DEMOGRAPHICS

Personal Demographics are the identifiable characteristics of individuals and groups of people. Personal demographic variables include: age, sex, family size, income, occupation, and education. **Geographic Demographics** are the identifiable characteristics of towns, cities, states, regions, and countries. Geographic demographics include: county size, city or SMSA (Standard Metropolitan Statistical Area) size, population density, and climate.

BEHAVIORAL DIMENSIONS

The behavior of individual consumers within target markets can be influenced by social factors, psychological variables, and purchase situations. These sources of influence can be used to describe and identify target markets. **Behavioral dimensions** of markets include: purchase occasion, user status, user rate, and brand loyalty. Customer attitudes toward products and product benefits are also behavioral characteristics of markets.

Psychographics refer to those factors which influence consumers' patterns of living or life-style. These include activities, interests, opinions (AIOs), as well as social class, personality, and values.

MARKET SEGMENTATION

In most instances, the total potential market for a product is too diverse or **heterogeneous** to be treated as a single target market. **Market Segmentation** is the process by which the total potential market for a product is divided into smaller parts or segments. Segments are created by grouping customers together according to their characteristics or needs. The resulting segments are said to be **homogeneous** with respect to these dimensions. That is, potential buyers within each segment are more similar to each other on key dimensions than to buyers assigned to other segments. The objective is to identify groups which will respond in a similar manner to marketing programs.

The primary advantage to segmenting markets is that it allows marketers to better match products to the needs of different customer types. Developing a marketing mix tailored to a clearly defined target market will provide a competitive advantage for the firm. This advantage is gained by fitting the design of the product, promotional efforts, pricing, and distribution to the preferences of the customer.

The process of **segmenting** markets is performed in two steps. In the first stage, segmentation variables are chosen and the market is divided along these dimensions. This identifies groups of consumers who may require separate marketing mixes. The second stage requires profiling the resulting segments. Each segment is profiled according to its distinctive demographic and behavioral characteristics.

Once the segmentation process is complete, each resulting segment is evaluated in terms of its attractiveness for the firm. The firm's target market(s) are chosen based on this evaluation. This phase is referred to as **Market Targeting**.

In order to identify market segments which will respond in a homogeneous manner to marketing programs, three conditions must be satisfied:

1. The dimensions or bases used to segment the market must be **measurable**.

2. The market segment must be **accessible** or **reachable** through existing channels. These channels include advertising media, channels of distribution, and the firm's sales force.

3. Each segment must be **large enough** to be profitable. Whether or not a segment is potentially profitable will be affected by many factors including the nature of the industry, the size of the firm, and its pricing structure.

The most appropriate **variables** or **bases** for segmenting a market will vary from one product to another. The appropriateness of each potential factor in segmenting a market depends entirely on its relevance to the situation. The best segmentation bases are those which will identify meaningful differences between groups of customers.

Buyer behavior can seldom be adequately related to only one segmentation variable (**Single-Variable Segmentation**). It is usually more appropriate to use two or more variables or "bases." **Multi-Variable Segmentation** recognizes the importance of interrelationships between factors in defining market segments. Common interrelationships can be observed between demographic factors such as age, income, and education.

Several factors will affect the firm's selection of **target markets**. Many of the factors which can be used in evaluating the potential and appropriateness of alternative segments are listed below.

SEGMENT CHARACTERISTICS	COMPETITORS WITHIN SEGMENT	MATCH WITH COMPANY
Size Growth Potential Profit Potential	Number Size Strength Resources	Strengths Objectives Resources Channels

Managers may select one or more segments as their target markets. The decision to focus on one segment as a target market is called a **single-segment** or **concentration strategy**. The choice to pursue more than one target market with corresponding marketing mixes for each is called **multiple segmentation strategy**. This option is also sometimes called **differentiated marketing**. A third alternative is to treat the total potential market as a whole—one vast target market. This is referred to as **undifferentiated** or **mass marketing**.

CONSUMER BEHAVIOR

An understanding of consumer behavior is essential to the development of effective marketing programs. The creation of an appropriate marketing mix for a specific target market requires an understanding of consumer preferences and decision-making processes. Marketers also need to be aware of how they can influence consumers' decision-making through their use of marketing mix variables.

Consumers engage in many buying-related **behaviors**. Apart from purchasing products, consumers may spend significant time and effort in seeking out product information or shopping to compare alternative brands, stores, and prices. The primary determinant of how consumers reach purchase decisions is **involvement**. Involvement refers to the importance which consumers attach to the purchase of a particular product.

There are several factors which may influence a consumer's level of involvement in a purchase situation. The characteristics most often associated with **high involvement** decision-making behavior are presented below.

- The product is perceived to be personally important.

- The product is relatively expensive or high-priced.

- The consumer lacks relevant information about the product.

- The risks associated with making a bad decision are high.

- The product offers potentially great benefits to the buyer.

On balance, most buying decisions tend to be **low involvement**. This is characteristic of frequently-purchased, low-priced goods.

High Involvement Decision-Making can be characterized as a five-stage process. This process is shown below.

Need or Problem Recognition

Search for Relevant Information

Identification and Evaluation of Alternatives

Purchase Decision

Postpurchase Behavior

One possible outcome of the purchase decision is postpurchase **cognitive dissonance**. This state of mental anxiety can be caused by a consumer's uncertainty about a purchase. Virtually all high involvement decision processes generate a set of viable alternatives. Cognitive dissonance occurs when consumers continue to evaluate the advantages and disadvantages of alternatives after the sale has been made. Consequently, the buyer remains uncertain and less than fully satisfied with the final selection.

Low Involvement Decision-Making can be characterized as a three-stage process. This process is shown below.

```
┌─────────────────────────────────────┐
│                                     │
│      Need or Problem Recognition    │
│                                     │
│         Purchase Decision           │
│                                     │
│       Postpurchase Behavior         │
│                                     │
└─────────────────────────────────────┘
```

Since the consequences of low involvement decisions are less important to consumers, the processes of searching for relevant information and evaluating alternatives are generally omitted.

The distinction between high and low involvement decision-making is not intended to be absolute. High and low involvement represent the endpoints of a continuum. Many purchase decisions may share characteristics of both extremes. It is also worth noting that consumers are not all alike in this regard. What one may regard as an unimportant purchase may be very important to another.

Individuals' decision-making behavior is substantially influenced by many other factors within their environment. Consumer wants and perceptions are affected by social, psychological, and informational forces. Social factors include culture, social class, reference groups, and family members. Psychological factors involve consumer's motivations and personality. Informational forces provide decision makers with relevant views on products and brands in the marketplace. This information may stem from commercial sources (e.g., advertisers), independent sources (e.g., product rating services), or the consumer's social environment.

ORGANIZATIONAL AND INDUSTRIAL MARKETS

Organizational and industrial markets differ from consumer markets in the types of purchases made and the characteristics of the markets involved. Organizational buyers purchase materials for resale, operational needs, or for use in further production. Consumers most typically purchase finished goods for final consumption. Organizational consumers are fewer in number and are less geographically dispersed than final consumers.

One of the essential differences which separates organizational and consumer markets is **derived demand**. Organizational buyers derive their demand for materials from the anticipated demand by consumers for finished goods.

Some of the bases used to segment consumer markets also have applications in industrial and organizational markets (e.g., geographic demographics). There are three characteristics which are, however, used exclusively in segmenting nonconsumer markets: **Customer Type**, **Customer Size**, and **Buying Situation**. Customer Types include manufacturers, wholesalers, retailers, government agencies, and nonprofit institutions. Customer Size is based on the purchasing power of buyers rather than the number of buyers. The Buying Situation can be characterized as one of three types: New-Task Buying, Straight Rebuy, or Modified Rebuy.

New-task buying is the most complex of the three buy classes. The task requires greater effort in gathering information and evaluating alternatives. More people are involved in the decision-making process for new-task buying than for the other two classes. New-task buying processes are most frequently employed in the purchase of high cost products which the firm has not had previous experience with.

The **Straight Rebuy** process is used to purchase inexpensive, low risk products. In most instances, previous purchases are simply reordered to replace depleted inventory. Alternative products or suppliers are not typically considered or evaluated.

Modified Rebuy processes are used when the purchase situation is less complex than new-task buying and more involved than a straight rebuy. Some information is required to reach decisions and a limited number of alternatives may be evaluated.

The sequence of stages in organizational decision-making is similar to consumer purchasing. The high involvement decision-making process for consumers is comparable to new-task buying within organizations. The five stages are the same. The fundamental difference is that more people are typically involved in reaching organizational buying decisions. Similarly, the three-stage model of low involvement decision-making is comparable to organizational consumers' straight rebuy.

Organizational buying decisions are typically influenced by many people within the firm. Individuals who affect the decision-making process usually fit one of the categories listed below.

Buyers:	Individuals who identify suppliers, arrange terms of sale, and carry out the purchasing procedures.
Users:	People within the firm who will use the product.

Influencers: Those individuals who establish product requirements and specifications based on their technical expertise or authority within the organization.

Gatekeepers: People within the organization who control the flow of relevant purchase-related information.

Deciders: The individual(s) who makes the final purchase decision.

The **Buying Center** is not a specific place or location within an organization. It is an entity comprised of all the people who participate in or influence the decision-making process. The number of people making up the buying center will vary between organizations. Within an organization, it will change with the nature and complexity of the purchase under consideration. Large companies may establish a formal "buying committee" to evaluate purchasing policies and product line modifications.

3 PRODUCT PLANNING AND MANAGEMENT

Product Planning entails all phases of decision-making related to new product development and the management of existing products. The role of product-related factors in marketing is to provide goods and services which will satisfy the demands of the market and create a profit for the firm. The dynamics of product management are shaped by changing tastes and preferences within the market.

PRODUCT CLASSIFICATION

Products can be classified as either **consumer products** or **industrial products** depending on their markets. Consumer products are targeted toward individuals and households for final consumption. Industrial products, sometimes called **business products**, are typically purchased for resale, operational needs, or for use in further production.

Consumer goods can be further classified into one of three product types: Convenience, Shopping, and Specialty. **Convenience goods** are those purchased frequently and with a minimum of shopping effort (low involvement decision-making). **Shopping goods** are those for which consumers typically make price-quality comparisons at several stores before buying (high involvement decision-making). **Specialty goods** are those for which buyers have strong brand loyalty—they'll accept no substitutes. Shopping behavior for these products is characterized by doing "whatever it takes" to find and purchase their brand. The characteristics corresponding to each type of product are illustrated below.

PRODUCT CHARACTERISTICS	Type of Product		
	Convenience	Shopping	Specialty
Effort Expended in Shopping for Product	Very Little	Moderate	As Much As Needed
Information Search and Evaluation of Alternatives	Very Little	High	Very Little
Product Importance or Involvement	Low	High	Varies
Price	Usually Low	Usually High	Varies
Frequency of Purchase	High	Low	Varies
Willingness to Accept Substitutes	High	Moderate	None

An additional category used for a very unusual class of consumer products is **unsought goods**. Unsought goods are those for which no demand exists. This may be due to the fact these are new and unfamiliar product innovations or simply because consumers do not currently want them.

Industrial or **Business Goods** can be classified as belonging to one of six product categories. The categories are based on the uses of the products and purchase characteristics. **Raw Materials**, **Component Materials**, and **Fabricated Parts** are used in the production of finished goods or become part of them. **Accessory Equipment** and **Installations** are capital goods which are used in the production process (e.g., assembly line equipment, drill presses, lathes). **Operating Supplies** are low cost items which aid in the production process (e.g., lubricating oils, pencils, janitorial supplies). The characteristics corresponding to each type of product are illustrated in the table below.

PRODUCT TYPE	Unit Price	Frequency of Purchase	Becomes a Part of Final Product	Complexity of the Decision Making Process
Raw Materials	Very Low	High	Often	Low
Component Material	Low	Varies	Yes	Low
Fabricated Parts	Low	Varies	Yes	Low
Accessory Parts	Medium	Low	No	Medium
Installations	Very High	Very Low	No	Very High
Operating Supplies	Low	High	No	Low

Services are tasks performed by one individual or firm for another. Services may be classified as either **consumer services** or **industrial services**, depending on the customers served. Services may be provided in conjunction with goods (e.g., auto rental) or without (e.g., accounting services). There are three tendencies which are characteristic of services. Services are **often intangible**. Services are **usually perishable**. Unlike products, they cannot be stored for use at a later date. Services are **frequently inseparable** from the individual(s) who provide the service (e.g., accounting services). Many services (e.g., medical) also require that the customer receive the services at the site where they are provided.

PRODUCT CONCEPTS

Products are defined within marketing as bundles of attributes. These attributes include both tangible and intangible product features. Products may be goods or services. They are the consequence of the firm's efforts to satisfy both consumer and organization goals.

The **Tangible Product** consists of those features which can be precisely specified (e.g., color, size, weight). The **Extended** or **Augmented Product** includes both the tangible and intangible elements of a product. These intangible features would include brand image and accompanying service features.

A firm's **Product Line** consists of a group or set of closely-related items. Product lines usually share some attributes in common. Some of the features which may relate items within a line include product composition, customers, and distribution channels. A firm's **Product Mix** is comprised of all the product lines which it offers.

NEW PRODUCT PLANNING

New Product Opportunities can stem from the modification of existing products or the development of wholly new product innovations. New products can make important contributions to the growth, profitability, and competitiveness of the firm. The chart below illustrates the range of possible new product opportunities.

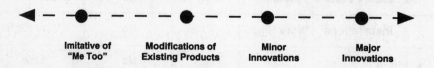

| Imitative of "Me Too" | Modifications of Existing Products | Minor Innovations | Major Innovations |

Imitative, "Me Too," or "Cloned" products are not typically regarded as innovative. They are not new to the market. They are only new to the firm attempting to enter a new market with a copy of competitors' products.

Idea Generation is the process of searching for new product opportunities. There are many methods used to generate new ideas including laboratory studies, market research, and "**brainstorming**." Brainstorming is a small group technique which encourages participants to voice creative ideas on a specified topic. The idea generation process may involve experts within the firm as well as consumers and experts from outside the company. Employees at all levels, suppliers, distributors, and others knowledgeable about the products and markets involved may participate in the process.

Product Screening and Concept Testing takes place after the firm has generated several ideas for new products. In the **Product Screening** phase, potential products are sorted relative to their strengths and weaknesses. After those failing to meet the firm's standards are eliminated from further consideration, the remaining concepts are tested. **Concept Testing** subjects new ideas to consumer scrutiny. Potential customers for the new product are asked to evaluate the concept. Their attitudes toward the idea partially determine whether or not there is sufficient consumer interest and sales potential to warrant further development of the product.

Business Analysis and Product Development are the next two stages in the process for those product concepts which survive the screening and concept testing phases. **Business Analysis** is a detailed evaluation of the concept's commercial feasibility. The criteria examined at this stage include: product costs, competitors' strengths in relevant markets, projected market demand, needed investment, and potential profitability. **Product Development** is the stage at which viable ideas are first produced in tangible form and the initial marketing strategy is created. Initial product models may continue to undergo testing and refinement at this stage as well.

Test Marketing and Commercialization are the final stages in the process of developing new products. **Test Marketing** provides a series of commercial experiments to test the acceptance of the product and the appropriateness of the proposed marketing strategy. These limited studies are conducted in one or more isolated geographic markets. Information from test markets is used to further refine the marketing strategy and, if needed, the product itself. If product sales have been adequate in test markets, the next stage is **commercialization**. Commercialization marks the start of full-scale production and the implementation of the complete marketing plan. This step corresponds to the Introductory stage of the Product Life Cycle for the product.

PRODUCT ADOPTION AND DIFFUSION

After a product has been introduced, the firm's initial objective is to gain consumer acceptance. The **Product Adoption Process** describes the stages which consumers go through in learning about new products. The process begins with a prospect's initial awareness of the product. If interested, the prospect will evaluate the perceived merits of the product and develop an opinion or attitude toward trying the product. If this attitude is sufficiently positive, the individual may buy the product (initial product trial). This trial will either confirm or reverse the buyer's initially positive impression. **Product Adoption** takes place when the buyer decides to continue using the product regularly. Despite having adopted the product, buyers seek regular reassurance or confirmation that their decision to adopt the product was a correct one.

The **Diffusion Process** describes the typical rate of adoption exhibited by consumers in response to new products. There are five categories of adopters.

- **Innovators** are the first to buy a new product. They comprise approximately three percent of the relevant market. They tend to be younger, more affluent, and more cosmopolitan than later clusters of buyers.

- **Early Adopters** are the next to buy. They make up approximately 13 percent of consumers. Early Adopters tend to be more locally-oriented than innovators and are typically well respected within their communities. They are opinion leaders who influence others' buying patterns.

- The **Early Majority** represent about 34 percent of the target market. They tend to be slightly above average in both social and economic standing. They are influenced by advertising and sales people, as well as Early Adopters.

- The **Late Majority** represent another 34 percent of the market. They are more resistant to change and risk taking than previous groups. They tend to be middle aged or older and somewhat less well off than average in socioeconomic terms.

- **Laggards** make up 16 percent of the market and are the last to buy. They tend to be price conscious, low-income consumers. By the time Laggards have adopted the product, it has reached the Maturity stage of the Product Life Cycle.

PRODUCT MIX MANAGEMENT

Product Positioning refers to the process of developing a product or brand image in the consumer's mind. The image is defined as a **position** relative to competing brands and products. Positioning is based on consumer perceptions of product features relative to their preferences. **Ideal points** identify consumers' perception of the perfect bundle or combination of attributes.

Firms may expand their product mix by adding new lines or increasing the depth of existing product lines. **Mix expansion** provides the firm with new opportunities for growth. Firms may also consider reducing or **contracting** the product mix. This can be accomplished either by eliminating entire lines or reducing the variety within lines. This weeding out process is usually intended to eliminate products which provide low profits.

The relationship between product lines within the same firm can be used to secure competitive advantages in the marketplace. A **wide product mix** represents a diversification strategy. Offering several different product lines enables the firm to meet several different types of customer needs. **Deep product mixes** focus the firm's resources on a smaller number of product lines. In turn, this allows the development of several products within each line. The firm can then target several segments within the same market.

PRODUCT LIFE CYCLE

The Product Life Cycle describes a pattern of changes which is characteristic of most products from their inception to their eventual departure from the market. The life cycle is divided into four stages: Introduction, Growth, Maturity, and Decline. The product's movement through each stage is described in terms of its sales, profits, and competitors.

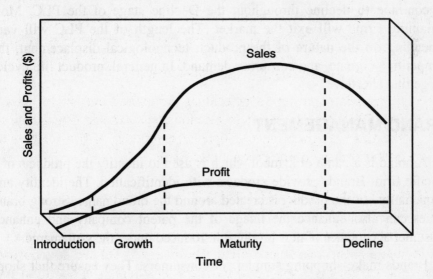

Introduction

This stage of the Product Life Cycle (PLC) corresponds to the commercialization of a new product. The rate of new product failures during this stage remains high. Sales, beginning at $0, increase steadily through-out the Introduction stage, though profits remain negative. Innovators are the initial buyers of the product. There is very little direct competition in this phase.

Growth

The beginning of the Growth stage is marked by the point at which profitability becomes positive. Sales growth continues at an increasing rate and new firms will enter the market, attracted by high profit potential.

Maturity

The initial phase of the Maturity stage is characterized by slowing sales. Eventually industry sales level off as the market becomes saturated. Consumer demand peaks during this stage. Price competition is greater during maturity than during the preceding stages. Some manufacturers may be forced out of the market as total industry profits decrease through-out maturity.

Decline

Industry sales decline and many firms leave the market. Industry prof-its continue to decline throughout the Decline stage of the PLC. Most remaining firms will exit the market. The length of the PLC will vary depending on the nature of the product, technological displacement, the competitive climate, and consumer demand. In general, product life cycles are getting shorter.

BRAND MANAGEMENT

A brand is a name or symbol which is used to identify the products of a specific firm. Brands provide products with identification. The identity and "personality" of the product is created around the brand name. Strong brand names can also enhance the image of the parent company and enhance consumer acceptance of new products introduced under the same name.

Brands make shopping simpler for consumers. They ensure that shop-pers can repeat purchases of products which they prefer (brand loyalty). The brand name provides implicit assurance that the quality will remain unchanged over time. Brand images also serve to differentiate competi-tors. Consequently, price comparisons become less critical in consumers' decision-making and other differences enter into the evaluation process.

Consumers also tend to feel more confident and secure when buying a familiar brand. Distinctive brands can provide the centerpiece around which marketing strategies are developed.

Different types of brands are classified according to their origin. **Manufacturer brands** are created by product manufacturers. These are sometimes called "National Brands." **Dealer Brands** are created by intermediaries (e.g., retailers). These are sometimes referred to as "Private Brands."

Characteristics of Good Brand Names:

- Suggests something about the product's benefits.
- Short and simple.
- Easy to spell, read, and pronounce.
- Pleasant sounding.
- Distinctive and memorable.
- Appropriate to new products which may be added to the line at a later date.
- Legally available for use.

Brand Familiarity exists on five different levels:

- Brand Insistence occurs when consumers are absolutely brand loyal and will accept no substitutes.
- Brand Preference means that target consumers will usually choose one specific brand over others.
- Brand Recognition exists when consumers remember the brand name.
- Brand Non-Recognition means that consumers do not recall the brand name.
- Brand Rejection exists when consumers recognize, but refuse to buy, specific brands.

Marketers of more than one product have several branding strategies to consider. A **Family Brand** strategy is used when the same brand is applied to several products. Family branding is most appropriate when all of the products are of comparable type and quality. **Individual Brands** can be assigned each product when there exists significant variation in product type and quality. Generic products are those which have no brand name at all. Intermediaries often market low-priced generic products to cost-conscious consumers.

A **Licensed Brand** is a well-established brand name which other sellers pay to use. This allows sellers to take advantage of existing brand recognition and preferences.

Trademarks are brand names, marks, or characters used to identify products. Registered trademarks are legally protected entities—reserved for the exclusive use of their owners.

PACKAGING

Packaging serves valuable functions for both buyers and sellers. The three primary functions of product packaging are **Protection**, **Promotion**, and **Information**.

Effective packaging can prevent product damage and spoiling. The costs associated with good packaging are partially offset by the resulting reduction in goods damaged in transit. Child-proof and tamper-resistant protective packaging can also provide additional benefits to the final consumer.

Packaging can be an effective promotional tool. Consumers are exposed to product packaging at the point-of-purchase. Consequently, it represents the last opportunity to influence their decision-making. Distinctive packages which reinforce positive brand images help sell the product.

Benefits provided by the packaging itself can also enhance consumer preference. Improved dispensers, reusable containers, and greater convenience are examples of how packaging can increase the value of the purchase.

Product Information and Labeling permit consumers to critically evaluate products and compare brands. Consumers are increasingly concerned with product contents, nutritional information, and the environmental consequences of the products and packaging they purchase.

4 DISTRIBUTION SYSTEMS

CHANNELS OF DISTRIBUTION

Channels of distribution are designed in response to the needs of the sellers in executing the marketing mix. Environmental factors considered within this context include company resources, buyer behavior, competitors' strategies, and the product itself. Channel structure, the relative intensity of distribution, and the number of members within the channel are among the critical decisions made in establishing a distribution channel.

CHANNEL FUNCTIONS

The physical distribution of products is the primary function served by channels. Distribution includes transportation, inventory management, and customer service functions. Intermediaries can also perform other tasks which contribute to greater channel efficiency and market development. These include market research, promotion, and product planning.

In many channel systems, members participate in the **sorting** process. This includes accumulation, sorting, and assorting functions. **Accumulation** is the process of assembling and pooling relatively small individual shipments so that they can be transported more economically. **Sorting** is the process of separating goods by quality, color, or size. **Assorting** is typically performed at the retail level. It is the process of acquiring a wide variety of merchandise to meet the diverse preferences of consumers.

CHANNEL STRUCTURE

Channel systems which move goods from the producer to the final consumer without using independent intermediaries or "middlemen" are termed **Direct Channels**. Those which move goods with the cooperation and assistance of independent intermediaries are **Indirect Channels**.

Channel width refers to the number of independent members at one level of the distribution channel (e.g., producer, wholesaler, retailer, final consumer). **Channel length** refers to the number of levels used to create a distribution channel.

The intensity of a distribution system is determined by the number of intermediaries involved at the wholesale and retail levels of the channel. An **Intensive** distribution strategy is one in which a firm sells through every potential outlet which will reach its target market. With **Selective** distribution, a firm will sell through many, but not all, potential wholesalers and retailers. An **Exclusive** distribution strategy limits the number of outlets employed to one or two intermediaries within each market.

Three types of systems can be used to coordinate distribution functions within indirect channels. In a **Corporate** channel of distribution, one firm owns either all channel members or the firms at the next level in the channel. The control of operations within the channel is maintained through ownership.

Two arrangements can be used to coordinate the functions of independent members within indirect channels. **Contractual** arrangements specify performance terms for each independent channel member. Legal contracts specify terms governing the matters related to the physical movement of goods, pricing policies, and system efficiency. **Administered** arrangements coordinate channel operations through a dominant channel member. The market power of the dominant firm is sufficient to secure the voluntary cooperation of other channel members.

Vertical Integration is the process of acquiring firms which operate at different channel levels. One possible outcome of this strategy is the development of a corporate channel system. In this instance, vertical integration has the effect of increasing operational control and stability of the channel. **Horizontal Integration** is the process of acquiring firms which operate at the same channel level. This strategy allows the firm to increase its competitive strength, market share, and power within the channel system.

MULTIPLE CHANNELS

Multiple Channels (also called dual distribution) exist when a firm develops two or more separate and distinct distribution channels. This strategy may be pursued for several reasons. The firm may use multiple channels as a means of increasing market coverage or to reach new market segments. New channels may also be created to distribute new products.

CHANNEL BEHAVIOR

Channel Control refers to the ability to influence the actions of other channel members. This control may be established by the decision-making structure of the channel (e.g., corporate ownership) or from the relative market power of the members.

Channel Conflict exists when disagreements arise between members over channel practices and policies. Horizontal conflicts take place between firms at the same channel level. Vertical conflict occurs between firms at different levels of the same distribution system.

PUSHING vs. PULLING STRATEGIES

Manufacturers have two strategy alternatives to consider as a means of ensuring that products (especially new products) reach the final consumer. **Pushing** a product through the channel utilizes promotional efforts to secure the cooperation of intermediaries. Sales promotions, personal selling, and advertising are directed toward persuading intermediaries to cooperate in the marketing of the product. A **Pulling** strategy generates consumer demand for the product as a means of securing support within the channel. Promotional efforts are initially directed toward the final consumer. Pulling is most appropriate for new products seeking to gain access to an existing channel.

PHYSICAL DISTRIBUTION SYSTEMS

The most fundamental physical distribution tasks are transportation, materials handling, order processing, and inventory management. The goals of physical distribution systems are most critically concerned with two interrelated issues: costs and customer service. Cost control and reduction can be achieved through more efficient transportation practices and improved inventory management. Customer service and customer satisfaction depends on the efficient processing of orders and the reliable delivery of goods.

The **Total-Cost Concept** recognizes that minimizing costs and satisfying customer demands can represent conflicting objectives. The goal of the Total-Cost approach to system efficiency is to provide a level of customer service at the lowest total costs. These costs include lost sales resulting from customer dissatisfaction. The Total-Cost Concept takes into account that sacrificing some marginal sales opportunities can result in lower total system costs. Consequently, the ideal physical distribution system must strike a balance which preserves both high sales opportunities, customer satisfaction, and the lowest possible distribution costs.

Providing one centrally-located stock of inventory for all markets provides for better inventory control, requires less total inventory, and reduces handling costs. This strategy may, however, create very high transportation costs and delivery delays for customers. Using too many dispersed inventory sites poses the opposite problems.

The **Distribution-Center Concept** recognizes that the most effective strategy may be a compromise between these two extremes. The resulting **distribution centers** are a type of warehouse planned in relation to specific markets. They provide key locations at which all operations take place. Each center is an integrated system which takes orders, processes them, and makes delivery to the customer.

5 WHOLESALING AND RETAILING

WHOLESALING

Wholesaling consists of all the activities related to the resale of products to organizational buyers, other wholesalers, and retailers. These functions typically include warehousing, transporting, and financing. Wholesalers participate in the sorting process by accumulating an assortment of merchandise and redistributing large product volumes in smaller units. Wholesalers provide a salesforce which enables manufacturers to reach many customers at relatively low costs.

Manufacturer Wholesaling exists when the product's producer performs the wholesaling functions. These are carried out through the manufacturer's branch offices and sales offices. **Merchant Wholesalers** are independent firms which take title and possession of the products they sell. These firms are also sometimes referred to as distributors or jobbers. Merchant wholesalers may be full- or limited-service wholesalers.

Full Service Merchant Wholesalers perform the complete range of wholesaling functions. They store, promote, and transport merchandise. They provide sales support, merchandising assistance, customer service, and market research information to both their suppliers and customers. They can often provide assistance in financing transactions by extending trade credit. **Limited Service Merchant Wholesalers** may not provide merchandising or market research assistance. In most instances, they will not extend credit to facilitate transactions.

Rack Jobbers are full-service merchant wholesalers which provide the display racks used to merchandise the product. **Drop Shippers** are limited-service merchant wholesalers which buy products from manufacturers and arrange for the delivery to retailers. They take title of the merchandise, but do not take physical possession of it.

Agents are independent wholesalers that do not take title of the products that they handle. They derive their compensation through sales commissions or manufacturer fees. **Brokers** act as temporary wholesalers. Their primary function is to bring buyers and sellers together and facilitate the transaction process. They do not take title of merchandise.

RETAILING

Retailing consists of all the activities related to the sale of products to final consumers for individual or household consumption. Retailers are the final link in the channel of distribution.

There are three forms of **Ownership** which can be used to classify retailers. **Corporate Chains** are comprised of several (usually 10 or more) stores which are owned and managed by the same firm. They are typically standardized with respect to product lines, merchandising, and operational policies.

Vertical Marketing Systems provide a collective means of enhancing the market power of individually-owned retail units. Vertical Marketing Systems (VMSs) link stores together in voluntary chains or cooperatives. These contractual arrangements allow the group to compete more effectively and provide members with the advantages enjoyed by chain stores. The VMS provides members with assistance in merchandising, personnel training, inventory management, accounting, and promotion.

Independent Stores are single retail units which are not affiliated with a corporate chain or cooperative. They tend to have higher prices than affiliated stores, less market power, and rely more heavily on customer service for a competitive edge.

Franchise Systems are a specific type of Vertical Marketing System. Under this form of VMS, the parent company (franchisor) provides franchisees with the legal right to use company trademarks. The franchisor may also provide franchisees with assistance in site selection, personnel training, inventory management, and promotional strategy. This system allows franchisees to take advantage of well-known product and brand names. Participants may also benefit from the direct acquisition of proven store layouts and operational procedures.

Retail stores may pursue one of several store mix strategies. These strategies are based on product assortment, pricing strategy, and the level of customer service provided. The table below classifies each store according to the width and depth of its product assortment, pricing strategy, and level of customer service relative to other store types selling similar products.

STORE TYPE	PRODUCT ASSORTMENT	PRICING STRATEGY	CUSTOMER SERVICE
CONVENIENCE STORE	Narrow/Shallow	High Prices	Low
SUPERMARKET	Wide/Deep	Low-Moderate	Moderate
DEPARTMENT STORE	Wide/Deep	Moderate	Moderate/High
DISCOUNT STORE	Wide/Shallow	Low	Low
SPECIALTY STORE	Narrow/Very Deep	High	High
CATALOG SHOWROOM	Wide/Shallow	Low	Low
SUPERSTORES & HYPERMARKETS	Very Wide/Deep	Low	Low

Nonstore Retailing describes retail transactions which occur outside of traditional store settings. The techniques of nonstore retailing include direct selling, direct marketing, and vending sales. These activities account for about 20 percent of retail sales.

The selection of a **retail store location** is a function of the target market, location of competitors, and site costs. Location options include planned shopping centers, unplanned business/shopping districts, and isolated store locations.

A store's **atmosphere** is comprised of those characteristics which contribute to consumers' general impression of the store—its image. The dimensions which contribute to store atmosphere include the exterior appearance, interior design, product display, and store layout.

Scrambled Merchandising takes place as retailers add products which are not related to their traditional lines. Retailers engaged in this practice are seeking to add any products which sell quickly, increase profitability, and build store traffic. Scrambled merchandising can attract different target markets and often creates competition between unrelated retail stores.

Wheel of Retailing is a concept which describes the evolution of retail stores. The theory states that new retailers enter markets as low-status, low-price competitors. If successful, they tend to evolve into more traditional forms—adding customer-service features and raising prices to meet higher operating costs. This moving-up process creates opportunities for new retailers to enter the market with "low-end" strategies.

6 PROMOTIONAL STRATEGY

PROMOTION PLANNING

The process of Promotion Planning requires that the firm identify the most appropriate Promotion Mix, Objectives, and Budget. The Promotion Plan serves to coordinate elements of the firm's promotional efforts with the total marketing program. Elements within the promotional mix must be both internally consistent and jointly supportive of the strategic direction of the other marketing mix variables.

Promotion Mix is comprised of those elements which contribute to the firm's overall communications program. The mix includes: advertising, personal selling, publicity, public relations, and sales promotions.

Promotion Objectives may address three goals within the marketing mix. Promotion can be used to **inform** both intermediaries and end-users about new products. For products which are already established, promotion can be used to persuade buyers. The objective is to influence brand preference and purchase behavior. Promotion may also serve to **remind** buyers about the availability of very well established products.

Communication Channels provide the medium through which promotional messages are sent and delivered. The elements of a typical channel of communication are shown below.

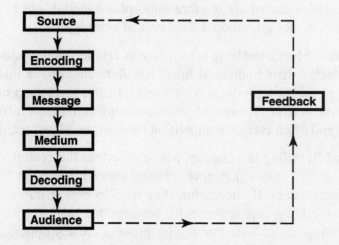

This process may be interfered with or break down at any point along the sequence due to **noise**. Noise may result in poorly encoded/decoded messages or weak audience response.

Several different techniques can be used to establish promotion **budgets**. The **Percent-of-Sales** technique allocates a fixed percentage of the previous year's sales for promotional programs. The **Competitive Parity** approach establishes a budget based on the actions of the firm's closest competitors. This strategy seeks to mirror rivals' changes in promotional intensity. The **Objective and Task** procedure relies on the matching of promotional objectives to the funding required to achieve specific, objective-related tasks.

New firms often spend as much as they can afford when initially establishing a promotion budget. Once all other elements of the marketing plan have been funded, the **All Available Funds** technique allocates remaining resources to promotional activities.

ADVERTISING PLAN

Advertising **objectives** are determined by the marketing strategy for the product or firm. These objectives may include:

- New Product Introduction—Build Brand Awareness
- Establish Brand Preference (Selective Demand)
- Create and Maintain Brand Loyalty
- Market Development
- Build Primary Demand, Industry Sales
- Increase Product Uses or Rates of Usage
- Support the Firm's Salesforce
- Enhance the Firm's Image

Several of these objectives are typically combined in the development of an advertising plan.

The **Advertising Budget** stems from the budget developed in the Promotion Plan. The determination of a specific dollar allocation reflects the costs associated with alternative media and production costs.

Two different levels of decision-making relate to **media planning**: the choice of media-type and the selection of specific vehicles within each medium. Once appropriate vehicles have been identified, the process of developing advertising schedules and buying media begins.

The alternative media available to advertisers include: television, radio, newspapers, magazines, outdoor advertising, and direct mail. Each medium has distinctive characteristics which may pose an advantage or problem—depending on the creative requirements of the ad and the nature of the product.

MEDIUM	STRENGTHS	WEAKNESSES
Television	Combines action and sound. Extensive market coverage.	Very expensive. Viewers' short attn. span.
Radio	Station formats can provide access to target markets.	Audio only. Very passive medium.
Newspapers	Flexible—short lead times. Concentrated market.	Poor quality printing. High ad clutter.
Magazines	High-quality color printing. Very selective means of access to specific audiences. Long life, good pass-along value.	Less flexible scheduling of ads—long lead times.
Outdoor Ads	High intensity coverage within geographic market area. Large size, brief messages.	Low impact. Public criticism of "landscape pollution."
Direct Mail	Highly selective—no wasted circulation.	Low rate of consumer acceptance. Very expensive.

The selection of specific vehicles within each medium can be influenced by several factors. The evaluation of alternative vehicles is based on the cost and market coverage measures listed below.

Reach refers to the percentage of a target audience that is exposed to an ad through a given vehicle, within a specified time frame. The time frame used is typically four weeks.

Advertising costs are evaluated according to the cost of reaching one thousand prospects through a given vehicle–**Cost-per-Thousand**. Establishing this common measure of efficiency allows for comparisons across media and within media types.

Frequency refers to the average number of times that members of the target audience are exposed to an ad through a given vehicle. Like Reach, Frequency is usually based on a four-week period.

Gross Rating Points (GRPs) are calculated by multiplying Reach times Frequency. GRPs indicate the "total weight" of advertising delivered over a four-week period.

The **Creative Platform** provides the overall concept and theme for an advertising campaign. Themes may relate to the product, the consumer, or the firm. Product themes emphasize performance characteristics and the brand's competitive advantages. Consumer themes stress benefits of using the brand or illustrate how the product can enhance the buyer's life. Ads emphasizing the firm are typically intended to improve the image of the company.

Advertising Effectiveness can be assessed by both direct and indirect measures. Sales, store traffic, and coupon redemption rates provide direct measures of advertising effects. Indirect measures use consumers' recall of ads to estimate their impact.

PUBLICITY AND PUBLIC RELATIONS

Publicity is a form of nonpersonal communication which is not paid for by an identified sponsor. Publicity efforts initiated by firms include: news features, articles in business and trade publications, and editorials. Publicity about a firm may be either positive or negative. The content of publicity pieces can be influenced, but not controlled, by a firm. Both positive and negative publicity is characterized by high audience attentiveness and high credibility.

Public Relations may be paid or nonpaid and includes both personal and nonpersonal communications. Public relations is primarily concerned with enhancing the image of the firm. Institutional advertising, personal appearances, and publicity represent various forms of public relations.

PERSONAL SELLING

There are three types of salespeople corresponding to the essential tasks of personal selling. **Order Getters** are responsible for securing new business for the firm. **Order Takers** service customer accounts which have already been established.

There are two types of **Support Salespeople** who provide assistance to both the order getters and order takers. Missionary salespeople work for producers. They foster goodwill and work to maintain productive relationships with intermediaries and their customers. Technical Specialists support the efforts of order getters and order takers by providing customers with expert technical assistance.

The process of recruiting salespeople begins with determining the number of people needed and the qualifications desired. These factors may include education, intelligence, technical knowledge/skills, job experience, and personality traits. Based on a written job description, a pool of qualified applicants is reviewed and the best qualified candidates should be selected.

Salesforce training programs differ, according to the needs of the employer. Virtually all salespeople need some training. The most fundamental issues in training programs include company policies, product information, and selling techniques.

Sales potential, the maximum possible sales within a territory, will vary according to several considerations. Some of these factors include: the number of potential buyers, the size of accounts, the relative dispersion of buyers, and the geographic characteristics of the market.

Salesforce Allocation to specific territories should attempt to match the talent and ability of salespeople to the characteristics of the customers within the territory. Ideally, each salesperson should be assigned to the territory where his or her relative contribution to the firm's profitability is the greatest. Sales managers will endeavor to minimize the ratio of selling expense to total sales for each territory.

Selling Process is a sequence of stages which are essential to effective personal selling.

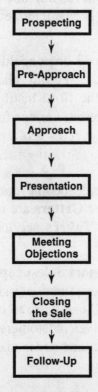

Prospecting is the process of seeking and identifying prospective buyers or "leads." In addition, the prospect must be "qualified" to buy. In **Qualifying Leads** the salesperson determines whether the prospect is both willing and able to buy.

The **Pre-Approach** takes place prior to meeting with a qualified prospect, when the salesperson must decide how to best initiate a face-to-face meeting. This includes an analysis of available information about the prospect's buying behavior and an evaluation of competitors' products.

The **Approach** takes place when the seller first meets the prospective buyer. The goal at this stage is to gain the interest and attention of the buyer. Since there are several possible strategies which can be effective, careful pre-approach planning should indicate which ones are most likely to succeed.

The **Presentation** of the sales message may take the form of a prepared ("canned") presentation or take an interactive (needs-satisfaction) approach. The message is intended to persuade buyers to purchase based on the attributes and benefits of the seller's product.

Meeting Objections, part of the presentation process, is an important sales skill. Objections raised by a prospect may represent a request for clarification or additional information. Well-prepared salespeople will anticipate objections and be prepared to overcome them.

Closing the Sale is the stage at which the seller tries to gain a purchase commitment from the prospect. Salespeople who are uncertain that it is an appropriate time to "close the deal" may use a trial close. If a trial close seems to be going well, it can be pursued to a complete close. If not, it can be withdrawn without detracting from the effectiveness of the meeting.

The **Follow-Up** step in the process represents the salesperson's efforts to assure customer satisfaction after the sale. These efforts provide an important basis for building goodwill and future sales. It may also be used to suggest additional sales of the product or related goods.

Canned sales presentations are memorized messages. Salespeople using canned presentations deliver the same prepared statement to each prospect. **Interactive** presentations rely heavily on learning more about each prospect's needs and preferences through direct interaction. Salespeople using this "needs-satisfaction" approach tailor each sales message to each customer. By allowing the potential buyer to speak initially about his or her needs, the salesperson can respond by explaining how the product will address those needs. It is a problem-solving approach to selling. Many salespeople employ parts of both strategies.

Salesforce Compensation plans may take one of three basic forms: **Straight Salary, Straight Commission,** or **A Combination Plan**. The appropriateness of each option is determined by balancing the need to provide income security (salary) versus sales incentives (commission). Combination Plans provide for some measure of both.

The **Drawing Account Method** is a modification of the straight commission plan. Under this method, sales commissions are credited to each individual's drawing account. Salespeople may withdraw a fixed amount each period against their current balance or as an advance against future commissions. In most instances, employees are responsible for any indebtedness incurred under this plan. Some employers, however, provide a **guaranteed draw** where the salesperson is not obligated to pay back the difference when the draw exceeds commissions earned over a specified period.

A great deal of information about the performance of salespeople can be obtained from Sales Reports. Sales Reports describe each individual's schedule of calls and sales results. Key measures of a salesperson's performance include: revenue per call, number of calls per day, time per contact, cost per call, percentage of "successes" per call, and the number of new customers created.

Ratios are often used in the **evaluation process**. Among the most common evaluation ratios are: Sales/Sales Potential, Sales Expense/Sales, Total Accounts/Total Potential Number of Accounts, and Total Number of Calls/Number of Accounts. Comparisons may be made to the same salesperson's performance in previous periods or to the performance standards established by others.

Qualitative measures are also used to evaluate salespeople. Customer satisfaction can be measured through telephone interviews or mail questionnaires. Many firms also provide for formal assessment of salespeople's knowledge of the company, its products, customers, and competitors.

SALES PROMOTION

Sales Promotion is comprised of all paid marketing communications other than advertising, public relations, and personal selling. In contrast to advertising, sales promotions are usually intended to provide short-term boosts in product sales. The types of sales promotions typically aimed at final consumers and intermediaries are listed below.

CONSUMER-DIRECTED—Coupons, Contests, Sweepstakes, Rebates, Premiums, Refunds, Point-of-Purchase Displays, Product Samples,

Trading Stamps, Cents-Off Deals, Multi-Pack Offers, Demonstrations, Free Trial Offers.

INTERMEDIARY-DIRECTED—Push Money, Trade Allowances, Quantity Discounts, Sales Contests, Trade Shows, Point-of-Purchase Display Materials, Trade Rebates.

7 PRICING POLICIES AND STRATEGIES

PRICE ELASTICITY OF DEMAND

Price elasticity of demand is the percentage change in the number of units demanded divided by the percentage change in the price of the product. It reflects the degree to which the level of product sales is dependent on price. Specifically, it relates the rate at which demand changes in response to price changes. The mathematical formula for price elasticity of demand is shown below.

$$\text{Price Elasticity of Demand} = \frac{(Q_1 - Q_2)/Q_1 + Q_2}{(P_1 - P_2)/P_1 + P_2}$$

Where:
- Q_1 = Initial Quantity Demanded
- Q_2 = New Quantity Demanded
- P_1 = Initial Price
- P_2 = New Price

Elastic Demand exists when the value of the price elasticity of demand formula is less than -1. If demand is elastic, an increase in price will produce a decrease in demand and a decrease in total revenue. (Total Revenue is the product of price times the number of units sold.) Price decreases will increase demand and **increase** total revenue.

Inelastic Demand exists when the value of the price elasticity of demand formula is greater than -1. If demand is inelastic, an increase in price will produce a decrease in demand and an **increase** in total revenue. Price decreases will increase demand and **decrease** total revenue. If demand does not decrease at all in response to price increases, it is said to be perfectly inelastic.

Unitary Elasticity exists when the value of the price elasticity of demand formula is -1. In this instance, the change in demand is directly proportional to the change in price. When unitary elasticity exists, total revenue does not change in response to price increases or decreases.

The **Price Elasticity of Demand Coefficient (E_d)** is equal to the **absolute value** or non-negative value of the Price Elasticity of Demand formula (Section 8.1). The interpretation of E_d is provided in the table below.

Value of E_d	Effect of an Increase in Price on Quantity Demanded (Q_d) and Total Revenue (TR)
if E_d = 0 (Perfectly Inelastic)	No Change in Q_d, TR Increases
if E_d < 1 (Inelastic)	Q_d Decreases, TR Increases
if E_d = 1 (Unitary Elasticity)	Q_d Decreases, No Change in TR
if E_d > 1 (Elastic)	Q_d Decreases, TR Decreases
if E_d = ∞ (Perfectly Elastic)	Q_d = 0, TR = O

The price elasticity of demand for a given product may change significantly at different price levels. Consequently, the value of E_d should be evaluated at several different prices.

PRICE FIXING AND PRICE DISCRIMINATION

The Sherman Act (1890) prevents businesses from restraining trade and interstate commerce. Pricing policies which are predatory or otherwise contribute to the monopolization of markets and conspiracies contrary to competitive pricing are illegal under the provisions of this law.

The Robinson-Patman Act (1936) prohibits any form of price discrimination which has the effect of reducing competition among wholesalers or retailers. The law provides that the same seller cannot provide the same products to competing buyers (resellers) at different prices unless those price differentials can be justified on the basis of cost savings or good faith efforts to meet competitors' prices. The Robinson-Patman Act also prohibits producers from providing a higher level of service to large customers.

PRICING STRATEGY

Price Skimming is a strategy that introduces new products at relatively high prices. Higher initial prices enhance the perceived quality of the product and maintain demand at a level consistent with the firm's production capacity. The higher profit margins may offset some R&D costs and protect the firm from failing to cover costs.

After the initial introductory period, the firm often lowers its price gradually in response to competitive pressures and the need to reach new market segments. In this way the firm can "skim" layers of profitability from each successive price level. Initially high prices are paid by the least price-sensitive segment of the market. Lowering product prices over time provides the expansion of the market and growth.

Penetration Pricing is an alternative pricing strategy for new product introductions. This option uses low introductory prices to gain a large share of the market more quickly than price skimming would allow. This is especially appropriate for new products which are very similar to competing brands. The lower price strategy may have several advantages. It provides for quick entry into new markets and often discourages potential competitors from entering. Building relatively high volume sales can also reduce the firm's unit costs through economies of scale. The disadvantages stem from lower unit profit margins and less pricing flexibility.

PRICING DECISIONS

Pricing decisions are often characterized as belonging to one of three categories: cost-based, demand-based, or competition-based pricing. In practice, most pricing decisions integrate elements from each of these categories. Prices typically reflect marketers' consideration of product-related costs, consumer preferences, and competitors' prices.

Cost-Based Pricing establishes product prices as a function of product costs. Cost-based pricing techniques include cost-plus pricing and return-on-investment pricing. Cost-plus pricing determines prices by adding a predetermined level of profit to product costs. Return-on-investment pricing sets product prices that will enable the firm to achieve a specified rate of return. This method requires forecasting sales volume over the life of the investment period. Virtually all price-setting strategies must take costs into account as part of the process.

Demand-Based Pricing attempts to set prices based on consumer responses to product prices. Demand-based pricing techniques include prestige pricing, odd-even pricing, price lining, and leader pricing. These methods of setting prices are sometimes referred to as psychological pricing. Market research on consumer attitudes and preferences often identify the range of acceptable prices specific to each market segment.

Competition-Based Pricing sets prices according to those charged by the firm's closest competitors. This may result in prices above, below, or at market levels. Competition-based pricing strategies include customary pricing and price leadership. In certain markets, competitors have converged on a narrow range of price points. This traditional basis for setting prices is referred to as Customary Pricing. Price Leadership exists when one firm is usually the first to change prices from previous levels and this change is routinely followed by the rest of the industry.

A **One-Price** policy offers the same price to all buyers for purchases of essentially the same quantities in comparable situations. **Flexible Pricing** permits the seller to charge different prices to different buyers in similar circumstances. This strategy is most common in personal selling contexts. Flexible pricing allows the salesperson to adjust prices in response to competitive shifts and customer requirements.

Geographic Pricing policies reflect different levels of transportation and other costs related to the physical distance between buyers and sellers. Sellers may quote F.O.B. (free-on-board) prices which do not include shipping charges. Zone pricing sets separate prices for different geographic regions—incorporating average transport costs for each area into the quoted prices of the product.

Unit Pricing provides consumers with information on the price per unit on or near the product. This practice is intended to simplify comparisons between brands and various package sizes.

PRICE-QUALITY CORRELATION

In many instances, consumers believe that higher prices represent superior product quality. In the absence of specific product information, buyers often rely on price as an indicator of quality and use this measure when evaluating brands. This price-quality correlation is strongest when buyers have little confidence in their ability to judge product quality and they suspect substantial differences in quality between brands.

PSYCHOLOGICAL PRICING

Prestige Pricing establishes retail prices which are high, relative to competing brands. The higher price is intended to suggest higher product quality, consistent with the strength of the price-quality association in consumers' minds. It may also provide the product with a measure of prestige or status relative to competing brands.

Odd-Even Pricing sets prices just below even dollar values (e.g., $99.99 or $99 v. $100). There are several possible explanations for consumers' apparent preference for certain odd prices, rather than even ones.

Buyers may implicitly believe that odd prices are the consequence of a price reduction from a higher even price. They may prefer odd prices because they seem substantially lower (the difference between $100 and $99 seems far more than one dollar.) It may also provide shoppers with a reference point when trying to stay within price limits. On balance, consumers seem to feel that odd prices provide greater value for their money.

Consumers may also seek "even" prices under some circumstances. When prices for a product category (e.g., candy bars, chewing gum) have remained relatively stable over extended periods, buyers may have very adverse reactions to any increase. When confronted with rising costs, marketers may try to maintain these **customary prices** by reducing the size of each package or changing the ingredients used in production.

Price Lining simplifies consumers' evaluation of alternative products by establishing a limited number of price points for groups or lines of products. Product groups of similar quality are all sold at the same price, thereby allowing shoppers to evaluate alternatives based on other considerations. A retailer may, for example, price various styles and lines of shirts at three price levels: $24, $29, and $36.

When establishing a price line, the seller must be certain that price points are far enough apart so that buyers perceive different levels of merchandise quality. Price lining may minimize consumers' confusion when comparing brands while allowing retailers to maintain a wider assortment within specified price ranges.

Leader Pricing occurs when a firm sells select products below their usual price as a means of gaining attention or building store traffic. In retail settings, leader pricing tends to feature popular brands of frequently-purchased products. The expectation is that sales of regularly-priced merchandise will benefit from increased traffic and that the image of the store as a price leader will be enhanced. When items are sold below cost they are termed "loss leaders."

PROFIT MARGIN

Markups are percentages or dollar amounts added to the cost of sales to arrive at the product's selling price. Many retailers and wholesalers use a standard percentage markup to set selling prices. Markups are usually calculated as a percentage of the selling price, rather than a percentage of the cost.

$$\text{Markup Percentage (On Selling Price)} = \frac{\text{Selling Price} - \text{Product Cost}}{\text{Selling Price}}$$

Example: Product Cost = $50   Selling Price = $80

$$\text{Markup Percentage (On Selling Price)} = \frac{\$80 - \$50}{\$80} = \frac{\$30}{\$80} = .375 \text{ or } 37.5\%$$

$$\text{Selling Price} = \frac{\text{Product Cost}}{(100 - \text{Markup Percent})/100}$$

Example: Product Cost = $30   Markup Percentage = 60%

$$\text{Selling Price} = \frac{\$30}{(100 - 60)/100} = \frac{\$30}{.4} = \$75$$

Markdowns are retail price reductions. Managers typically markdown retail prices in response to low consumer demand. Like markups, markdowns are usually expressed as a percentage of the selling price.

$$\text{Markdown Percentage (Off Original Price)} = \frac{\text{Original Selling Price} - \text{Reduced Price}}{\text{Original Selling Price}}$$

Example: Original Selling Price = $85   Reduced Price = $60

$$\text{Markdown Percentage (Off Original Price)} = \frac{\$85 - \$60}{\$85} = .294 \text{ or } 29.4\%$$

Discounts are reductions from list prices which are given by sellers to buyers. These price reductions may be based on several factors.

Trade Discounts are reductions from the list price given to intermediaries in exchange for the performance of specified tasks. Trade discounts may compensate buyers for promotional considerations, transportation, storage costs, extending credit and order processing.

Quantity Discounts arise from the economies and improved efficiency of selling in large quantities. As order size increases, the fixed costs related to order processing and customer service remain substantially unchanged. Consequently, the associated per unit costs are reduced for the seller. In turn, some financing and storage costs may also be shifted to the buyer. Quantity discounts may be cumulative over a specified period of time or noncumulative.

Cash Discounts are given to encourage buyers to provide payment promptly. 2/10 net 30, for example, is a common policy which gives buyers a two percent discount if the account is paid within 10 days. "Net 30" indicates that the balance is due within 30 days. If the account is not paid within 30 days, interest may be charged.

Seasonal Discounts are used to encourage buyers to make their purchases off-season. This strategy may provide needed cash to the seller, reduce inventories or help to smooth out production scheduling.

Allowances are price reductions which are intended to achieve specific goals. Trade-in allowances may make financing a purchase easier for the buyer. Promotional allowances are used to secure reseller participation in advertising and sales support programs intended to boost product sales.

Break-Even Analysis allows managers to estimate the impact of alternative price levels on profits. The Break-Even Point is the price at which total revenue just equals total costs. When sales exceed the break-even level for a given price, each successive unit sold generates profit.

Total Revenue = Price x Quantity Sold

Total Costs = Fixed Costs + (Variables Cost per Unit x Qty. Sold)

$$\text{Break-Even Pt. (Units)} = \frac{\text{TOTAL FIXED COSTS}}{\text{PRICE} - \text{VARIABLE COST PER UNIT}}$$

Each price level has its own break-even point. The value of break-even analysis stems from its usefulness in evaluating pricing options. It should not, however, be relied on as the sole basis for setting prices. The assumptions implicit in using straight line total revenue and total cost curves are not realistic. If they were, profits would continue to grow indefinitely once the break-even point was surpassed. Break-even analysis represents one additional perspective on price setting that should be incorporated with other cost-based, demand-based, and competition-based pricing strategies.

8 MARKETING EVALUATION AND CONTROL

SALES ANALYSIS

Sales analysis provides a study of the firm's net sales and total sales volume. This type of analysis is performed for each product line and for each significant market, sales territory, or market segment. This type of in-depth analysis uncovers the core strengths and weaknesses of the firm. Once areas of concern are identified, management can obtain additional information to identify the causes of success and failure. Information obtained through this process can subsequently be applied to decisions regarding similar situations.

Two types of comparisons provide useful means of evaluating the sales performance of marketing units: **Sales v. Goals** and **Market Share Analysis**. Comparing sales results to sales goals indicates the firm's level of success against its own standards. To assess the strength of a firm relative to its competitors, market share analysis is used. Both the current position and recent trends in sales and market share are important considerations. These comparisons may be used for individual product lines, markets, or sales territories.

9 MARKETING APPLICATIONS IN SPECIAL FIELDS

INTERNATIONAL MARKETING

Any firm which markets products outside its own country is engaged in international marketing. The essentials of marketing are applicable throughout the world. Success in international marketing is contingent on creating a marketing mix which matches the needs and preferences of the target market. The complexity of international marketing operations stems from the need to understand differences between countries and cultures. Among the cultural differences which may impact on the marketing plan of a firm are language, family structure, social customs, religion, and educational systems. Government policies may also pose substantial barriers to trade with other countries.

There are several types of intermediaries which can be used to enter foreign markets. Firms may engage the services of import-export intermediaries who provide expertise in international operations. This option requires very little investment on the part of the exporter. Firms willing to commit more resources to international ventures may establish company-owned sales branches in foreign countries. Firms committed to operations in a foreign country may establish wholly-owned foreign subsidiaries.

NONPROFIT MARKETING

Marketing principles and practices are applied within a wide range of nonprofit organizations. Nonprofit marketing applications include the marketing of **Persons, Ideas**, and **Organizations**. In contrast to business firms, nonprofit organizations pursue nonfinancial, social, and service objectives. They also differ from "for-profit" ventures by their need to attract volunteer labor and financial contributions. Consequently, nonprofit groups need to satisfy two distinct target markets: donors/supporters and clients/recipients of their services. In addition, their objectives often include gaining the approval and support of society at-large for their causes as well as their organizations.

DIRECT MARKETING

Direct Marketing refers to any system which distributes products or services from the producer to the consumer without the use of channel intermediaries. It provides a direct channel of distribution. Direct Marketing relies heavily on advertising media to initiate sales contacts with prospective buyers. The most frequently-used media options include direct mail (e.g., catalog sales), telephone solicitation ("telemarketing''), and direct response broadcast advertising. Direct response broadcast advertising utilizes radio and television messages which feature toll free (1-800) telephone numbers. Print media may also be used in conjunction with toll free telephone numbers and reply cards as means of securing customer orders. In-home television shopping channels and interactive computer shopping services are also increasing in popularity.

All types of organizations use direct marketing methods to sell a growing array of products. One of the primary advantages of direct marketing is greater efficiency in targeting prospects. Mailing lists, for example, can narrowly target virtually any market of interest. In contrast to traditional forms of promotion, direct marketing techniques provide sellers with more immediate response as a measure of effectiveness.

PRACTICE
TEST 1

CLEP PRINCIPLES OF MARKETING
Test 1

(Answer sheets appear in the back of this book.)

Section 1

TIME: 45 Minutes
50 Questions

> **DIRECTIONS**: Each of the questions or incomplete statements below is followed by five possible answers or completions. Select the best choice in each case and fill in the corresponding oval on the answer sheet.

1. The production of a new car model includes which of the following activities?

    (A) Predicting the types of cars different types of people will buy

    (B) Actually making the car

    (C) Determining the features of the car

    (D) Selling the car

    (E) Developing a sales promotion campaign for the car

2. The term "micro-macro dilemma" means that

    (A) people have a hard time making choices between products.

    (B) every economy needs a macro-marketing system but not necessarily a micro-marketing system.

    (C) what is good for some producers may not be good for society as a whole.

    (D) satisfying a customer's wants and needs is difficult because the consumer may not know what his/her wants and needs are.

    (E) it is difficult to determine consumer tastes in the globally diverse marketplace.

3.　The standardization and grading functions of marketing involves

(A)　conducting surveys to gather information.

(B)　storing products until customers can use them.

(C)　determining the sizes and fonts of type which will be used in creating advertisements.

(D)　distribution of products from one place to another.

(E)　sorting products according to size and quality.

4.　Ogden Parts Inc. has named a new sales manager with responsibilities for market planning. Ogden's president thinks the sales manager should sell more parts and outsell the competition. It seems that this company is run as if it were in the

(A)　sales era.

(B)　production era.

(C)　marketing company era.

(D)　simple trade era.

(E)　marketing department era.

5.　The "four Ps" of a marketing mix are

(A)　Product, Price, Profit, Promotion.

(B)　People, Product, Place, Promotion.

(C)　Promotion, Production, Price, Place.

(D)　Product, Price, Place, Promotion.

(E)　Profit, Place, Price, Product.

6.　The role of price in a market-directed economy is to

(A)　determine the sale prices of clearance items in a retail store.

(B)　serve as a rough measure of the value of resources used to produce goods and services.

(C)　ensure no consumer pays prices that are too high.

(D)　determine the amount of losses that can be sustained by a company.

(E)　allocate profits to companies even though they may not be providing the most desirable goods and services.

7. Which of the following statements about marketing is FALSE?

   (A) Marketing attempts to affect the products and services you buy.

   (B) Marketing does not apply to non-profit organizations.

   (C) Advertising and sales-promotion marketing functions.

   (D) Marketing can affect the prices you will pay for a product.

   (E) Marketing includes decisions about how to sell products.

8. Family units in Smallisland Country make all the products they consume. This is an example of

   (A) an economy where marketing is efficient.

   (B) a pure market-oriented economy.

   (C) a planned economy.

   (D) an economy where the role of middlemen is important.

   (E) a pure subsistence economy.

9. Tariffs are

   (A) taxes on imported products.

   (B) predetermined prices planned by several competing companies.

   (C) rules on the amount of products which can be imported.

   (D) extra money paid to officials for favored status.

   (E) illegal in the United States.

10. As XYZ Company produces larger quantities of watches, the cost of producing each watch goes down. This is known as

    (A) micro-marketing.   (D) marketing concept.

    (B) possession utility.   (E) transaction efficiency.

    (C) economies of scale.

11. The Magnuson Act of 1975 says that

    (A) producers of goods must warrant their products as merchant-able.

(B)   a written warranty reduces the responsibility of a producer.

(C)   producers must provide a clearly written warranty.

(D)   each product must be identified with a readable electronic code.

(E)   goods must be clearly labeled and easy to understand.

12.   When marketers focus on comparing their product versus a competitor's product; they

(A)   formulate a SWOT analysis.

(B)   should be concerned with total product offering.

(C)   look at the relative quality.

(D)   Both B and C.

(E)   All of the above.

13.   One would consider an intangible deed performed by one party for another party at a cost as a

(A)   supply.   (D)   perishable good.

(B)   service.   (E)   Both B and D.

(C)   good.

14.   Which of the following is NOT true about the three types of convenience products (staples, impulse products, and emergency products)?

(A)   Staples are products which are bought routinely, without much thought.

(B)   With impulse products, much of the buyer's behavior affects place utility.

(C)   Customers shop extensively when purchasing these items.

(D)   Emergency products are purchased when urgently needed.

(E)   With staples, branding helps customers cut shopping efforts.

15.   New product planning is becoming increasingly important in a modern economy because

(A)   most profits go to innovators or fast companies that quickly copy products from other companies.

(B)   it is not always profitable JUST to sell "me-too" products.

(C)   the failure rate of new products is becoming increasingly low.

(D)   every product must pass FTC laws to be bought and sold.

(E)   All of the above are true.

16.   A capital item (a necessary element in setting price) is

(A)   a building or other type of major equipment.

(B)   office supplies purchased by the individuals.

(C)   raw materials that become part of the physical good.

(D)   long-lasting products that can be depreciated.

(E)   Both A and D.

17.   Which of the following symbols is a trademark?

(A)   (D)   All of the above.

(B)      (E)   None of the above.

(C)

18.   Which of the following are characteristics of a good brand name?

(A)   Always timely (does not become out-of-date)

(B)   Adaptable only to television media

(C)   One that has no "jingle" to it

(D)   Can not be remembered easily

(E)   Makes labeling and packaging incompatible

19.   Packaging is of importance to marketers because

(A)   it provides better shelf placement in grocery stores.

(B) packaging costs over 95% of a manufacturer's selling price.

(C) the Federal Packaging and Labeling Act holds restrictions on packaging sizes.

(D) new packages can make a difference in a new marketing strategy.

(E) labels are inaccurate, and no one reads them anyway.

20. What level of familiarity exists when a consumer buys paper clips for the office, and she/he does not notice the brand name of the product?

(A) Brand rejection (D) Brand preference

(B) Brand recognition (E) Brand insistence

(C) Brand non-recognition

21. Some customers feel that certain brands of refrigerators are very similar and have the same attributes. By shopping for the best price, or lowest price, what kinds of products are these?

(A) Specialty products (D) Regularly-sought products

(B) Heterogeneous products (E) Homogeneous products

(C) Convenience products

22. A company that needs to buy cushioning protection for their porcelain figurines for shipping had only two alternatives in the past. The company could either buy plastic air bubble sheets or styrene peanuts from various firms. Recently, the company became aware of Renature—a new (2 months in production), one-hundred percent biodegradable, protective cushioning product. Renature was listed in the Federal Trade Commission report as being solely produced by a German firm named Storopack. In product testing, Renature was found to be quite pleasing to a growing number of environmentally-conscious consumers. The company decided to use Renature. In general, in what part of the product life cycle would Renature be placed?

(A) Market growth (D) Market awareness

(B) Market maturity (E) Sales decline

(C) Market introduction

23. Which of the following statements is NOT true about the product life cycle?

    (A) As industry sales rise, industry profits also rise.

    (B) Each stage may have a different target market.

    (C) In general, competition tends to move toward pure competition.

    (D) Industry profits start to decrease in market growth.

    (E) A and D.

24. Which statement is correct about the market growth stage?

    (A) Industry profits tend to increase in the beginning of the stage.

    (B) Industry profits decrease toward the end of the stage.

    (C) More companies enter into the industry.

    (D) Industry sales increase.

    (E) All the above are correct statements.

25. When "E.T." was the major motion picture hit of the season in 1985, marketers sold tremendous amounts of "E.T." related merchandise. However, the "E.T." buying frenzy sharply declined to zero when the movie was no longer playing in theaters. Which of the following terms best describes what occurred with the buying of "E.T." merchandise?

    (A) Fashion   (D) A and B

    (B) Style   (E) B and C

    (C) Fad

26. Which of the following is NOT true?

    (A) A patent must be registered to be legally recognized.

    (B) Patent infringement lawsuits can take months and sometimes years to get settled.

    (C) Patents seem to be often disregarded by foreign producers.

    (D) Patents offer 100% protection for producers.

    (E) All of the above are true.

27. Mingilton Meats increased the price of their bologna from $2.00 a pound to $3.00 a pound. After doing this they noticed a decrease in total revenue. This is because

   (A) the demand for the meat is elastic.

   (B) the demand for the meat is inelastic.

   (C) the demand is unitarily elastic.

   (D) the meat was too old to purchase.

   (E) Cannot tell from the information given.

28. The Yearous Group saw an increase in total revenue when they decreased the price of their golf bags. The marketing manager can assume that the demand is

   (A) unitarily elastic.   (D) All of the above.

   (B) elastic.   (E) None of the above.

   (C) inelastic.

29. A potato farmer in Alamosa, Colorado, would be likely to have which type of demand for his potato crop?

   (A) Inelastic demand

   (B) No demand; everyone buys potatoes from Idaho

   (C) Elastic demand

   (D) Unitary elasticity of demand

   (E) All of the above.

30. Bob opened a new restaurant featuring "Crab Legs Ala Bob." As he experimented with the price of the offering he found that no matter if he raised or lowered his price, the total revenue from the "Crab Legs Ala Bob" stayed the same. He could conclude that his product had what kind of elasticity?

   (A) He can draw no conclusions from the information given.

   (B) His demand is elastic.

   (C) His demand is inelastic.

   (D) He has a situation where there is unitary elasticity.

   (E) He should sell shrimp.

31. Bliss Art Supplies is trying to decide whether they should sell paint to end users or final consumers. Currently, 60% of their business goes to organizations that utilize the paint to produce other products. This figure would change to 45% if the business decides to sell to the final consumer, who would receive 55% of the business. If Bliss decides to sell to the final consumer they would be going into a new line of business called

    (A) wholesaling.   (D) service selling.

    (B) retailing.   (E) personal selling.

    (C) rack jobbing.

32. Given the following choices, which is NOT considered a retailing activity?

    (A) The Alpha Kappa Psi Fraternity sells coffee to faculty members in the morning at a local college.

    (B) Because your car broke down you are forced to call a "Tow Truck" to tow your car to be fixed, for which you are charged $50.

    (C) A soap company salesperson comes to your door and sells you $10 worth of soap.

    (D) You purchase a new suit at Macy's Department Store for $259.00.

    (E) All of the above are examples of retailing.

33. Which of the following are true?

    (A) For a product to be considered new by the FTC, the product must be less than a year old.

    (B) The majority of new product ideas do not make it to market.

    (C) Most firms need to continually develop new products to survive.

    (D) A and C.

    (E) B and C.

34. Ben and Jerry's is in the idea evaluation stage of a new ice cream flavor called "candied apples." In this stage the company needs to

    (A) make estimates of the costs and profits associated with the new flavor.

    (B)   use concept testing for the "candied apples" flavor.

    (C)   produce the "candied apple" flavor ice cream and test market it.

    (D)   A and B.

    (E)   All of the above are true.

35.   Disposable diapers, which are not biodegradable, are what type of new product opportunity?

    (A)   Desirable products   (D)   Deficient products

    (B)   Pleasing products   (E)   Salutary products

    (C)   Performance products

36.   Which of the following statements could occur in market maturity?

    (A)   Industry sales become stable.

    (B)   Profits can increase for an individual company.

    (C)   Individual firms drop out of the industry.

    (D)   Promotion costs rise.

    (E)   All of the above.

37.   An easily biodegradable plastic wrap would be which of the following?

    (A)   Desirable product   (D)   Deficient product

    (B)   Pleasing product   (E)   Salutary product

    (C)   Performance product

38.   John Randall is a purchasing agent for a rather large delivery service. John has just agreed to purchase a 1992 Chevy van from his brother's construction company, although he has never driven it or seen it. This buying approach would be an example of

    (A)   description buying.

    (B)   test buying.

    (C)   inspection buying.

    (D)   sampling buying.

    (E)   negotiated contract buying.

39. Which of the following is NOT part of the Multiple Buying Influence, when making a decision to buy a new copy machine in a business?

    (A) General public

    (B) Influencer

    (C) Buyer

    (D) Decider

    (E) Gatekeeper

40. By definition, "Price" is

    (A) the sticker on a product that suggests a price.

    (B) what is charged for something (product or service).

    (C) calculated by dividing cost with retail selling price.

    (D) the term used by marketers defining the cost of a product.

    (E) profit-oriented.

41. Sally Rudolph is selling a new shirt, which she made, to her friend for $1,000. The shirt cost Sally $400. What is her markup?

    (A) $40

    (B) $100

    (C) $300

    (D) $400

    (E) $600

42. If Bob Peters sells a set of steak knives for $1,000, and he has a markup (or selling price) of $600, what is his markup percent?

    (A) 10%

    (B) 20%

    (C) 50%

    (D) 60%

    (E) Cannot be determined from the information given.

43. What is the retail price if the cost of a product is $400, and the markup percent on retail selling price is 60%?

    (A) $1,000

    (B) $2,000

    (C) $450

    (D) $550

    (E) $600

44. Ron and Dee own a floor tile retail outlet. They want to achieve a 40% markup at retail for all of the merchandise that they sell. If one style of floor tile retails at $3 per tile, what is the maximum that Ron and Dee can pay for the tile?

   (A) $3.10

   (B) $3.00

   (C) $2.00

   (D) $1.80

   (E) Cannot be determined from the information given.

45. Pake Productions wants to markdown a new line of speakers that they have in the stores. After they are marked down, Pake Productions wants to calculate the markdown percentage. If the original price of the speakers was $200, and the new price of the speakers is $160, what is the markdown percent?

   (A) $40.00

   (B) $50.00

   (C) 25%

   (D) 20%

   (E) Both C and D are correct.

46. Ogden & Ogden receive an invoice for $100, which they pay in nine days. The terms on the invoice indicate 2/10 net thirty. How much money did Ogden & Ogden send to the seller?

   (A) $100   (D) $2.00

   (B) $98   (E) $96.45

   (C) $102

47. Making goods and services available in the right quantities and locations when the customer wants them is the definition for which one of the following marketing mix variables?

   (A) Promotion   (D) Price

   (B) Place   (E) None of the above.

   (C) Product

48. Alarid Company purchases goods from a manufacturer who then turns around and sells them to a retailer who sells them to final customers. The Alarid Company is participating in a(n)

    (A) Regrouping Activity.   (D) Bulk-Breaking Project.

    (B) Accumulating Activity.   (E) None of the above.

    (C) Channel of Distribution.

49. A type of channel system is

    (A) Direct.   (D) Both A and C.

    (B) Middlemen.   (E) None of the above.

    (C) Indirect.

50. Companies that make little or no effort to cooperate with each other and do what is considered to be in their own best interest describes what type of channel system?

    (A) Corporate channel system

    (B) Vertical integration

    (C) Administered channel system

    (D) Traditional channel system

    (E) None of the above

Section 2

TIME: 45 Minutes
         50 Questions

DIRECTIONS: Each of the questions or incomplete statements below is followed by five possible answers or completions. Select the best choice in each case and fill in the corresponding oval on the answer sheet.

51. ABC Corporation sells only to wholesalers who give their product special attention. ABC Corporation is practicing what type of distribution?

(A) Selective distribution

(D) Ideal market exposure

(B) Intensive distribution

(E) None of the above.

(C) Exclusive distribution

52. A selective distribution policy might be used to avoid selling to wholesalers or retailers who

(A) have a poor credit rating.

(B) have a reputation for returning too many products.

(C) place orders that are too small.

(D) do not do a satisfactory job in selling products.

(E) All of the above.

53. Turner Corporation sells its product to several competing channels that will reach the same target market. Turner Corporation is using what type of distribution?

(A) Exclusive distribution

(D) Both A and B.

(B) Intensive distribution

(E) None of the above.

(C) Dual distribution

54. Which statement best describes why Dual Distribution is becoming more common with producers and retailers?

(A) It is best applicable for convenience products and business suppliers.

(B)   Retailers want large quantities with a lower price per unit.

(C)   Present channel members are doing an excellent job.

(D)   Both A and C.

(E)   All of the above.

55.   Which statement best describes the duties of a channel captain?

(A)   A manager who helps direct the activities of a whole channel.

(B)   One who tries to avoid channel conflicts.

(C)   Arranges for the necessary functions to be performed.

(D)   All of the above.

(E)   None of the above.

56.   What are the two basic types of conflicts in channels of distribution?

(A)   Horizontal and vertical

(B)   Discrepancy of quantity and assortment

(C)   Assorting and sorting

(D)   Both B and C.

(E)   None of the above.

57.   Within the industrial mix, the product variable places a great deal of emphasis on

(A)   price.   (D)   distribution.

(B)   services.   (E)   sales promotion.

(C)   environmental influences.

58.   In regard to industrial marketing, the following example best exemplifies what type of pricing? "The seller determines the price (or a series of prices) for a given product, and the customer pays that specified price."

(A)   Bid pricing   (D)   Retail pricing

(B)   Negotiated pricing   (E)   Economic pricing

(C)   Administered pricing

59. Services that cannot be seen, touched, tasted, smelled, or possessed are examples of what kind of services?

    (A) Perishable   (D) Intangible

    (B) Not-for-profit   (E) Inseparable

    (C) Heterogeneous

60. Advertising can make industrial customers aware of

    (A) new products or brands.   (D) representatives.

    (B) product features.   (E) All of the above.

    (C) organizations.

61. Which of the following statements is NOT true when developing a marketing strategy?

    (A) It allows flexibility in providing for customer service.

    (B) It allows the hiring of high quality personnel.

    (C) It may help to resolve problems in regard to service.

    (D) It provides for the use of high technology, allowing for lower cost services.

    (E) None of the above.

62. If an organization is conducting marketing activities other than for the goals of profit, market share, or return on investment (ROI), these marketing activities are referred to as

    (A) a waste of time.   (D) promotional marketing.

    (B) non-business marketing.   (E) non-marketing activities.

    (C) strategic marketing.

63. Which channel of distribution is being utilized if products are sold directly from the producer of the goods to the final consumer?

    (A) Industrial distribution   (D) Horizontal distribution

    (B) Production distribution   (E) Intermediary distribution

    (C) Direct distribution

64. What psychological influences within an individual are best described as basic forces that motivate a person to do something?

    (A) Drive

    (B) Needs

    (C) Wants

    (D) Attitudes

    (E) Self-esteem

65. Which of the following choices is NOT a level in the hierarchy of needs?

    (A) Money needs

    (B) Safety needs

    (C) Physiological needs

    (D) Social needs

    (E) All of the above are levels in the hierarchy of needs.

66. Which of the following choices best defines a change in a person's thought processes caused by prior experience?

    (A) Cue

    (B) Response

    (C) Learning

    (D) Belief

    (E) Reinforcement

67. In marketing, an analysis of a person's day-to-day patterns of living is referred to as a person's AIOs, which are also known as

    (A) Awareness, Interests, Opinions.

    (B) Activities, Interests, Opinions.

    (C) Actions, Incentives, Objections.

    (D) Actions, Integrity, Observations.

    (E) Awareness, Incentives, Observations.

68. The people to whom an individual looks when forming attitudes about a particular topic is a definition of

    (A) social class.

    (B) opinion leaders.

(C) reference groups.

(D) culture groups.

(E) None of the above are correct for the given definition.

69. Which of the following is NOT one of the five steps in a problem-solving process?

(A) Memorize your plan of action.

(B) Recall and gather information on solutions.

(C) Evaluate alternative solutions.

(D) Evaluate the decisions.

(E) Become aware of the problem.

70. Which of the following is the best example of a product a consumer would consider under the extensive problem-solving process?

(A) Milk   (D) Toilet paper

(B) Washing machine   (E) T-shirt

(C) Pair of shoes

71. Which of the following is NOT one of the steps in the adoption process?

(A) Confirmation   (D) Decision

(B) Trial   (E) Payment

(C) Awareness

72. Which of the following is NOT a function of channels of distribution?

(A) Alleviating discrepancies in assortment

(B) Alleviating discrepancies in quantity

(C) Providing customer service

(D) New product development

(E) Creating utility

73. Which of the following is NOT a regrouping activity used by channel specialists to adjust discrepancies?

    (A) Assorting   (D) Bulk-Breaking

    (B) Accumulating   (E) Sorting

    (C) Transforming

74. The use of two or more channels to distribute the same product to the same target market is known as

    (A) Direct distribution.

    (B) Indirect distribution.

    (C) Dual distribution.

    (D) Strategic distribution.

    (E) None of the above are correct for the definition provided.

75. _____ is the combining of two or more stages of the channel under one management where each channel member is seen as an extension of their own operations.

    (A) Strategic Alliances

    (B) Horizontal Channel Integration

    (C) Reverse Channels

    (D) Oligopoly

    (E) Vertical Channel Integration

76. Which type of distribution would best be used for products such as soap, food, and personal care products when consumers desire wide availability of the products?

    (A) Intensive distribution   (D) Horizontal distribution

    (B) Exclusive distribution   (E) Selective distribution

    (C) Vertical distribution

77. Which type of distribution technique used a single outlet in a fairly large geographic area to distribute a product or service such as Jaguar and Rolls-Royce Automobiles?

(A) Selective   (D) Exclusive

(B) Universal   (E) None of the above.

(C) Intensive

78. A group of individuals and organizations that direct the flow of products from producers to customers are

(A) marketing intermediaries.   (D) marketing management.

(B) middlemen.   (E) None of the above.

(C) marketing channels.

79. Forbidding an intermediary to carry products of a competing manufacturer is known as

(A) tying agreement.   (D) strategic channel alliance.

(B) monopoly.   (E) vertical marketing system.

(C) exclusive dealing.

80. _____ can be described as the ability of one channel member to influence another member's goal achievement.

(A) Reward power   (D) Referent power

(B) Expert power   (E) Channel power

(C) Legitimate power

81. When designing products, the most fundamental level of a product which answers the question: What is the buyer really buying? is

(A) tangible product.   (D) brand name.

(B) core product.   (E) quality level.

(C) augmented product.

82. Tangible goods that normally survive many uses (last long) and may require more personal selling and service, command a higher margin, and require more seller guarantees are called

(A) convenience goods.   (D) durable goods.

(B) nondurable goods.   (E) shopping goods.

(C) unsought goods.

83. Goods that the consumer does not know about or knows about but does not normally think of buying, such as cemetery plots, are called:

    (A) convenience goods.

    (B) nondurable goods.

    (C) unsought goods.

    (D) durable goods.

    (E) shopping goods.

84. A brand or part of a brand that is given legal protection because it is capable of exclusive appropriation is called:

    (A) brand name.

    (B) copyright.

    (C) brand mark.

    (D) trademark.

    (E) None of the above.

85. Which of the following choices is an example of a manufacturer's brand?

    (A) Heinz ketchup

    (B) Diehard batteries

    (C) Craftsman tools

    (D) Kenmore appliances

    (E) All of the above.

86. A strategy that consists of the seller's development of two or more brands in the same product category is called

    (A) brand repositioning decision.

    (B) brand extension decision.

    (C) multibrand decision.

    (D) family brand decision.

    (E) brand quality decision.

87. A product's immediate container is called the

    (A) primary package.

    (B) shipping package.

    (C) secondary package.

    (D) cardboard box containing a bottle.

    (E) labeling.

88. Another name for manufacturer's brand is

(A) private brand.

(D) distributor brand.

(B) dealer brand.

(E) middleman brand.

(C) national brand.

89. Which of the following statements is NOT a reason for downward stretching the product line?

(A) The company is attacked at the high end and decides to counterattack by invading the low end.

(B) The company finds that slower growth is taking place at the high end.

(C) The company at the lower end of the market may want to enter the higher end.

(D) The company initially entered the high end to establish a quality image and intended to roll downward.

(E) The company adds a low-end unit to plug a market hole that would otherwise attract a new competitor.

90. The set of all product lines and items that a particular seller offers for sale to buyers is called

(A) marketing mix.

(D) tangible products.

(B) product mix.

(E) augmented products.

(C) packaging.

91. A tariff is a(n)

(A) limit on the amount of goods the importing country will accept in certain product categories.

(B) tax levied by the foreign government against certain imported products.

(C) total ban on some kinds of imports.

(D) method of entering a foreign market in which the company enters an agreement with a license.

(E) tax levied by the government against certain exported products.

92. The two major economic factors that reflect a country's attractiveness as an export market are

    (A) industrial structure and income distribution.

    (B) political stability and attitudes.

    (C) cultural environment and government bureaucracy.

    (D) joint venturing and direct investment.

    (E) contract manufacturing and management contracting.

93. Which of the following economies creates a new rich class and a small, but growing, middle-class that both demand new types of imported goods?

    (A) Subsistence economy

    (B) Raw-material-exporting economy

    (C) Industrialized economy

    (D) Industrializing economy

    (E) None of the above.

94. Which of the following market income distributions would best suit sales of a Lamborghini (an automobile costing in excess of $50,000)?

    (A) Very low family incomes

    (B) Mostly low family incomes

    (C) Very low and very high family incomes

    (D) Low, medium, and high family incomes

    (E) Mostly medium family incomes

95. The simplest way to enter a foreign market is through

    (A) joint venturing.   (D) direct investment.

    (B) licensing.   (E) exporting.

    (C) management contracting.

96. Marketing a product in a foreign market without any change to the product is called

(A) straight extension.

(B) product adaptation.

(C) product invention.

(D) communication adaptation.

(E) dual adaptation.

97. Which form of entry into a foreign market causes the most risk?

(A) Exporting

(D) Licensing

(B) Joint venturing

(E) Direct investment

(C) Joint ownership

98. Which type of joint venturing offers a low-risk method of getting into a foreign market, and yields income from the beginning?

(A) Licensing

(D) Joint ownership

(B) Contract manufacturing

(E) Both A and B are correct.

(C) Management contracting

99. With the high regulation of the U.S. government before the 1980s, carriers of products did not compete in the area of _____ as they do now.

(A) promotion

(D) product

(B) price

(E) service

(C) place

100. Which of the following types of products would have the highest percentage of total cost in transportation?

(A) Electronic equipment

(D) Gravel

(B) Pharmaceuticals

(E) Phone service

(C) Manufactured food

CLEP PRINCIPLES OF MARKETING
TEST 1

ANSWER KEY

Section 1

1.	(B)	14.	(C)	27.	(A)	39.	(A)
2.	(C)	15.	(B)	28.	(B)	40.	(B)
3.	(E)	16.	(E)	29.	(C)	41.	(E)
4.	(A)	17.	(D)	30.	(D)	42.	(D)
5.	(D)	18.	(A)	31.	(B)	43.	(A)
6.	(B)	19.	(D)	32.	(E)	44.	(D)
7.	(B)	20.	(C)	33.	(E)	45.	(E)
8.	(E)	21.	(E)	34.	(D)	46.	(B)
9.	(A)	22.	(C)	35.	(B)	47.	(B)
10.	(C)	23.	(A)	36.	(E)	48.	(C)
11.	(C)	24.	(E)	37.	(A)	49.	(D)
12.	(D)	25.	(C)	38.	(A)	50.	(D)
13.	(B)	26.	(D)				

Section 2

51.	(A)	64.	(B)	77.	(D)	89.	(C)
52.	(E)	65.	(A)	78.	(C)	90.	(B)
53.	(C)	66.	(C)	79.	(C)	91.	(B)
54.	(B)	67.	(B)	80.	(E)	92.	(A)
55.	(D)	68.	(C)	81.	(B)	93.	(D)
56.	(A)	69.	(A)	82.	(D)	94.	(C)
57.	(B)	70.	(B)	83.	(C)	95.	(E)
58.	(C)	71.	(E)	84.	(D)	96.	(A)
59.	(D)	72.	(D)	85.	(A)	97.	(E)
60.	(E)	73.	(C)	86.	(C)	98.	(C)
61.	(E)	74.	(C)	87.	(A)	99.	(B)
62.	(B)	75.	(E)	88.	(C)	100.	(D)
63.	(C)	76.	(A)				

DETAILED EXPLANATIONS OF ANSWERS

TEST 1

Section 1

1. **(B)** The key word in the question is "production." Because production involves the making of the product, choice (B) is correct. Predicting the types of cars different people will people will buy (A), determining the features of the car (C), selling the car (D), and developing a sales promotion campaign for the car (E) are marketing activities and are not correct answers.

2. **(C)** Macro-marketing looks at the marketing function in relation to society as a whole while micro-marketing looks at activities of individual organizations. The dilemma occurs when marketing efforts of individual producers may not be good for society, therefore (C) is the correct choice. Answers (A), (B), (D), (E), while in part may seem to be correct statements, do not relate to society as a whole. Thus, they are not examples of the macro-micro dilemma.

3. **(E)** There are eight universal functions of marketing: buying, selling, transporting, storing, standardization and grading, financing, risk taking, and market information. The standardization and grading function involves sorting products according to size and quality. Therefore, (E) is the correct answer. Answers (A), (B), and (D) relate to other functions of marketing, and (C) is a creative decision in advertising.

4. **(A)** With an emphasis on selling more parts and outselling the competition, the company is run as if it were in the sales era. (A) is the correct choice. The production era (B) focused on the production of products. The marketing company era (C) is a time when companies embraced the marketing concept. The simple trade era (D) was when middlemen were introduced in the early role of marketing involving simple distribu-

tion. The marketing department era (E) tied together various marketing efforts under one department.

5.   **(D)**   The "four Ps" of a marketing mix are product, price, place, and promotion. These are the controllable variables a company applies in their marketing strategy. (D) is the correct choice. The remaining answers (A), (B), (C), and (E), while they contain portions of the marketing mix and elements important in marketing strategy, are not correct answers.

6.   **(B)**   Prices in a market-directed economic system vary to allocate resources and distribute income according to consumer preferences, so price is a rough measure of the value of resources used to produce goods and services. (B) is the correct answer. The remaining choices (A), (C), (D), and (E) relate to decisions which may be utilized in some pricing strategies and tactics but do not relate to the role of price at the macro-level of a market-directed economy, and are incorrect choices.

7.   **(B)**   Marketing applies to both profit and non-profit organizations. Although a non-profit's primary objective may not be to seek profit, the firm still wants to satisfy customer needs, consequently the priorities will be different than a for-profit organization. The correct answer is (B). The remaining sentences about marketing are true. Marketing affects products and services that are bought (A) as well as product prices (D). Advertising and sales promotion are areas in the marketing mix (Promotion) (C) and marketing decisions would include how to sell products.

8.   **(E)**   In a pure subsistence economy family units make all the products they consume, therefore (E) is correct. In this type of economy no marketing takes place because marketing doesn't occur unless two or more parties are willing to exchange something for something else, consequently, (A) is incorrect. In a planned economy, government makes all decisions about the production and distribution of products and services, therefore (C) is not the correct choice. In a pure subsistence economy, there is no need for middlemen, since marketing does not occur. (D) is not a correct choice.

9.   **(A)**   Tariffs are taxes on imported products, therefore (A) is the correct choice. Answer (B) describes "price-fixing" an action sometimes taken by companies which is considered illegal in the United States. Quotas are quantities of products which can be moved in or out of a country (C) and is not the correct answer. Extra money paid to officials for favored

status is bribery and is illegal in the United States, therefore (D) is not a correct answer. Tariffs are legal as long as all regulations are followed. (E) is not the correct answer.

10. **(C)** The question relates to a definition. Economies of scale means that as a company produces larger quantities of an item, the cost of producing each watch goes down. (C) is the correct answer. Micro-marketing looks at marketing as a set of activities, (A) is incorrect. Possession utility is having the right to use a product, (B) and is not correct. The marketing concept looks at satisfying customers needs. (D) is not correct. Transaction efficiency is not an "official" marketing term although it may be used to describe a process, thus, (E) is not correct.

11. **(C)** Along with the FCC guidelines, the Magnuson Act of 1975 ensures that warranties are clear and definite—not deceptive or unfair. The Act states that producers must provide a clearly written warranty, therefore (C) is the correct choice. U.S. Common Law says (A) producers of goods must warrant their products as merchantable. Although it may reduce the responsibility of the firm (B) that was not the ruling of the Magnuson Act. The UPC code which identifies products with a readable electronic code was developed to speed the handling of fast-selling products (D). The Federal Fair Packaging and Labeling Act of 1966 required goods to be clearly labeled and understandable (E).

12. **(D)** When marketers compare their product to competitors' offerings they are concerned with the quality and satisfaction of the total product (B, C). A SWOT analysis (A) is a comparison of a company's strengths vs. weaknesses, and opportunities vs. threats, rather than comparing single products. This eliminates (A) and (E) as possible correct answers.

13. **(B)** A deed performed by one party for another at a cost is a service. (B) is the correct choice. (A) Supplies are expense items that do not become a part of a finished product and are tangible. You can't "hold" a service, therefore, (C) would be an incorrect answer. (A) is not the correct choice. A perishable good (D) is one that is subject to spoil, such as food. Consequently (D) is not the correct choice. Because the correct answer is (B), choice (E) is not correct.

14. **(C)** Convenience products are products a customer needs but is not willing to shop around for, therefore (C) is an incorrect choice, be-

cause when it comes to convenience products, customers DO NOT shop extensively. The three types of convenience products are staples, impulse products, and emergency products. Staples are products which are bought routinely without much thought. Therefore (A) is a correct statement. If a buyer does not see an impulse product at the right place, the sale will be lost. Therefore (B) is a true statement, buyer behavior does affect place utility with impulse products. Because they are usually purchased in emergency situations, emergency products are purchased when urgently needed. (D) is a correct statement. (E) is also true. Branding does help customers cut shopping efforts and encourages repeat buying of satisfactory brands.

15.   **(B)**   In today's modern economy, market competition and product life cycles are changing at a fast pace. The product life cycle shows a firm needs different marketing mixes as a product moves through the cycle. It may no longer be profitable *just* to sell "me-too" products; firms need to expand their offerings, therefore B is the correct choice. Most of the profits do not go to innovators (A) as profits rarely occur in the product introduction phase. Moreover, the failure rate of new products is high, not low (C), since only 2% of new products make it to market. The FTC ensures that products are safe for public use, (D) but does not play a part in the planning of a new product. Since (D), (A), and (C) are incorrect choices, (E) would be eliminated as a correct answer.

16.   **(E)**   Customers pay for the capital items when they buy it, but for tax purposes the cost is spread over a number of years. Therefore a long-lasting product that can be depreciated (D) is a capital item. An example of a capital item is an installation, buildings, land rights, or major equipment in any business or company (A), thus (E) is the correct answer. Office supplies purchased by individuals are not long lasting, nor would a person depreciate office supplies over a number of years, therefore, (B) is not correct. Raw materials (C) are not considered capital items, rather they are expense items.

17.   **(D)**   All of the symbols are legally registered for the use of a single company. A trademark includes those words, symbols, or marks like (A), (B), and (C). By officially registering their seal, a company is protected legally from those who try to copy the label. Trademarks do not even need to be a word, they can be a symbol (C). (E) is incorrect because all the symbols are trademarks.

18. **(A)** Brand names help build brand familiarity and that is why marketers want to create a brand that is always timely, and promotes a positive image. (A) is the correct answer. Brand names should be adaptable to all advertising mediums, not just to television (B). A brand with no jingle (D) makes it harder for consumers to recognize the product. Last, (E) is incorrect since a product should be adaptable in its packaging and labeling needs. The easier a company can convert its brand name onto all of its products and create brand familiarity, and recognition, the better the brand name is. The purpose of a brand is to help consumers remember the product, so (D) is not the correct choice.

19. **(D)** By meeting customers needs better, a better package can help create a "new" product for a "new" market. The packaging of a product (A) does not provide better shelf placement. Consumer demand and extra money paid for shelf space dictate the shelf placement of a product. (B) The average packaging costs are between 1 and 70% rather than over 95%. The Federal Packaging and labeling act (C) does not hold restrictions on packaging—rather its various laws provide general guidance on packaging issues and the producers can choose whether or not to abide by them. If consumers do not understand the terminology, labeling can become misleading, but the statement that labels are inaccurate and no one reads them (E) is not true. Many labels are correct and many people do read labels.

20. **(C)** Brand nonrecognition means that final consumers do not recognize a brand at all. (C) is the correct answer. Brand rejection (A) occurs when a customer refuses to buy a certain brand. Brand recognition (B) happens when customers remember the brands they buy. Brand preference (D) means that customers choose one brand over other brands, perhaps out of habit. Brand insistence (E) occurs when customers insist on a firm's branded products and are willing to search for it by any means. Hence the example in the question clearly demonstrates a customer who is exhibiting brand nonrecognition (C).

21. **(E)** Shopping products the customer sees as basically the same are homogeneous—customers do not think the brand differences are important, they just look at the price. (E) is the correct answer. Specialty products (A) are those that the customer really wants and makes a special effort to find—it does not involve comparing prices or brands. Convenience products (C) are those that a customer needs but is not willing to spend much time shopping for—often bought on an impulse, no compar-

ing is used here either. Regularly sought products (D) is not a division of product class. This term may be confused with regularly unsought products which are a division of product class.

22. **(C)** Market introduction is the correct answer. Renature is a new product which means the product must be less than six months old according to the FTC, and thus being new Renature is not all that widely known. In addition, Renature is only produced by the firm Storopack. A product that is new as well as having only one producer, a monopoly, characterizes the market introduction phase of the product life cycle. (A), market growth, is not correct because in market growth there would be more than one producer of Renature. (B) is not correct because in market maturity the product should be well-known in addition to having more than one producer. (D) is not correct because market awareness is not a stage in the product life cycle. (E) Sales decline is also not the correct product life cycle state for Renature. However, if we were classifying styrene peanuts or plastic air bubble sheets, the sales decline stage would be correct, since in this stage many competitors exist in addition to new products, such as Renature, replacing the old.

23. **(A)** is the correct answer because it is the only statement that is entirely not true. Just because industry sales rise doesn't mean that industry profits will also rise. Increased competition among individual companies within the industry could prompt lower selling prices in the industry which would lead to lower profits for the industry. Increased sales could also prompt expensive investments in capital equipment which would decrease profits if the individual firms are already operating at full capacity. (B) is not the correct answer because the statement is true. Customers' attitudes as well as needs will change over time. Thus, a customer who bought the product in the past may no longer have need for the product, or a customer who previously didn't have a need for the product may acquire a need for the product (target markets may change). (C) is also not correct because the statement is true. Once a product proves its profit potential, everybody will want to sell the product to get a piece of the "profit pie." (D) is also incorrect because the statement is true. Growth refers to sales growth, not necessarily profit growth. Remember, competition enters in this stage, which, in general, tends to decrease profits. (E) is also not correct because although (D) is true, (A) is not true.

24. **(E)** is correct because all of the above statements are correct. Industry profits initially do increase (A), but later industry profits start to

decline (B). Also, more companies enter the industry because they see that industry profits initially are increasing (C). Furthermore, industry sales increase (D) because of heightened consumer awareness. (A), (B), (C), and (D) are all correct, consequently, (E) is the correct answer.

25. **(C)** Fad is the correct answer because a fad only attracts a certain group of people for a fairly short time. In the case of "E.T.," the merchandise attracted children—but only for a short time. (A) is not correct because a fashion is longer lived than a fad. (B) is also not correct because a style tends to come back over time. (D) is an incorrect choice since neither (A) or (B) are correct choices. (E) is incorrect because while the merchandise was a fad, it wasn't a style.

26. **(D)**   is not a true statement because although patents do offer some protection for producers, they do not offer 100% protection, especially when foreign producers often disregard U.S. patents. Because the questions asks for the statement that is not true, (D) is the correct answer. Choice (A) is a true statement and therefore an incorrect choice, because a patent must be registered to be legally recognized. Patent courts are tremendously backlogged. By the time the case is settled, the offending company could already be out of business, consequently, (B) is a true statement and not a correct choice. Patents seem to be flagrantly disregarded by foreign producers, therefore (C) is an incorrect choice. (E) is not correct because while (A), (B), and (C) are true statements, (D) is not true.

27. **(A)** The demand is elastic. Any increase in price that creates a decrease in total revenue is said to be elastic. (B) is not correct, because in order for the demand to be inelastic the total revenue would have to have increased. (C) Unitary elasticity occurs when the total revenue stays the same when the price of a product is changed. (D) There is not enough information given to know whether or not the meat is old. (E) Elasticity can be determined from the information given, so (E) is incorrect.

28. **(B)**   is the correct answer, the demand is elastic. When a firm or organization reduces their price, and total revenues increase (or stretch), the demand is said to be elastic. (A) is incorrect. In order for the demand to be unitarily elastic, the revenue would have to stay the same. (C) Inelasticity would occur if the total revenue decreased in conjunction with a decrease in price. (D) and (E) are both incorrect. You cannot have elasticity and inelasticity at the same time, and in the example, revenue of the Yearous Group showed an increase, while the price was dropped.

29.   **(C)**   is the correct answer. The farmer's crop would most likely be elastic. If the farmer dropped his price, more people would buy his potatoes. Potatoes are a commodity where people shop for the "best buy." (A) is incorrect because the total revenue would, in all likelihood, increase, not decrease, with a price reduction. (B) is incorrect because people shopping for potatoes are price conscious, and shop for the least expensive. (D) is incorrect because the total revenue would not stay the same with an increase or decrease in price for this type of product. (E) cannot be true because demand must be elastic, inelastic, or have unitary elasticity.

30.   **(D)**   Bob would find himself in a situation with unitary elasticity. When raising or lowering the price of your product has no effect on total revenue, the situation is said to have unitary elasticity of demand. (A) is wrong because Bob can make a conclusion about demand. (B) is also incorrect because if the demand were elastic, if the price was dropped, total revenues would increase, and if the price were raised total revenues would decrease. (C) is also wrong because if it were inelastic, when Bob tried to lower his price he would find that his total revenue would also be lower, yet if he raised his price, his total revenue would increase. (E) With the information given, we don't know whether he should sell shrimp.

31.   **(B)**   Any organization that sells over 50% of their total product revenue to the final consumer is said to be a retailer, by US government definition. Wholesaling is selling the majority of the business's product or service to intermediaries, which is what Bliss is doing currently, so (A) is incorrect. Rack jobbing is performed by intermediaries, usually in a supermarket or grocery store, so (C) is incorrect. (D) is incorrect because the art supply store is not selling a service, per se, they are selling a physical product. And although Bliss is utilizing personal selling to help push the product, they are actually not in the line of business called personal selling, so (E) is incorrect.

32.   **(E)**   All of the above are examples of retailing. Retailing refers to the selling of products and services to the final consumer. (E) is correct. (A) is a good example of retailing at a college level, with the final consumer being the faculty at the college. (B) is also a type of retailing, although not a pleasant one for the car owner. (C) is door-to-door retailing involving selling a product to a final consumer. (D) is probably the most common type of retailing, where the final consumer goes directly to the point-of sale for a product.

33. **(E)** is correct because both (B) and (C) are true. Because of the difficulties encountered with bringing new product ideas to market, the majority of new product ideas never reach consumers (B). For most firms, if they don't develop new products, all the firm's products will eventually become obsolete, and the company will be forced to go out of business, so (D) is also correct. (A) is not true because the FTC requires a product to be less than six months old to be considered new. (D) is not true because while (C) is true, (A) is not true.

34. **(D)** is correct because Ben and Jerry's must look at the costs and estimated profits to decide if the flavor is feasible (A). In addition, in concept testing, Ben and Jerry's must determine if the customers not only think that the "candied apples" flavor will be appealing but also if they would be willing to pay a premium price for this flavor of ice cream. Concept testing is an integral part of idea evaluation (B). (A) and (B) are true, consequently, (D) is correct because it states that both answers are true. (C) is not true because making and test marketing the actual product is the development stage. (E) is not correct because while (A) and (B) are true, (C) is false.

35. **(B)** is correct because pleasing products are not good for the long run consumer welfare but do give immediate satisfaction. Disposable diapers satisfy the parents' need for convenience but are not good for the environment and thus are not good for the long run consumer welfare. (A) is not correct because a desirable product gives immediate satisfaction and is good for long run consumer welfare. (C) is not correct because performance products are not a type of new product opportunity. (D) is not correct because deficient products do not satisfy long run consumer welfare or provide immediate satisfaction. (E) is not correct because salutary products are good for long run consumer welfare but do not give the consumer immediate satisfaction.

36. **(E)** is the correct answer because industry sales do level off in market maturity (A). Profits can increase for a particular company if they have a marketing mix that appeals to consumers (B). (C) is correct because some firms are not efficiently using their product and thus can't compete in the price wars of their more efficient competitors, so they drop out of the industry. Promotion costs rise (D) because firms want to promote their product as different, or they want to remind consumers about the product and its uses to keep sales from falling.

37. **(A)** is correct because biodegradable wrap is good for the environment in the long run and provides immediate satisfaction for our need to cover our food in the microwave as well as the refrigerator. Desirable products are good for the long run consumer welfare and provide immediate satisfaction. (B) is not correct because pleasing products are not good for the long run welfare but do provide immediate satisfaction. (C) is not correct because performance products are not a new type of product opportunity. (D) is not correct because deficient products neither satisfy long run consumer welfare nor provide immediate satisfaction. (E) is not correct because salutary products are good for long run consumer welfare but do not provide immediate satisfaction.

38. **(A)** This is a question of evaluating which type of buying method is being used in the process of purchasing a product for this company. The descriptive buying method is a form of buying a product through a written or verbal description and is often done without inspection. This purchase is usually based on a mutual trust between buyers and sellers and is used to reduce the cost of buying; (A) is the correct choice. There is no such thing as test buying, although it does sound good, so (B) is an invalid answer. Inspection buying is the process of inspecting every item before you buy it; (C) is not the best choice. Sampling buying means looking at only part of the potential purchase, making the assumption that the whole purchase will be of the same standards; (D) is not correct. Negotiated contract buying means agreeing to a contract to purchase, but the contract allows for changes in the purchasing arrangements; (E) is an incorrect choice.

39. **(A)** The Multiple Buying Influence means several people—perhaps even top management—share in making a purchase decision. Because the question pertains to a business, the general public would not influence the decision to purchase a copier. (A) is the correct choice. The next four choices are all part of the Multiple Buying Influence. An influencer (B) could be an engineer or research person who helps to write specifications or supply information for evaluating alternatives. A buyer (C) could be a purchasing agent who has the responsibility for working with suppliers and arranging terms of the sale. Deciders (D) are people in the organization who have the power to select or approve the supplier. A Gatekeeper (E) is a person who controls the information throughout the whole organization.

40. **(B)** The business exchange function in a market driven society involves giving an object or service to someone in exchange for money.

Money is the price. (A) is incorrect because it is a starting point for price negotiation. Many times wholesalers and retailers are willing to change the "Price" in exchange for quantity purchases, to get rid of out-of-season merchandise, and many other reasons. Price is not calculated by dividing cost by selling price, thus (C) is incorrect. Cost is how much the product or service "costs" or is paid for, by the intermediary or manufacturer. Adding a markup to that figure gives a price, thus (D) is not correct. And (E) is not correct because price may be driven by something other than profit, such as sales.

41.   **(E)**   is the correct choice. The shirt would be marked up $600. To calculate the amount of markup, you use the formula Amount of Markup = Selling Price − Cost. If the shirt sold for $1,000, and the cost to Sally was $400, then $1,000 − $400 = $600. (A), (B), (C), and (D) are incorrect.

42.   **(D)**   is the correct answer. Percent markup based upon selling price is calculated by taking the amount of the markup and dividing into that the selling, or retail, price. (A) is incorrect because 600/1,000 = 60%, not 10 percent. Likewise with (B) and (C). Amount of Markup/Selling Price − Percent Markup, thus the answer can be determined, and (E) is incorrect.

43.   **(A)**   is the correct choice. If the cost of a product is $400, and the markup percent on the retail selling price is 60%, then, by formula, the selling price is $1,000. The calculation can be made by taking the cost of the product and subtracting out 1 minus the percent of selling price. Thus (B), (C), (D), and (E) are incorrect. $400/1 − .60 = $1,000.

44.   **(D)**   is the correct answer. In order to calculate the minimum cost, the formula Retail Sales Price = Cost + Markup is used. (A) is incorrect since the amount is over the retail price. Likewise (B) is incorrect because the retail price is $3, so Ron and Dee cannot make any money if they sell the product for $3. (C) is incorrect since (.4 = $3 − Cost/$3) which equals ($1.20 = $3 − Cost). $3.00 − $1.20 = $1.80. $1.80 is the maximum amount that Ron and Dee can pay per tile and still expect to achieve at least a 40 percent markup. (E) is incorrect because the maximum amount per tile can be calculated utilizing the above information.

45.   **(E)**   is the correct answer. If Pake Productions utilizes the new price for the speakers, $160, then their markdown would be 25%. If they utilize the original price as the denominator, then the markdown percentage is 20%. (A) and (B) are both incorrect as they are dollar amounts, not

percentages. While 25% (C) is a good answer for calculating the markdown percentage on the new selling price (Amount of Markdown/New Sales Price, or, $40/$160), it is not the most correct. Likewise with (D); if Pake calculated the markdown on the original price ($40/$200) this would be the correct answer, although it is not the correct answer for the question. The markdown calculation depends on the accounting system being used. Both markdown methods are common.

46. **(B)** is the correct choice. The terms on an invoice 2/10 net 30, indicate that the buyers will get a two percent discount if they pay the bill early. This is to increase the amount of cash flow for the seller, and to encourage early payment of bills. (A) is not the correct choice. If Ogden & Ogden had paid the bill after the ten day period, this would have been the amount they owed. (C) is also incorrect. However, if Ogden & Ogden had paid the bill after the 30 day net, they may have owed this interest depending on the payment terms agreed upon with the buyer and seller. (D) and (E) are simply not correct. The Ogden & Ogden Company would not have paid that amount based upon the terms of the invoice.

47. **(B)** Place is the correct answer. By definition, Promotion (A) is communicating information between seller and potential buyers. Product (C) is the need satisfying offering of a firm. Price (D) is what is charged for something. Consequently, making goods and services available in the right quantities and locations describes Place (B), the correct choice and (E) is therefore not correct.

48. **(C)** A channel of distribution is any series of firms or individuals who participate in the flow of goods from producer to final user, therefore, (C) is the correct choice. Regrouping activities (A) adjust the quantities and assortments of products handled. Accumulating (B) involves collecting products from many small producers. Bulk-breaking (D) involves dividing larger quantities into smaller quantities. Because (C) is the correct choice, (E) would be incorrect.

49. **(D)** Two types of distribution are direct and indirect. In a direct system, the manufacturer or service provider sells directly to the end user. In an indirect system, the manufacturer or service provider sells to the end users through the use of intermediaries. Both (A) and (C) are correct answers. Middlemen (B) are considered the wholesalers of the industry, (B) is not a correct answer. (E) is incorrect because the best answer is (D).

50. **(D)** Traditional channel systems make little or no effort to cooperate with each other. (D) is the correct answer. A corporate channel system (A) occurs when the corporation owns the businesses along the channel. Vertical integration (B) describes a company that has acquired firms at different levels of channel activity. An administered channel system (c) occurs when the channel members formally agree to cooperate with each other. Because (D) is the correct answer, (E) cannot be correct.

Section 2

51. **(A)** Selective distribution occurs when a company only sells through middlemen who will give the product special attention, consequently, (A) is the correct answer. Intensive distribution (B) occurs when a company sells a product through all responsible and suitable retailers who will stock and sell the product. Exclusive distribution (D) occurs when a company sells through only one middleman in a particular geographic area. Ideal market exposure (D) makes a product available widely enough to satisfy target customer's needs. Because (A) is the correct choice (E) cannot be correct.

52. **(E)** All of the factors listed are reasons for a company to have a selective distribution policy. These factors can harm a business if their customers are companies that continually practice these actions. When a company chooses selective distribution, they have a preference to deal with other companies that do not have the traits as described in (A), (B), (C), or (D).

53. **(C)** Dual distribution occurs when a producer uses several competing channels to reach the same target market, (C) is the correct answer. Exclusive distribution (A) means that a company sells through only one middleman or one channel. Intensive distribution (B) means selling products through all responsible and suitable sellers. Since (A) and (B) are both incorrect, (D) would not be correct. (E) would also be an incorrect answer because (C) is correct.

54. **(B)** Dual distribution occurs when a producer uses several competing channels to reach the same target market. A reason this occurs is that retailers want large quantities with a lower price per unit, (B) is the best choice. Dual distribution is not needed for convenience products and

business suppliers, these types of products are best served by intensive distribution because customers want these products available everywhere. One of the reasons a producer moves toward dual distribution is that current channel members are doing a poor job, so (C) is not a correct answer. (D) is not correct because both (A) and (C) are incorrect and therefore, (E) cannot be correct either.

55. **(D)** All of the above statements describe the duties of a channel captain. Their responsibility is to control and/or avoid channel conflicts. They help direct activities of the channel as a whole. Because (A), (B), and (C) are correct, (E) cannot be a correct answer.

56. **(A)** Horizontal and vertical conflicts are the two basic types of conflicts in channels of distribution. Horizontal conflicts occur between firms at the same level in the channel of distribution. Vertical conflicts occur between firms at different levels of the channel of distribution. (A) is the correct answer. Discrepancy of quantity (B) means the difference between the quantity of products it is economical for a producer to make and the quantity final users or consumers want. Discrepancy of assortment means the difference between the lines a typical producer makes and the assortment final consumers or users want. Assorting (C) means putting together a variety of products and sorting means separating products into grades. (D) is not a correct choice because both (B) and (C) are incorrect and (E) is not correct because (A) is the correct answer.

57. **(B)** is the correct choice. Services included are on-time delivery, quality control, custom design, nationwide distribution systems along with technical advice. (A) is incorrect because prices are often elastic, requiring the firm to price at or near the prices of their competitors. This keeps prices stable. (C) is also incorrect. Industrial marketing is unique for environmental services, but is not the MOST emphasized area. The distribution emphasis is just to make sure products are available, so (D) is not the correct answer. And even though there is an element of sales promotion in an industrial setting, this is not the most emphasized element of the industrial mix, thus (E) is incorrect.

58. **(C)** The example shows administered pricing so (C) is the correct choice. In administered pricing the seller sets the price and the buyer pays that listed price. If a price is determined through the use of sealed or open bids, it is called bid pricing. Thus, (A) is incorrect. In negotiated pricing, there is a stated list price; however, discounting is used to entice

purchases. (B) is therefore incorrect. This is not a retail situation, so retail pricing is an incorrect answer (D). (E) economic pricing is where the business' environment has an impact on the amount of price set more so than the seller, so this is a wrong choice.

59. **(D)** If you cannot see, touch, taste, smell, or possess a service it is said to be intangible, thus (D) is the correct choice. Perishable services cannot be stockpiled or inventoried, yet they may be touched, smelled, or tasted, so (A) is not the best answer. (B) Not-for-profit organizations may offer services, but this is not a services category. Furthermore, a service offered by a not-for-profit group MAY have the traits of touch, smell, etc., thus (B) is an incorrect choice. Heterogeneity (C) refers to not performing consistently, and is wrong. Inseparability (E) refers to the fact that services are normally produced at the same time they are consumed, so it is not the best answer.

60. **(E)** Advertising can make customers aware of all of these areas, thus (E) is the correct answer. Advertisements allow customers to become aware of new products or brands which they may not otherwise be aware of (A). Additionally, advertising allows the customer to become exposed to product features (B). Advertising can expose potential customers to organizations (C) and customer representatives (D). In summary, advertising is used to reach customers for all of the reasons listed in the answer.

61. **(E)** None of the above. Marketing strategy can help to develop flexibility in providing additional customer service, so (A) is incorrect. Marketing strategy provides a road map, giving the marketers a direction and showing what types of expertise are needed, thus facilitating the hiring of high quality personnel (B), so this answer is not correct. Effective strategy planning is proactive in giving solutions to potential problems, thus (C) is also not true. An effective marketing strategy plan can provide for the utilization of high technology to decrease overall service costs to customers, so (D) is also not true.

62. **(B)** Marketing activities undertaken by groups without an objective of profit, ROI, or market share are called non-business marketing activities. An example of such an activity may be a beer manufacturer running an ad campaign to reduce teen age drinking. (A) is incorrect because they are not, or should not, be a waste of time. They may be providing useful information to the listener or viewer. (C) is incorrect, although they may be strategic in nature the purpose is non-business.

Promotional marketing activities (D) refers to activities and processes undertaken as a part of the promotional mix (i.e., advertising, public relations, sales promotion, selling) and is incorrect. (E), non-marketing activities, is incorrect, because these are marketing functions and activities.

63. **(C)** Any goods sold directly from the producer to the final consumer is said to be a direct distribution channel. Direct distribution is not used as much as indirect distribution with consumer goods, because of the high cost associated with it. Direct distribution from an intermediary to a final consumer would be more common. Industrial distribution (A) refers to an independent business organization that takes title to products, and carries inventory, and is an incorrect choice. Production distribution (B) is also incorrect. Horizontal distribution (D) refers to the "type" of distribution channel and level of business, and is incorrect. Intermediary distribution (E) would deal with intermediaries, or middlemen, and would not be a direct method of distributing a product, and is thus wrong.

64. **(B)** This question deals with psychological influences in an individual that are of great interest to marketers. Needs (B) are basic forces that motivate a person to do something, therefore (B) is the best answer. A drive (A) is a strong stimulant that encourages action to reduce a need. Wants (C) are needs that are learned during a person's life. Attitudes (D) are defined as a person's point of view toward something. Self-esteem (D) deals with how an individual perceives him/herself.

65. **(A)** Although many people think money is very important, it is not a level in the hierarchy of needs. (A) is the correct choice. Safety needs (B) are concerns about personal protection and well-being and are a level in the hierarchy of needs. Physiological needs (C) are needs for food, drink, rest, and sex and are a level in the hierarchy of needs. Social needs (A) are needs for love, friendship, status, esteem, and acceptance by others and are also a level in the hierarchy of needs. Since (A) is the answer, (E) would be an incorrect choice.

66. **(C)** The definition of learning is a change in a person's thought processes caused by prior experience, therefore (C) is the correct answer. A cue (A) is a product sign, ad, or other stimuli in the environment. Responses (B) are efforts to satisfy a strong stimulus that encourages action. A belief (D) is a person's opinion about something. Reinforcement (E) occurs when a response is followed by satisfaction. Cue, response, belief, and reinforcement all occur during the learning process.

67. **(B)**   In psychographics or lifestyle analysis, marketers use AIO to analyze people's day-to-day patterns of behavior. A stands for Activities, I stands for Interests, and O stands for opinions, making (B) the correct choice. Any other combinations as in (A), (C), (D), and (E) would be incorrect choices.

68. **(C)**   By definition, reference groups are people to whom an individual looks when forming attitudes about a particular topic, therefore (C) is correct. The definition of a social class is a group of people who have approximately equal social position as viewed by others. Opinion leaders (B) are people who influence others. Culture groups (D) are whole sets of beliefs, attitudes, and ways of doings things in a homogeneous group. Because (C) is the correct choice, (E) cannot be correct.

69. **(A)**   Memorize your plan of action is not included in the five-step problem-solving process, therefore (A) is the correct choice. The five-step process is as follows: Become aware of the problem (E), Recall and gather information on solutions (B), Evaluate alternative solutions (C), Decide on the appropriate solutions, and Evaluate the decision (D).

70. **(B)**   Extensive problem-solving occurs for a completely new or important need involving high involvement in how to satisfy it. The best answer is a washing machine (B), because there is typically high involvement in such a major purchase. Milk (A) and toilet paper (D) are routinized behaviors requiring little involvement. Buying a pair of shoes (C) and T-shirts (E) involve limited problem-solving.

71. **(E)**   The adoption process are the steps people go through on the journey of accepting or rejecting a new idea. Payment (E) is not one of these steps. The six steps are as follows: Awareness (D), Interest, Evaluation, Trial (B), Decision (D), and Confirmation (A).

72. **(D)**   New product development deals with developing ideas for new products and is not a function of channels of distribution, therefore, (D) is the correct answer. Alleviating discrepancies in assortment (A) and in quantity (B) are both function of distribution channels. Because providing customer service is integrated in all aspects of marketing, (C) is also a function. Creating channels of distribution create time, place, and possession utility, so (E) is also a function of distribution.

73. **(C)**   Transforming is not used as a regrouping activity by channel

specialists, therefore (C) is the correct choice. Regrouping activities adjust the quantities and assortments of products handled. Assorting (A) means putting together a variety of products. Accumulating (B) involves collecting products from many small producers. Bulk-breaking (D) involves dividing larger quantities into smaller quantities. Sorting (E) means separating products into grades and qualities desired by the target market.

74. **(C)** Dual distribution is the use of two or more channels to distribute the same product to the same target market. (C) is the correct choice. Direct distribution (A) is an incorrect answer because it involves channels in which products are sold directly from producer to consumer. Indirect distribution (B) is incorrect because there is no classification in channels of distribution called indirect distribution. Strategic distribution (D) occurs when the products of one organization are distributed through the marketing channels of another organization. Because (C) is the correct answer, (E) cannot be correct.

75. **(E)** Vertical channel integration is the combining of two or more stages of the channel under one management. (E) is the best answer. A strategic alliance (A) is a partnership formed to create a competitive advantage on a worldwide bases. Horizontal channel integration (B) deals with combining institutions at the same level of operation. Reverse channels (C) are used to retrieve products that consumers no longer want. An oligopoly is a competitive structure existing when a few sellers control the supply of a large proportion of a product.

76. **(A)** The best type of distribution for this scenario would be intensive distribution, because sellers want the product to be easily reached by everyone. Exclusive distribution (B) is using a single outlet and would not answer the request for availability. Vertical distribution (C) and horizontal distribution (D) are not types of distribution. Selective distribution (E) means using only some available outlets to distribute a product, which also would not satisfy the availability factor.

77. **(D)** The definition of exclusive distribution is using a single outlet in a fairly large geographic area to distribute a product or service, therefore (D) is the correct answer. Exclusive distribution also creates the "mystique" marketers want to make the product more appealing. (A) Selective distribution is used when you want middlemen to give a product special attention. Selective distribution uses many outlets to distribute the product but not as many as intensive. Universal distribution (B) would not

be correct because it is not a distribution classification. Intensive distribution (C) would not be correct because sellers do want the product to be easily reached by everyone. In exclusive distribution, sellers only want the product to be available to those that can afford the product.

78.   **(C)**   A marketing channel is a group of individuals and organizations that direct the flow of products from producers to customers. A marketing intermediary (A) is similar to a middleman, linking producers to buyers, and is not the best choice. Middlemen (B) can be part of a channel, but it does not reflect the entire definition and is not the best choice. Marketing management (D) deals with establishing objective and planning activities in a broad sense. Because (C) is correct, (E) cannot be a correct choice.

79.   **(C)**   Exclusive dealing forbids an intermediary to carry products of a competing manufacturer. A tying agreement (A) requires a channel member to buy other products from a supplier besides the one preferred by the channel member. A monopoly (B) involves a market structure that exists when an organization produces a product that has no close substitutes and becomes the sole source of supply. A strategic channel alliance (D) is a marketing channel that exists when the products of one organization are distributed through the marketing channels of another organization. A vertical marketing system occurs when channel activities are coordinated by a single channel member to achieve efficient, low-cost distribution aimed at satisfying the target market.

80.   **(E)**   Channel power is the ability of one channel member to influence another member's goal achievement. Consequently, (E) is the correct answer. Reward power (A) is one of the five non-economic sources of power and is gained by providing financial benefits. Expert power (B) is also one of the five sources of power which occurs when other channel members believe that the leader provides special expertise required for the channel to function property. Legitimate power (C) deals with displays of power in a superior to subordinate relationship. Referent power (D) occurs when other members strongly identify with and emulate the leader, but it does not deal with the ability to influence channel members.

81.   **(B)**   This question is about the development of a product, where the product planner needs to think about the product on three levels. The most fundamental level is the core product. Choice (B) is correct. A tangible product (A) is what the core product is turned into. The augmented

product (C) is the additional services and benefits that the product planners envision. A brand name (D) is a characteristic of a tangible product. The quality level (E) is also a characteristic of a tangible product.

82.　**(D)**　This question deals with product classification according to their durability or tangibility. Durable goods (D) are the type of goods that can survive many uses, such as refrigerators, stereo systems, and computers. (D) is the correct choice. Convenience goods, unsought goods, and shopping goods are types of goods classified on the basis of consumer shopping habits, not tangibility, which makes choices (A), (C), and (E) incorrect. Nondurable goods (B) are tangible goods, but are normally consumed in one or a few uses so choice (B) is incorrect.

83.　**(C)**　This question deals with a type of good that is classified on the basis of consumer shopping habits. Unsought goods are goods such as smoke detectors which are unsought until the consumer is made aware of them. (C) is the correct choice. Convenience goods (A) are based on consumer shopping habits but are goods purchased frequently, immediately, and with minimum effort. Both nondurable (B) and durable (D) goods are products classified according to their durability or tangibility, not shopping habits. Shopping goods (E) are based on consumer shopping habits but are goods that the consumer knows about and compares with other products.

84.　**(D)**　This question deals with branding which can add value to a product and is an important aspect of product strategy. A trademark protects the seller's rights to use the brand name or brand mark. (D) is the correct choice. A brand name (A) is that part of the brand that can be vocalized. A copyright (B) is the legal right to reproduce, publish, and sell the matter and form of a literary, musical, or artistic work. It is not a brand or part of a brand. A brand mark (D) is that part of the brand which can be recognized but is not able to be vocalized. Because trademark is the correct answer, (E) is incorrect.

85.　**(A)**　This question deals with brand sponsor decisions. Manufacturers' brands dominate the American scene, such as Heinz ketchup. Many manufacturers create their own brand and some even rent well-known brand names by paying royalties. Choices (B), (C), and (D) are all private brands owned by Sears. Sears (a retailer) does not produce many of their products, but rather, contracts with manufacturers to produce these products on their behalf. Thus these are incorrect choices. Because (A) is the best answer, (E) cannot be correct.

86. **(C)** This question deals with the broad topic of brand decisions. A company may be able to use any one of these decisions for their products. The strategy described in this question relates to the multibrand decision, so (C) is the correct answer. Brand repositioning (A) may be needed if a competitor launched a brand that competes directly with an existing product. Brand extension decisions (B) relate to any effort to use a successful brand name to launch product modifications or new products. Family brands (D) are manufacturers who brand their products. Brand quality (E) supports the brand decision in the target market.

87. **(A)** This question deals with product packaging. The primary package is the product's immediate container. (A) is the correct answer. The shipping package (B) refers to the packaging necessary for storage, identification, or transportation. The secondary package (C) is the material that protects the primary package. A cardboard box containing a bottle (D) is an example of a type of secondary package. Labeling (E) is part of the packaging that consists of printed information.

88. **(C)** This question deals with brand sponsor decisions. Manufacturer's brand and national brands are the same. (C) is the correct choice. If a manufacturer sells the product to middlemen, the product is on a private brand (A). Dealer brand (B), distributor brand (D), and middleman brand (E) are all other names for private brand.

89. **(C)** This question pertains to a company's product line-stretching decisions. Line stretching occurs when a company lengthens its product line beyond its current range. A company may stretch downward for any of the above reasons except (C). Therefore, (C) is the correct answer. When a company decides to stretch upward it may be because the company at the lower end of the market may want to enter the higher end (C).

90. **(B)** An organization with several product lines has a product mix. (B) is the correct choice. The marketing mix is the product, price, place, and promotional aspects of marketing decisions. Packaging (C) is the activity of designing and producing the container or wrapper for a product. Tangible products (D) are those products which may have certain characteristics, such as quality level, feature, brand name, styling, and packaging. Augmented products (E) are additional services and benefits.

91. **(B)** is correct. A tariff is a tax levied by the foreign government against certain imported products. (A) is incorrect because that is a quota,

not a tariff. (C) a total ban on some kinds of products is known as an embargo, so it is the wrong answer. When a company enters a foreign market with a license, that is known as licensing, so (D) is not the correct choice. (E) is not the correct choice because it is a tax levied by the government against certain *exported* products, not imported.

92. **(A)** is the right choice because the industrial structure shapes a country's product and service needs, income, and employment levels. The income distribution determines if the income of the population in that country would create a market for the product. These things are economically important. (B) political stability and attitudes and (C) cultural environment and government bureaucracy are not really economic factors that reflect the country's attractiveness. Rather they are factors that are involved in the political-legal attractiveness of the country environmentally. (D) and (E) do not deal with why one does business in a foreign country, they are actually dealing with HOW one does business.

93. **(D)** is correct. An industrializing economy needs more imports of certain products as manufacturing increases. A subsistence economy (A) offers few market opportunities and a rich class seldom exists. A raw-material-exporting economy (B) gains much of their revenues from exporting one particular natural resource, therefore their economy has either a poor class or wealthy upper class. An industrialized economy (C) has varied manufacturing activities and a large middle class. Answer (E) is incorrect because one of the above is true.

94. **(C)** Very low and very high family incomes is the best choice. This is the only income distribution mentioned that has a very high family income, which is needed for the purchase of this product. A family has to have enough wealth, and be status-conscious, to afford and want luxury cars. Very low incomes (A) and Mostly low incomes (B) do not have enough income to provide for a market. (D) is incorrect; even though there is some high family income, it is not high enough to make the purchase of this product. Mostly medium family incomes (E) could not afford these cars.

95. **(E)** Exporting is the simplest way to enter a foreign market because all of the goods are manufactured or produced in the home country. In joint venturing (A) the company has to join with a partner to set up production facilities abroad which help to complicate entry, and dilute control. Licensing (B) and Management contracting (C) are methods, or types, of joint venturing and are not correct. Direct investment (D) has the

biggest involvement because the company develops foreign-based assembly or manufacturing facilities. This makes the entry into the foreign market much more difficult, not simple.

96. **(A)** is correct. Straight extension is the only strategy for marketing a product in a foreign market without any product changes. Product adaptation (B) by definition involves changing the product to meet the local conditions. Certain aspects of the product such as packaging, branding, or labeling can be changed. Product invention (C) consists of creating something new. Both communication adaptation (D) and dual adaptation (E) are promotional strategies, not product strategies, and are incorrect choices.

97. **(E)** direct investment involves the highest risk. Direct investment risks include devalued currencies, falling markets, and government takeover (nationalization). Exporting (A) involves very little risk because the company can passively export surpluses from time to time, or it can actively commit to the country. While joint venturing (B) often gives a company less control, it doesn't involve as much risk as direct investment. (C) joint ownership is a type of joint venturing, and is incorrect. Licensing (D) is also a type of joint venturing, so it is incorrect.

98. **(C)** Management contracting is the best answer because the domestic firm is exporting services rather than products. With licensing (A), the company may give up not only potential profits, but it could also create a competitor when the contract ends. Control manufacturing (B) provides less control over the manufacturing process and a loss of potential profits. Joint ownership (D) provides the risk that the partners could disagree over issues such as investment and marketing strategies. (E) is incorrect since both (A) and (B) are not correct answers.

99. **(B)** Before the 1980s regulation of the country's transportation systems was intense. The federal government set the rates that could be charged by the carriers. Therefore carriers could not compete on price as they do now. The carriers had to compete with the other variables of the marketing mix, and often had increases in promotion (A). The government did not tell the carriers where to ship (C), so that is incorrect. Product offerings (D) and Service offerings (E) are also incorrect because the carriers were competing in these areas to make up for the lack of differences in cost.

100. **(D)** The costs for transportation are usually high for products that are heavy and of low value such as minerals and other raw materials like gravel. While electronic equipment (A) or pharmaceuticals (B) may seem like they would be expensive to ship, they have a relatively high value compared to their light weight. Manufactured food (C) may be considered to have high transport cost because of refrigeration, but these costs don't compare to the high percentage costs related to the transportation of heavy low value goods such as gravel. Phone service (E) transportation costs are almost non-existent as a percentage of total cost.

PRACTICE
TEST 2

CLEP PRINCIPLES OF MARKETING
Test 2

(Answer sheets appear in the back of this book.)

Section 1

TIME: 45 Minutes
50 Questions

DIRECTIONS: Each of the questions or incomplete statements below is followed by five possible answers or completions. Select the best choice in each case and fill in the corresponding oval on the answer sheet.

---

1. Based upon retail selling price, if John Doe wants to figure out the actual amount of markup of a product he plans to retail, he should

    (A) divide the selling price by the cost.

    (B) divide the cost by the selling price.

    (C) subtract the cost from the selling price.

    (D) subtract the cost from the markup.

    (E) Cannot be determined from the information given.

2. With a selling price of $2,000, and a cost of $800, what would the markup (at retail) be for this product?

    (A) $1,000   (D) $800

    (B) $2,000   (E) $1,250

    (C) $1,200

3. Joe Fisherman wants to know his percent markup on retail of a pair of shoes for which he paid $1,000 for. He knows the amount of markup was $600. Which of the following would answer his question?

(A) 40%   (D) 60%

(B) 150%   (E) 100%

(C) 50%

4. The MOLE, a toy retailer, wants to calculate the selling price for some of their stuffed dolls. They know that they paid $400 each for the dolls, and they want a 60% markup on selling price. What should their selling price be?

(A) $640   (D) $1,000

(B) $350   (E) $5,300

(C) $750

5. Jan and Bob Winfield want to calculate the cost of a new chair they just bought. Jan told Bob that the retail selling price of the chair was $1,000, and that the markup percent on the selling price was 60%. What would their cost be?

(A) $1,000   (D) $400

(B) $600   (E) $150

(C) $625

6. The McHenry Store, a retailer of fine clothing, wants to calculate both the cost and selling price of a new suit they received from a fine clothing tailor. The amount of markup on selling price is 20%, and the amount of markup is $100. Can they calculate both the cost and the selling price of the product?

(A) Definitely not; they must have more information.

(B) Certainly; the selling price is $500 and the cost is $400.

(C) Certainly; the selling price is $1,000 and the cost is $400.

(D) Of course they can; the selling price is $500 and the cost is $200.

(E) Yes; the cost is $100 and the selling price is $120.

7. When trying to calculate markup based on product cost, Doc and Den wanted to determine the markup on a product that cost $150 and sold for $200. What is their markup?

(A) $25   (D) $60

(B) $40   (E) $110

(C) $50

8.   What is the percent markup based upon cost for a product that costs $150, and has a markup of $50?

(A) 33.33%   (D) 50%

(B) 35%   (E) Cannot be determined.

(C) 25%

9.   Judy and Dale want to calculate the selling price (on COST) of an item that has a cost of $10.00 and a markup percent on cost of 40%. What is their selling price?

(A) $16.67   (D) $12.00

(B) $10.00   (E) $14.00

(C) $10.50

10. If the retail selling price of an object is $100 and the markup percent on cost is 70%. What is the cost?

(A) $100   (D) $54.45

(B) $65.45   (E) $17.95

(C) $58.82

11. When entering a foreign market, a marketer may need to adapt or modify which of the following promotional methods to meet the culture norms of the target market?

(A) Theme   (D) Media

(B) Copy color (E) All of the above.

(C) Product's name

12. When preparing to market internationally, what is the typical chronological progression (or order) that most companies would follow?

(A) Export department; international division; multinational organization

(B) International division; export department; multinational organization

(C) Multinational organization; international division; export department

(D) Multinational organization; export department; international division

(E) Export department; multinational organization; international division

13. Sugar Bear Fresh Farm Produce is a premium item sold in exclusive stores where freshness and quality are crucial. Which form of transportation should Sugar Bear Fresh Farm Produce utilize in order to get their goods from Colorado to Pennsylvania?

(A) They shouldn't ship that far.

(B) Air

(C) Water

(D) Train

(E) Pipeline

14. Which of the following is not associated with getting the lowest cost by combining small shipments to make one full shipment?

(A) Freight forwarders

(B) Pool car service

(C) Piggyback service

(D) None of the above.

(E) All of the above are true.

15. Which of the following is the best choice when large volumes of goods must be stored regularly?

(A) Private warehouse

(B) Public warehouse

(C) Distribution center

(D) Containerization

(E) All of the above should be utilized to store goods regularly.

16. When Tommy realized his new home did not have a fire detector, he went out immediately and bought a fire protection system. This is an example of

(A) social needs.   (D) safety needs.

(B) physiological needs.   (E) friendship needs.

(C) personal needs.

17. You finally decided (after some coaxing from your friends) that a good way to get into shape is rollerblading. You **suddenly** become aware of television and radio advertisements about rollerblade products. This is an example of

(A) selective retention.   (D) selective exposure.

(B) selective perception.   (E) None of the above.

(C) selective response.

18. Advertising belongs to which aspect of the marketing mix?

(A) Product   (D) Promotion

(B) Price   (E) Perception

(C) Place

19. Which of the following statements is true about advertising?

(A) It can help position a firm's marketing mix to better reach the target market.

(B) It does NOT aid in informing and persuading customers.

(C) It is more flexible than personal selling.

(D) It does NOT have the potential to reach large numbers of prospective customers.

(E) It will become less important as the economy grows.

20. Which of the following will be the best and most effective advertising objective?

(A) To help introduce new products

(B) To increase shelf space in our cooperating retail outlets by 25% during the next 5 months

(C) To help expand market share

(D) To increase interest

(E) To promote the product

21. Which of the following types of advertising develops primary demand for a product category as opposed to demand for a specific brand?

(A) Institutional

(D) Reminder

(B) Competitive

(E) Pioneering

(C) Product

22. Which of the following is the best medium to use to increase interest in a product that requires demonstrating that product's benefits?

(A) Newspaper

(D) Direct mail

(B) Television

(E) Magazine

(C) Radio

23. Which of the following is the best medium for a marketer that wants to target specific individuals directly?

(A) Television

(D) Direct mail

(B) Radio

(E) Outdoor (billboard)

(C) Newspaper

24. Best Value Hardware, a national franchise, embarks on a nationwide ad campaign to run for two months. Rick Esquibel, an owner of a small Best Value Hardware in Allentown, PA, has seen an increase in his store's net sales in the first months of the campaign. Rick has paid a set amount toward the cost of the campaign. This situation is an example of which of the following types of advertising?

(A) Comparative

(D) Institutional

(B) Educational

(E) Pioneering

(C) Cooperative

25. When choosing the best medium to deliver a firm's message, the first and most important factor to be decided is

(A) the package design of the product.

(B) to specify the target market and target audience.

(C) to choose the most expensive medium because the most money spent will guarantee the greatest effectiveness.

(D) the products' placement in a store.

(E) the medium the competitive producers are using.

26. The effectiveness of an advertising medium depends on all of the following except

(A) a firm's promotional objectives.

(B) the funds available for advertising.

(C) the nature of the media.

(D) what target markets a firm wants to reach.

(E) the compensation of the sales representatives.

27. The message that the words and illustrations of an ad should communicate is described as the ad's

(A) advertising allowance.

(B) copy thrust.

(C) AIDA concept.

(D) target audience.

(E) medium.

28. Which type of new product test is most likely to answer the questions: "How does the customer perceive the product?" and "Who would use the product?"

(A) An internal test

(B) A concept test

(C) Commercialization

(D) Weighted point system

(E) Non-weighted point system

29. The process of offering a product for sale on a limited basis in a defined geographic area in order to gauge consumer reaction to the actual product is known as

(A) selected controlled markets.

(B) store audits.

(C) standard markets.

(D) test markets.

(E) None of the above.

30. What is meant by commercialization of a new product?

(A) Create a product prototype.

(B) Test the product and product strategy in the marketplace.

(C) Position and offer the product in the marketplace.

(D) Identify the new product niche.

(E) None of the above.

31. Which of the following are NOT examples of support goods?

(A) Services

(B) Supplies

(C) Installations

(D) Accessory equipment

(E) All of the above are examples of support goods.

32. The manufacturing of a telephone, using various raw materials, is an example of what type of utility?

(A) Task

(B) Possession

(C) Time

(D) Form

(E) Place

33. In macro-marketing, which of the following eight universal functions of marketing have to be performed?

(A) Buying

(B) Transporting

(C) Marketing information

(D) All of the above.

(E) None of the above.

34. The marketing concept came to the forefront of American business during which of the following eras?

    (A) Simple trade era

    (B) Marketing department era

    (C) Production era

    (D) Sales era

    (E) Marketing company era

35. Which of the following is NOT a step in the approach to segmenting *product-markets*?

    (A) Name the possible product markets.

    (B) List the potential customer needs.

    (C) Estimate the size of the product market segments.

    (D) Form a heterogeneous market.

    (E) All of the above are steps in the process.

36. Which of the following is the best example of product development?

    (A) American Express increased advertising expenditures to encourage customers to use the card when they went out to dinner, not just for shopping.

    (B) To reach new customers, Taco Bell opened new retail outlets in airports, office buildings, zoos, and hospitals.

    (C) Suave boosted sales by introducing a new line of shampoo products.

    (D) Nintendo purchased Cover Girl and expanded into cosmetic products.

    (E) None of the above are good examples of product development.

37. A routine repurchase that may have been made many times before is called

    (A) New-task buying.   (D) Purchase.

    (B) Straight rebuy.   (E) None of the above.

    (C) Modified rebuy.

38. Employers hire buying specialists. These specialists are called what?

    (A) Purchasing agents

    (B) Sales managers

    (C) Order takers

    (D) Order getters

    (E) Any of the above.

39. By evaluating suppliers and how they are working out for a company, buyers can make better (and more informed) decisions. A formal rating of suppliers on all relevant areas of performance is called a(n)?

    (A) evaluation.

    (B) check-list.

    (C) vendor analysis.

    (D) subjective interpretation.

    (E) buyer analysis.

40. Multiple buying influence means that several people share in making purchase decisions. These people are called

    (A) users.

    (B) buyers.

    (C) influencers.

    (D) gatekeepers.

    (E) All of the above.

41. What type of buying is required for non-standardized products that require careful examination?

    (A) Negotiated contract buying

    (B) Inspection buying

    (C) Sampling buying

    (D) Description buying

    (E) Routinized response buying

42. Which of the following is the first step in undertaking a marketing research project?

    (A) Define the problem.

    (B) Solve the problem.

    (C) Collect problem-specific data.

(D)   Analyze the situation.

(E)   Define a sample.

43.   Which of the following steps of the market research process typically takes over half of the time in completing the research?

(A)   Problem definition

(B)   Situational analysis

(C)   Data collection

(D)   Problem-solving

(E)   Alternative development

44.   A research proposal

(A)   is stated right after the problem is defined.

(B)   is a plan that specifies what information will be obtained and how.

(C)   can include information about costs.

(D)   Only (A) and (C) are correct.

(E)   Only (B) and (C) are correct.

45.   Which of the following research methods require the most care in interpreting the results?

(A)   Random sampling

(B)   Mail surveys

(C)   Telephone surveys

(D)   Personal interview surveys

(E)   All of the above.

46.   Marketing research

(A)   should be planned by research specialists who understand research techniques better than marketing managers.

(B)   consists mainly of survey design and statistical techniques.

(C) is only needed by producers who have long channels of distribution.

(D) is needed to keep isolated marketing managers in touch with their markets.

(E) should not be an on-going process.

47. Marketers are always concerned about demographics. In that regard, in the next 20 years, the world's population is expected to nearly double and the population of the United States is expected to

(A) be maintained at its current growth rate.

(B) slow dramatically—less than one percent a year during the decade.

(C) continue to grow at an increasing rate—more than one percent a year during the decade.

(D) stop altogether.

(E) grow at the rate of sixteen percent.

48. The birthrate in the United States is currently

(A) starting to drop because more couples are waiting to have children.

(B) rising sharply due to the returning Persian Gulf soldiers starting new families.

(C) rising sharply due to the abundance of women at the child-bearing age.

(D) dropping because more women are entering the workforce and there is less of a want for large families.

(E) Both (A) and (D) are correct.

49. The United States

(A) and England have the highest divorce rate in the world—about 45% of marriages end in divorce.

(B) has the lowest divorce rate in the world—about 12% of marriages end in divorce.

(C) has the highest divorce rate in the world—about 38% of marriages end in divorce.

(D) and England have the lowest divorce rate in the world—about 24% of marriages end in divorce.

(E) has a divorce rate of about 13%.

50. A widely available measure of the output of the whole economy and the total market value of goods and services produced in a year in the United States is called

(A) economic systems.

(B) gross domestic product.

(C) gross sales.

(D) gross margin.

(E) gross national product.

Section 2

TIME: 45 Minutes
          50 Questions

> **DIRECTIONS**: Each of the questions or incomplete statements below is followed by five possible answers or completions. Select the best choice in each case and fill in the corresponding oval on the answer sheet.

51.   The income that is left after taxes for a family to make payments on necessities is called

   (A)   gross profit.

   (B)   disposable income.

   (C)   net profit.

   (D)   discretionary income.

   (E)   family income.

52.   Sales promotion refers to promotion activities that stimulate interest, trial, or purchase by consumers. It would thus include activities other than

   (A)   advertising.

   (B)   publicity.

   (C)   personal selling.

   (D)   point-of-purchase materials.

   (E)   only (A), (B), and (C) are correct.

53.   The three basic promotional objectives are

   (A)   encoding, decoding, and receiving.

   (B)   personal selling, mass selling, and sales promotion.

   (C)   innovating, adopting, and nonadopting.

   (D)   attention, interest, and action.

   (E)   informing, persuading, and reminding.

54.   Managers who are satisfied with their current market share and profit situation sometimes adopt "status quo" objectives. Which of the following phrases would not be used in status quo pricing?

(A) Meet competition.

(B) Stabilize prices.

(C) Avoid competition.

(D) Slightly raise prices.

(E) Promote more aggressively.

55. During the communication process, the same message may be interpreted differently by the various audiences. How the message is translated by the buyer/receiver is called

(A) decoding.   (D) source.

(B) encoding.   (E) receiver.

(C) noise.

56. The adoption curve, which shows how products are adopted once introduced into the market place, defines several different groups, and how they accept ideas. The largest percentage of adopters fall into which group(s)?

(A) Innovators   (D) Late majority

(B) Early adopters   (E) Laggards or nonadopters

(C) Early and late majority

57. "Pulling" a product through the distribution channel refers to

(A) using normal promotional efforts in order to help sell the whole marketing mix to possible channel members.

(B) getting customers to ask intermediaries (or middlemen) for the product.

(C) promotion to employees.

(D) using only one promotion "blend" for all situations.

(E) using highly expensive and aggressive promotions.

58. Selective demand for a company's own brand would most likely occur in which stage of the product life cycle?

(A) Market introduction

(D) Sales decline

(B) Market growth

(E) Competition decline

(C) Market maturity

59. An example of a sales promotion activity aimed at a final consumer or user could be

(A) banners and streamers.

(D) bonuses.

(B) promotional allowances.

(E) training materials.

(C) sales contests.

60. Trucks are expensive, but much more flexible than other types of transportation modes. Approximately what percentage of consumer products travel from the producer to the final consumer by truck?

(A) 25%

(D) 66%

(B) 50%

(E) 75%

(C) 33%

61. By handling large quantities, railroads are able to transport goods at which of the following prices?

(A) Approximately 10-15 cents per ton

(B) Approximately 5-10 cents per ton

(C) Approximately 3-4 cents per ton

(D) Approximately 3-4 cents per half ton

(E) Approximately 13 cents per ton

62. Truckers compete with railroads for high-value items. In the United States, the cost of trucking is which of the following?

(A) 10-15 cents per ton

(D) 3-4 cents per half ton

(B) 5-10 cents per ton

(E) 13 cents per ton

(C) 3-4 cents per ton

63. The firm can vary its marketing mix through the storing function of physical distribution in which of the following ways?

(A)   Adjusting the time the goods are held

(B)   Sharing the storing costs

(C)   Delegating the job to a specialized storing facility

(D)   All of the above.

(E)   None of the above.

64.   Storing is the marketing function of holding goods. Which economic utility(ies) does it provide?

(A)   Time

(B)   Place

(C)   Possession

(D)   Ownership

(E)   All of the above.

65.   Which of the following examples is not a factor that affects physical distribution (PD) levels?

(A)   Advance information on delays

(B)   Back-order procedures

(C)   Time to enter and process the orders

(D)   All of the above affect physical distribution levels.

(E)   None of the above affect physical distribution levels.

66.   When groups of shippers pool their shipments together, what is this called?

(A)   Containerization

(B)   Piggyback service

(C)   Pool car service

(D)   Diversion in transit

(E)   Birdyback service

67.   When evaluating consumer behavior, which of the following is/are considered to be an economic need?

(A)   Economy of purchase or use

(B)   Efficiency in operation or use

(C)   Improvement of earnings

(D)   All of the above.

(E)   Only (A) and (B).

68. In relation to Maslow's hierarchy of needs, the need for self-esteem, accomplishment, fun, freedom, and relaxation are attributed to which of the following needs?

    (A) Physiological

    (B) Safety

    (C) Self-actualization

    (D) Love and belongingness

    (E) Esteem and love and belongingness

69. Differences in perceptions affect how consumers gather and interpret information from their environment. The selective processes influencing these perceptions include

    (A) selective retention.

    (B) selective perception.

    (C) selective exposure.

    (D) selective response.

    (E) Only (A), (B), and (C) are correct.

70. A response is an attempt to satisfy

    (A) a cue.   (D) an attitude or belief.

    (B) a learned behavior.   (E) All of the above.

    (C) a drive.

71. "Psychographics" is (are)

    (A) life-style analyses.

    (B) the study of "who wears the pants in the household" in terms of purchases.

    (C) an analysis of a person's day-to-day pattern of living expressed as activities, interests, and opinions.

    (D) an analysis of geographic areas for competitive study.

    (E) Only (A) and (C) are correct.

72. A reference group may influence one's purchases because

    (A) they are members of the same social class.

    (B) they are part of middle-class America.

    (C) people make comparisons between themselves and others, or try to imitate other's behavior or purchase decisions.

    (D) having a mink coat is considered a status symbol.

    (E) an opinion leader is a person who influences others in the group.

73. Which of the following statements about personal selling are (is) true?

    (A) There should be a desire to combine mass selling and sales promotion with personal selling.

    (B) It has flexibility.

    (C) It is direct spoken communication between buyer and seller.

    (D) It is expensive, especially per contact.

    (E) All of the above.

74. The AIDA model is best represented by which of the following?

    (A) Awareness, idea, desire, action

    (B) Attention, interest, desire, action

    (C) Association, interest, decision, adoption

    (D) Attention, interest, decision, adoption

    (E) Awareness, interest, decision, action

75. The adoption diffusion curve shows different groups accepting product trial. Which of the following is true about the innovators?

    (A) They consist of the majority of adopters.

    (B) They are first to adopt.

    (C) They are eager to try a new idea and willing to take risks.

    (D) (A) and (B) are true.

    (E) (B) and (C) are true.

76. Which of the following are characteristic(s) of early adopters?

    (A) They are distrusted by their peers.

    (B) They are often opinion leaders.

    (C) They tend to be old.

    (D) They are conservative.

    (E) They are the majority.

77. Opinion leaders

    (A) tend to have the greatest contact with salespeople.

    (B) are regarded as most important by marketers.

    (C) spread word-of-mouth information and advice among other consumers.

    (D) might have a negative influence on sales.

    (E) All of the above.

78. This group tends to avoid risk. They wait to consider a new idea or product until many others have tried and like the product (or idea). This group has a great deal of contact with mass media, salespeople, and opinion leaders who are early adopters. This group is called what?

    (A) Late majority   (D) Early majority

    (B) Laggards   (E) Innovators

    (C) Nonadopters

79. The marketing strategy of promoting sales through middlemen or intermediaries, and at the same time getting consumers to ask the intermediaries for the product, is called which of the following?

    (A) Putting-pulling   (D) Patting-pushing

    (B) Putting-pushing   (E) Pitching-pulling

    (C) Pushing-pulling

80. During the market introduction phase of the product life cycle, the basic promotional objective is informing. If the product is a really new idea, the promotion needs to develop and build demand. This demand is known as

(A) final demand.

(D) tertiary demand.

(B) primary demand.

(E) selective demand.

(C) secondary demand.

81. Which of the following is the best response for the statement, "Any-one seeking a profit maximization objective will charge high prices"?

(A) This is always true.

(B) This is not always true.

(C) Prices will always be higher than the competitor's.

(D) Prices tend to stay below the competitor's prices.

(E) None of the above relate to the statement.

82. A key point regarding sales-oriented objectives is

(A) a larger market share, if gained at too low a price, may lead to a success with no profits.

(B) aggressive companies often aim to increase market share.

(C) larger sales volume, by itself, does not necessarily lead to higher profits.

(D) it is never easy to measure a firm's market share when deter-mining if there is profit maximization.

(E) All of the above are correct.

83. The type of price policy that tries to sell the top of the demand curve utilizing a high price, before aiming at more price-sensitive consum-ers, is called

(A) skimming pricing.

(D) penetration pricing.

(B) flexible pricing.

(E) odd/even pricing.

(C) one-price policy.

84. Which of the following discounts refer to a list price reduction given to channel members for the specific jobs they are doing for the manufacturer or producer?

(A) Quantity discounts

(B) Cash discounts

(C) Trade discounts

(D) Cumulative quantity discounts

(E) Seasonal discounts

85. Which of the following terms allows a buyer to take a 4 percent discount off the face value of the invoice if the invoice is paid within 20 days, and if not, the full face value of the invoice becomes due in 60 days?

(A) 20/60, net 4   (D) 10/4, net 60

(B) 2/10, net 60   (E) 4/20, net 60

(C) 2/10, net 30

86. Which of the following makes illegal selling the same products to different buyers at different prices?

(A) Wheeler Lea Amendment

(B) Unfair Trade Practice Acts

(C) Robinson-Patman Act

(D) Magnuson-Moss Act

(E) Lanham Act

87. Price fixing falls under which Act or Amendment?

(A) Robinson-Patman Act

(B) Wheeler Lea Amendment

(C) Sherman Act

(D) Unfair Trade Practice Acts

(E) Lanham Act

88. According to the U.S. Bureau of the Census, wholesalers are defined as those who sell to

(A) retailers and other merchants.

(B) industrial users.

(C) institutional users.

(D) commercial users.

(E) All of the above.

89. Wholesalers perform a variety of activities that benefit their customers. Which one is NOT included in their activities?

(A) Regroup goods

(B) Carry stocks

(C) Deliver goods

(D) Create product designs

(E) Anticipate needs

90. Which of the following activities do wholesalers perform?

(A) Store inventory

(B) Supply capital

(C) Reduce credit risk

(D) Provide market information

(E) All of the above.

91. Marine-Unlimited buys tropical fish from local fish growers. The company takes title to the tropical fish for some period of time before selling to the many pet shops around the area on a cash or credit basis. Marine Unlimited is called a

(A) cash-and-carry wholesaler.

(B) rack jobber.

(C) Producers' cooperative.

(D) mail-order wholesaler.

(E) merchant wholesaler.

92. Service wholesalers provide all the wholesaling functions. Service wholesalers include

(A) general merchandise wholesaler.

(B) single-line (general-line) wholesaler.

(C)   specialty wholesaler.

(D)   All of the above.

(E)   None of the above.

93.   A service wholesaler that carries a wide variety of non-perishable items such as hardware, electrical supplies, furniture, drugs, etc. is called a

(A)   single-line wholesaler.

(B)   general merchandise wholesaler.

(C)   specialty wholesaler.

(D)   rack jobber.

(E)   limited-function wholesaler.

94.   A service wholesaler that carries a narrow range of products and offers more information and service than other service wholesalers is a

(A)   limited-function wholesaler.

(B)   specialty wholesaler.

(C)   single-line wholesaler.

(D)   general merchandise wholesaler.

(E)   drop shipper.

95.   Some of the features of cash-and-carry wholesalers include

(A)   catering to retailers too small to be served profitably by service wholesalers.

(B)   accepting only cash.

(C)   delivering products that they stock in their own trucks.

(D)   taking title to the products they sell, but not actually handling stocking, or delivering them.

(E)   (A) and (B).

96.   Sylvia Garcia brings buyers and sellers together. She is called a

(A) selling agent.

(D) manufacturers' agent.

(B) commission merchant.

(E) rack jobber.

(C) broker.

97. They provide a place where buyers and sellers can come together to inspect products and bid on final prices to complete transactions. There aren't many of these companies, but they are important in certain lines such as livestock, fur, tobacco, and used cars. These companies are classified as

(A) sales finance companies.

(D) brokers.

(B) auction companies.

(E) factors.

(C) field warehouser.

98. Rick is doing his weekly grocery shopping and purchases bathroom tissue. Bathroom tissue is an example of which of the following types of products?

(A) Impulse

(D) Emergency

(B) Heterogeneous

(E) Specialty

(C) Staple

99. Annie loves her Guess jeans. She wants another pair of Guess jeans but if there is a brand that has a lower price with similar quality, she will buy that pair instead. This is an example of

(A) brand recognition.

(D) nonrecognition.

(B) brand preference.

(E) None of the above.

(C) brand insistence.

100. Kenmore appliances (sold by Sears) are an example of a(n)

(A) dealer brand.

(D) individual brand.

(B) manufacturers' brand.

(E) family brand.

(C) licensed brand.

CLEP PRINCIPLES OF MARKETING
TEST 2

ANSWER KEY

Section 1

1.	(C)	14.	(C)	27.	(B)	39.	(C)
2.	(C)	15.	(A)	28.	(B)	40.	(E)
3.	(D)	16.	(D)	29.	(D)	41.	(B)
4.	(D)	17.	(D)	30.	(C)	42.	(A)
5.	(D)	18.	(D)	31.	(E)	43.	(A)
6.	(B)	19.	(A)	32.	(D)	44.	(E)
7.	(C)	20.	(B)	33.	(D)	45.	(E)
8.	(A)	21.	(E)	34.	(E)	46.	(D)
9.	(E)	22.	(B)	35.	(D)	47.	(B)
10.	(C)	23.	(D)	36.	(C)	48.	(E)
11.	(E)	24.	(C)	37.	(B)	49.	(C)
12.	(A)	25.	(B)	38.	(A)	50.	(B)
13.	(B)	26.	(E)				

Section 2

51.	(B)	64.	(A)	77.	(E)	89.	(D)
52.	(E)	65.	(D)	78.	(D)	90.	(E)
53.	(E)	66.	(C)	79.	(C)	91.	(E)
54.	(D)	67.	(D)	80.	(B)	92.	(D)
55.	(A)	68.	(E)	81.	(B)	93.	(B)
56.	(C)	69.	(E)	82.	(C)	94.	(B)
57.	(B)	70.	(C)	83.	(A)	95.	(E)
58.	(B)	71.	(E)	84.	(C)	96.	(C)
59.	(A)	72.	(C)	85.	(E)	97.	(B)
60.	(E)	73.	(E)	86.	(C)	98.	(C)
61.	(C)	74.	(B)	87.	(C)	99.	(B)
62.	(E)	75.	(E)	88.	(E)	100.	(E)
63.	(D)	76.	(B)				

DETAILED EXPLANATIONS OF ANSWERS

TEST 2

Section 1

1.   **(C)**   When one wants to calculate the markup of a product, at retail, the correct formula is Amount of Markup = Selling Price – Cost. Thus (C) is correct. (A), (B), and (D) are incorrect formulas and won't yield the markup. (E) is incorrect because the answer is available from the given data.

2.   **(C)**   When trying to find the markup based upon selling price, the formula to use is Amount of Markup = Selling Price – Cost. In this example, since the selling price is $2,000 and the cost is $800, the answer is $1,200. (A), (B), (D), and (E) are incorrect calculations.

3.   **(D)**   In order to calculate percent of markup to selling price one would use the formula amount of markup/selling price = percent of markup to selling price. Since this comes out to 60%, (D) is correct. (A) is incorrect because $600/1,000 = 60%. (B), (C), and (D) are also incorrect for the same reason.

4.   **(D)**   Their selling price should be $1,000. (A) is incorrect because this gives a 60% markup as a percentage of the $400 cost. (B) cannot be correct because $350 is below cost, thus MOLE would be selling at a loss. (C) is incorrect because in order to calculate selling price, the formula to utilize is SP = COST – MARKUP (SP = C + M). Since the cost of $400 + 60%(SP) is not $750, this choice is wrong. (E) is also incorrect because the cost plus 60% of the selling price does not equal $5,300.

5.   **(D)**   The cost would be $400. (A) is incorrect; the cost will not be equal to or in excess of the selling price. (B) is incorrect, $600 is 60% × $1,000. (C) is incorrect because this is the markup percentage on cost of

60%. (E) is incorrect because Cost = Selling Price – Markup (C = SP – M). Thus 1,000 – 60%(1,000) = 400, and the cost of the product was $400.

6. **(B)** The cost is $400, and the selling price is $500. (A) is incorrect since the selling price and cost can be calculated. (C) is incorrect since Markup % on Selling Price × Selling Price = Amount of Markup. When calculated, the answer is C = $400 and SP = $500, thus (D) is also wrong. (E) is incorrect. If the amount of markup is $100, and the markup percent on selling price is $120, this answer cannot possibly be right.

7. **(C)** When figuring markup based upon cost. Selling Price = Cost + Markup. Since $200 = $150 + $50, (A), (B), (D), and (E) are all incorrect. Utilizing the formula, $200 – $150 = $50. Remember, this is the markup based upon cost, NOT retail selling price.

8. **(A)** Remember, this is a calculation based upon COST, not Retail Price, thus the amount of markup/cost = percent markup based on cost. 50/150 = 33.33%, so (B), (C), and (D) are incorrect. Choice (C) gives the markup as a percentage of price, not cost. (E) is incorrect because the answer can be determined and is 33.33%.

9. **(E)** The key to remember is that this calculation is being performed on COST, not retail price. (A), $16.67, is incorrect; this would be the answer if the question had asked for a 40% markup on retail price. (B) cannot be correct because it is at cost. (C) is not correct because Selling Price = Cost + Markup. So SP = $10.00 = .4($10), or $14.00. (D) is also an incorrect answer.

10. **(C)** In order to calculate cost, the formula Selling Price = Cost + Markup is used. Algebraically then SP/1 + Markup percent on cost, would also give the cost. Since 100/1.7 is equal to $58.82, (C) is the correct choice. (A) cannot possibly be correct since $100 is the retail selling price of the product and it has a 70% markup based upon cost. (B) is incorrect. Remember, the calculations are being performed on the cost, not the retail selling price. (D) and (E) are also incorrect, although (E) would offer the best profit.

11. **(E)** The company must consider each of the elements before entering a foreign market since not doing so could result in embarrassment for the marketer (or worse). Although theme is a correct answer (A), it of itself is not sufficient to support the promotional program. Copy color (B)

is important, and the impact of color for the foreign market should be studied, however, it is not the best choice. Product name (C) and The media mix (D) are also important considerations, and are correct, but by themselves they are not the best choice.

12.   **(A)**   The simplest step is to begin shipping out the goods. As the company gets more involved in exporting, they will create an international division to handle all of the international activities. Finally, they begin thinking of themselves as global marketers, and become a multinational organization. Answers (B), (C), and (D) are incorrect because they do not begin with the simplest step of exporting. Answer (E) is incorrect because creating an international division after becoming a multinational organization is backwards.

13.   **(B)**   Because of spoilage Sugar Bear may want to utilize air. In order to increase their market and serve their customers, Sugar Bear may well want to serve the Pennsylvania market, so (A) is incorrect. Water (C) is probably unavailable between Colorado and Pennsylvania, and even if it were, the mode of transportation is probably far too slow for a perishable product. Train (D) may be a viable method of transportation however, since the produce is a perishable product, the slower forms of transportation like train may not be the best choice for a long journey (unless refrigerated cars are used, and the customer service level is low). Pipelines (E) are not feasible options since fresh produce cannot be sent through this form of transportation.

14.   **(C)**   Piggyback service does NOT offer the option of getting the lowest cost by combining small shipments. Piggy back service is where a truck's trailer is loaded onto a railroad car. Freight forwarders (A) and pool car services (B) both operate on the principle that it is cheaper per unit to move full loads than less than full loads, and thus are true. They are incorrect answers because the question asks which are NOT associated with getting the lowest costs by combining. (D) is also incorrect because one of the above is indeed not associated with this practice. All of the above (E) are not true so this is an incorrect choice.

15.   **(A)**   Private warehousing would be the best choice. If a company stores large volumes of goods on a regular basis, they should probably use company-owned or private warehouses. Public warehouses (B) are best suited to seasonal use. (C) a distribution center's main function is to redistribute the stock, not to store it, so this would be an incorrect choice.

Containerization (D) refers to the grouping of individual items into economical shipping quantities, and is incorrect. All of the above should not be utilized given the situation, so (E) is not the best choice.

16. **(D)**   Safety needs are concerned with protection and physical well-being. Tommy is concerned with protecting himself and his home. When he realized his new home did not have a fire detector he immediately went out to buy one. (D) is the correct answer. Social needs (A) involve a person's interactions with others. Love, friendship, and status are examples of social needs. Physiological needs (B) are concerned with biological needs such as food, drink, and rest. Personal needs (C) deal with an individual's need for personal satisfaction such as self-esteem, accomplishments, fun, and relaxation. Friendship needs (E) are covered under social needs.

17. **(D)**   This question involves selective processes when one is exposed to stimuli. With selective exposure (D) our minds and eyes seek out and notice information that interests us. In the example, rollerblade products begin to interest you, so you notice ads about them more often. Selective retention (A) occurs when we remember only what we want to remember. This may occur after we have been exposed, suddenly, to the information. Selective perception (B) is when we screen out or modify ideas, messages, and information that conflict with previously learned attitudes and beliefs. Selective response (C) is incorrect because there is not a category called selective response. (E) is incorrect because one of the above, (D) is true.

18. **(D)**   Advertising falls under promotion, which is the communication between the seller and potential buyer to influence attitudes and behavior. Product (A), price (B), and place (C) are all parts of the marketing mix, but advertising does not fit under them. Perception (E) is not one of the "4 Ps" in the marketing mix.

19. **(A)**   Advertising can help position a firm's marketing mix to better reach the target market by informing and persuading people. This is one of the main objectives in advertising. Because advertising aids in informing and persuading customers, (B) is incorrect. Personal selling (C) is more flexible than advertising because a presentation can be altered in order to meet a specific customer's needs, where advertising cannot. Advertising reaches large numbers of customers, making (D) an incorrect choice. Advertising will become more important as the economy grows

because people will have more money to spend on goods which they may learn about through advertising, consequently (E) is an incorrect choice.

20.   **(B)**   This objective tells exactly what is wanted and when it should be done. They help to measure what is to be accomplished by the marketing program for a given time period. Answers (A), (C), (D), and (E) are too broad to be good advertising objectives. These answers are more suited as strategies. More specifics such as target market and time frames would make these effective advertising objectives.

21.   **(E)**   Pioneering advertising is usually done early in the product's life cycle and informs potential customers of the product and its benefits, generating primary demand for the category. Institutional advertising (A) promotes a specific organization, not a product. Competitive advertising (B) aims to develop customers' preference for a specific brand. Product advertising (C) aims to sell a product. Reminder advertising (D) aims to keep the product name before the public later in the product life cycle.

22.   **(B)**   A product must be seen in order to demonstrate it and television allows for the effects needed to demonstrate a product's intended benefits. The remaining answers, newspaper (A), radio (C), direct mail (D), and magazine (E) do not allow for the type of setting where a product can be seen in operation and motion.

23.   **(D)**   Direct mail allows the marketer to target any number of specific individuals through mailing sent directly to potential customers' homes or businesses. Television (A), radio (B), newspaper (C), and outdoor (E) are meant to reach very large numbers of people within a specific geographic area. These types of media cannot include some individuals and exclude others intentionally. However, with the increase in popularity of cable TV, the ability to segment has increased with this medium.

24.   **(C)**   Cooperative advertising involves middlemen and producers who share in the cost of advertising, so both may benefit, as in the above situation. Comparative advertising (A) involves a comparison of two different brands of the same product. Education advertising (B) is not a formal type of advertising. Institutional advertising (D) promotes an individual organization's image, reputation, or services, not a product or line of products. Pioneering advertising (E) is used to develop primary demand for some specific product category early in the product life cycle.

25. **(B)** Before any medium is chosen a firm must specify the target market and audience, and know their interests, habits, and behavior. Answers (A) and (D) do not have anything to do with the medium chosen. As many marketers will say, the most expensive medium (C) is not always the best if it does not target the correct audience. (E) is also incorrect, but should be researched after the target market and audience are identified.

26. **(E)** How much a sales representative is paid has more to do with sales management than advertising. Sales representatives are responsible for generating orders for the already advertised product which has little to do with advertising effectiveness. (E) is the correct choice. Answers (A), (B), (C), and (D) all play a key role in the ad medium's effectiveness. They are all part of the marketing strategy and will be important to how well the medium fits into that strategy.

27. **(B)** An ad's copy thrust is what the ad should communicate to the target audience. Advertising allowance (A) is a price reduction given to a firm along a channel to encourage them to advertise a supplier's product in their own local area. The AIDA (C) concept describes how a message should get one's attention, hold their interest, arouse a desire to buy, and obtain buying action. The target audience (D) is the specific consumers at whom the ad is directed. The ad's medium (E) is the media channel through which the ad is presented such as TV, radio, newspaper, etc.

28. **(B)** Concept tests usually rely on written descriptions of new products, and may be augmented with sketches of other literature. Several key questions are asked during the concept testing phase of new product development, including "How does the consumer perceive the product," and "who would use the product?". The firm would internally evaluate all new products and proposals to see if they "fit" the product strategy, so an internal test (A) is incorrect. (C) is not correct. A weighted point system (D) can establish criteria for product screening, but does not answer the above questions. Likewise, a non-weighted point system can establish criteria, but it doesn't provide answers to the above questions, thus (E) is incorrect.

29. **(D)** Test marketing is performed to see if consumers will actually buy the product. Additionally, changes can be made to the marketing mix variables in a controlled setting. Selected controlled markets are those markets in which the total test is conducted by an outside organization or

agency. The tests are conducted by paying retailers for shelf space, guaranteeing distribution to the most popular test market(s), so (A) is incorrect. (B) is not the correct answer. Store audits are conducted by groups (such as the A.C. Nielson Company) measuring sales in grocery stores and the number of cases ordered by the stores. Standard markets (C) is also incorrect because standard markets are those test sites where companies sell a new product through normal channels, and then monitor the results. (E) is incorrect because there is a correct choice.

30. **(C)** The final phase of the new product planning process is known as commercialization. This is where the product is positioned in the marketplace and launched. (A) is incorrect because prototype development occurs in the development phase. The market testing phase (B) of the new product development process involves exposing the actual product to consumers under realistic, yet somewhat controlled, conditions. The new product's niche (D) is defined during the initial strategic phase of the new product development cycle. Finally, (E) is not correct, because there is a correct answer.

31. **(E)** Support goods are those goods used to assist in producing other goods and services. Support goods may include services, supplies, installations, and accessory equipment, thus all of the above are correct. (A), (B), (C), and (D), are all examples of support goods, thus each are incorrect choices.

32. **(D)** Form utility deals with something that is made out of some other material(s), usually called raw materials, thus the manufacturing of a telephone creates form utility. Task utility (A) is incorrect because this is service-related and deals with a person providing a task for someone. (B) is incorrect because possession utility refers to having the right to use or consume a good or service. Time utility is having a product ready for the customer(s) when she or he needs or wants it, so (C) is incorrect. Place utility (E) refers to having a product for a customer where they want it, thus (E) is incorrect.

33. **(D)** All of the above functions must be performed. The buying function (A) is the purchase of products or services, and is essential in macro-marketing. Likewise, transportation (B) is a required function of macro-marketing, and includes physically moving products to various locations within a channel of distribution. Marketing information (C) is the communication function performed in macro-marketing and is one of the

eight universal functions that marketers perform. All three of these answers help make up the eight universal functions of marketing performed in a macro-marketing environment. (E) is incorrect because all are universal macro-marketing functions.

34. **(E)** The marketing company era saw the development of the marketing concept which states that marketers should strive to satisfy consumer wants and needs, AT A PROFIT! (A) is incorrect because the marketing concept was not developed or practiced during this era. (B) is incorrect. During the marketing department era, all marketing functions were brought together under one department, but this was not a company-wide practice. (C) is incorrect because during the production era no consideration was given to the market or what customers wanted. (D) is incorrect. During the sales era a company stresses selling over marketing because of the increase in competition.

35. **(D)** Forming heterogeneous markets is the opposite of what one wants to do in the development of product-market segments. The marketer, or product manager, should be looking for homogeneous market segments. (A) is incorrect. The marketer should strive to find a name for the possible segments. (B) is also incorrect because the marketer should list the potential customer needs (as well as wants) for each of the segments. (C) is incorrect because the marketer needs to know the approximate size of the market in order to assure profitability. Since (D) is a correct choice, (E) is incorrect.

36. **(C)** Product development deals with offering NEW or IM-PROVED products for current or present markets, thus (C) is correct. (A) is incorrect because American Express is trying to penetrate the market by attempting to increase current product usage. (B) is not correct because Taco Bell is expanding their market with a current product, and are therefore attempting market development. (D) is incorrect because NINTENDO is taking a whole new product into an entirely new market, or attempting new venture strategies. (E) is not the best choice because there is a correct answer.

37. **(B)** Straight rebuy is a routine purchase of an item that is commonly purchased. (A) is not correct because new task buying occurs when an organization has a new need and the buyer wants a great deal of information about the product prior to purchase. (C) is also incorrect. Modified rebuy is the in-between process of buying where some review is done,

although not as much as in a new-task buying situation. Purchase (D) is incorrect because the question relates to a repurchase. (E) is incorrect, because there is a correct answer.

38. **(A)** People who specialize in buying are called purchasing agents. (B) is the manager in the marketing area who is concerned with personal selling. Order takers (C) are sales people who get orders, or sell, to the regular or "typical" customer. Order getters (D) are salespeople who specialize in generating new business. Finally, any of the above (E) is incorrect. There is only one most correct choice.

39. **(C)** Vendor analysis is the process used to evaluate suppliers and how they are working out for the company. An evaluation (A), is not the most correct answer. An evaluation is less formal and not as detailed as a vendor analysis. A check-list (B) may be part of a vendor analysis but more information is needed to make an assessment of the vendor than is provided for in a check-list, so this answer is incorrect. Subjective interpretation (D) may be used in analyzing the vendor, but objective measurement is also needed, making this a poor choice. Buyer analysis (E) could be performed by the vendor, but is not needed by the buyer analyzing the vendor, therefore this answer is not correct.

40. **(E)** Many people are involved in certain purchase decisions. All of the people listed could have a possible buying influence through the concept of multiple buying influences. Users (A) is a correct choice, however, not the most correct, since all of the individuals listed may have an influence on the final purchase decision. Buyers (B) are those involved in the purchase process, however the process may have been initiated by a user or someone else. Thus even though by itself this would be correct, it is not the best answer. Influencers (C) are those that influence the purchase decision and may share in the purchase decision, however this is not the most correct answer. Gatekeepers (D) may also be influencers, such as secretaries and other administrative assistants, however this is not the most correct choice.

41. **(B)** Every item should be inspected if non-standardized products have been ordered. (A) is not correct because negotiated contract buying is agreeing to a contract that allows for changes in the purchase agreement. (C) is also incorrect; sampling buying means looking at only a small part of the potential purchase, and would not be the best method of purchase in this situation. Description buying (D) is the purchase of a product based

on a verbal or written description. A routine response buying situation (E) is where the purchaser is making a normal purchase of products purchased before, and should not be used in this situation.

42. **(A)** Defining the problem is the first step that should be undertaken. Solving the problem (B) is the final step that should be undertaken, and is thus incorrect. Collecting problem-specific data (C) cannot be undertaken until the problem is defined. Analyzing the situation (D) is the second step, and therefore is incorrect. Defining a sample (E) shouldn't be undertaken until after the situation has been analyzed.

43. **(A)** Trying to ascertain what the problem is takes the majority of time in the process. (B) is incorrect. Although situational analysis may be time consuming, it does not take as much time as problem definition, and rarely would it require as much as half of the research time. Data collection (C) is time-consuming but does not take as much time as problem definition. Problem-solving (D) takes place after data collection, and usually doesn't require the time and effort that the other phases do, thus it is incorrect. The development of alternative solutions (E) again takes time, but the problem definition takes the most time, and in a lot of cases, takes well over half the research time. Therefore (E) is incorrect.

44. **(E)** A research proposal is a plan that specifies what information is needed and how it will be obtained. In addition, most proposals have information as to the cost of the data collection. (A) is incorrect. A research proposal is stated after the situational analysis, not after the problem definition. (B) is a definition of a research proposal, and is included in the body of the proposal, but is not the best answer. (C) usually is part of the research proposal, but is not the best answer. (D) is incorrect. Both (A) and (C) are NOT correct.

45. **(E)** All survey results require care in result interpretation. The researcher should be trained in this area. (A), (B),(C), and (D) all require care but are not the best answers for the question. Each must be analyzed carefully, and the results accurately stated with care.

46. **(D)** Research is needed to help keep marketing managers in touch with their markets. (A) is incorrect, because research should be planned by both specialists and marketing managers to make sure the user needs are being met. (B) is incorrect because marketing research is much more than just survey design and statistics. (C) is incorrect. Marketing

research is used by everyone involved in the marketing process. (E) is incorrect. Marketing research should be an on-going process.

47.   **(B)**   The population of the United States has slowed, and is expected to slow dramatically, less than one percent during the decades. The population has not maintained its current growth rate, so (A) is incorrect. (C) is incorrect. The U.S. population is still growing but not at an increasing rate of one percent. (D) The U.S. population has definitely not stopped growing and isn't expected to do so, thus (D) is incorrect. (E) is the least correct choice, the growth rate hasn't, nor is it forecasted to, grow anywhere near sixteen percent.

48.   **(E)**   The U.S. birthrate is starting to drop now with more couples waiting longer to have children and more women entering the work force, and there is less of a want for larger families. (A) is true, however it is not the best choice, because "D" is also correct. (B) is incorrect. The only time the birthrate rose sharply due to returning soldiers was during the post-World War II "baby boom" which lasted about 15 years into the early 1960s. (C) is incorrect because the birthrate is simply not rising sharply. This is affected by the fact that there is not an abundance of women at the child-bearing age. (D) is true, but not the most correct answer because (A) is also correct.

49.   **(C)**   The United States does have the highest divorce rate in the world—about 38% of the marriages in the U.S. end in divorce. England has nothing to do with divorce rates in the United States. There divorce rate is lower than the U.S. rate, thus (A) is incorrect. (B) is incorrect. The U.S. does not have the lowest divorce rate in the world, the opposite is true. (D) is also incorrect. Not only does England not have the lowest divorce rate, but the percentage given is incorrect. The United States does not have a divorce rate of 13%, it is closer to 38%, thus (E) is not the most correct choice.

50.   **(B)**   The economy's gross domestic product (GDP) is a widely available measure of the output of the whole economy and the total market value of goods and services for the United States (produced in a year). The economic system (A) is the way an economy organizes to use scarce resources to produce the goods and services and then distribute them to society for consumption, thus "A" is incorrect. Gross sales (C) is the total amount charged to all customers during a given time period, and is incorrect. Gross margin (D) refers to businesses, and the money they have to

cover expenses of selling and other business operations. (E) is incorrect. The term used to be used to define the output of the economy, but was dropped in favor of gross domestic product.

Section 2

51. **(B)** Disposable income is the income left after paying taxes which is used to make necessary expenditures such as housing and car payments. (A) refers to business transactions and is the money left over, for a business, to cover the expenses associated with running that business (i.e., sales expenses and operating expenses) and is incorrect. (C) is also incorrect. Net profit is what a company has earned from their operations during a specified time period. Discretionary income (D) is that income left over after taxes, and after payments for necessities, so it is incorrect. Family income (E) is that money which the family, or household, earns and is incorrect.

52. **(E)** Advertising, publicity, and personal selling are promotion activities and are not a form of sales promotion, thus sales promotion would not include those activities. Advertising (A) is part of the promotion mix, however, it is not the best choice of those given, and thus is incorrect. (B) is also incorrect, although it is a promotion mix, it is not part of sales promotion. (C) is also incorrect, because it is not the best choice of those given. Point-of-purchase materials (D) would be a form of sales promotion used to stimulate interest, trial, and purchase of products at the point-of-sale, therefore it is incorrect.

53. **(E)** All promotion objectives should strive to effect buyer behavior by providing information, persuading, and reminding. (A) is incorrect. These three items have to do with the communication process, the process of what the seller says, and how they translate this into consumer language. (B) shows the promotion mix, and is incorrect. (C) lists the different groups in the adoption diffusion process and is thus incorrect. (D) is a list of the jobs promotions should perform, following the AIDA model of promotion.

54. **(D)** Raising prices in the above situation would most likely boost your competitor's position, and reduce your customer base. (A) meeting competition would be likely with a status quo objective and is incorrect. (B) is also incorrect because maintaining stable prices may discourage

price competition and leave the situation in the status quo. (C) should not be selected because the manager utilizing a status quo objective does want to avoid price competition. Finally (E) is incorrect because it's a promotional function that would not be used in a status quo situation.

55. **(A)**   Decoding is the process that the receiver uses to translate the seller's message, and is a correct choice. Encoding (B) is how the seller translates ideas and thoughts about selling the product into words and/or symbols and is an incorrect choice. Noise (C) is incorrect. Noise refers to those distractions in the environment which may create an error in the communication process. (D) refers to the sender, or the seller, of the message and is not a correct choice. Finally, (E) is the potential consumer, not how the message is translated, so it too, is incorrect.

56. **(C)**   Both the early and late majority(s) make up approximately 34% (per group) of the adopting public. Innovators (A) make up around $2\frac{1}{2}$% of the adopting public, so this is incorrect. Early adopters (B) make up around 12% of the adopting public and is not the most correct answer. The late majority (D), as stated before, makes up about 34% of the adopting public and would be one of two groups who represent the largest adoption percentage, however, this is not the most correct choice. The laggards (E) represent anywhere from 5 to 16% of the adopting publics, if they adopt at all. This is an incorrect choice.

57. **(B)**   Pulling is getting the consumers to ask the intermediaries for products, thus forcing these channel members to request the product from the manufacturers. (A) is the process of "pushing" a product through the distribution channel and is incorrect. (C) is a type of internal marketing done to get the employees involved in selling specific products, so it is incorrect. (D) is incorrect. There is not one correct promotion mix for all selling situations. (E) is generally used when the intermediaries do not want to help, or cooperate, with the manufacturers.

58. **(B)**   In this stage, promotion emphasis shifts from trying to create primary demand to that of selective demand. The main objective is to convince consumers that the company's brand is the best choice for purchase. Market introduction (A) would have a promotion emphasis on building primary demand, not selective, and is incorrect. Market maturity (C) utilizes reminder advertising and promotion about the company's brand, and is not the most correct choice. Sales decline (D) utilizes targeted promotions for specific segments, or targets of the brand, and so is

incorrect. Competition decline (E) refers to the fact that the competition is leaving the market, so it is incorrect. Competition decline is not one of the phases of the product life cycle.

59.   **(A)**   Banners and streamers are examples of sales promotions aimed at the final consumer or end user to stimulate trial of the brand or product. (B) is an example of a sales promotion activity aimed at the intermediary and is not correct. (C) also is aimed toward intermediaries, trying to induce the middlemen to pay special attention to a particular product or brand, thus increasing sales. It is incorrect. Bonuses (D) are an internal sales promotion activity which attempts to motivate the company's own sales force. It is incorrect. (E) is incorrect, training materials are used as an internal method of sales promotion aimed at sales people, so that they pay particular attention to a given product or brand.

60.   **(E)**   Because of the flexibility of trucks, around 75 percent of all physical products transported by the producer to the end user travel by truck. (A), (B), (C), and (D) are simply incorrect choices, forcing the student to think about how the products they purchase are received and stocked by retailers and other merchants. Although somewhat expensive, products could not reach their final destination if it weren't for trucks.

61.   **(C)**   Railroads can transport goods at approximately 3-4 cents per ton. Railroads move large loads of product at the lowest costs to the manufacturers (over ground) and are considered the workhorses of the transportation industry. Railroads carry more freight over more miles than any other mode of transportation and are able to employ the concept of "economies of scale" to help reduce costs. (A), (B), and (D) are incorrect figures, and are not the most correct answer. (E) is the cost of transportation utilizing trucks, and is also incorrect.

62.   **(E)**   Trucks are more expensive than rail, however because of their flexibility they are essential in the transportation industry. The flexibility of trucks makes them better at moving smaller quantities of goods for shorter distances. (A), (B), (C), and (D) are incorrect choices.

63.   **(D)**   Storing is the marketing function of holding goods. Storing provides time utility for the firm and its customers. If consumption does not match production, storing is necessary. The storing of goods allows producers to achieve economies of scale for their products, helping to keep prices down. (A) is true, but not the correct choice. (B) is also true, but

again not the most correct answer. (C) is also true, but not the correct answer. None of the above (E) cannot be true since all of the above are in fact ways to alternate or vary the firm's marketing mix.

64. **(A)** Time utility is provided by storing, and is thus the correct choice. Goods must be ready when they are needed, wanted, or demanded by the consumer or else the firm loses sales. Place utility (B) is not achieved. Storage of goods at warehouses does not provide the consumer with a readily available product. Since the consumer does not get the possession of the product through the storage function, possession utility (C) is incorrect, as is ownership utility (D). All of the above are not correct, thus (E) is incorrect.

65. **(D)** The physical distribution concept focuses on the whole distribution system rather than just parts of the system. The PD concept says that all transporting and storing activities of a business, and not just a channel system, should be coordinated as one system. This seeks to minimize the cost of distribution for a given customer service level. Firms should spread this responsibility among different departments. The PD concept is much more than just (A), (B), and (C) although these are components of the system. Thus these are incorrect choices. None of the above (E) is incorrect.

66. **(C)** To offset the shortcomings of low speed and high cost, and still get business from small shippers, railroads allow groups of shippers to pool like goods into a full car. This term is called pool car service. Containerization (A) is incorrect. It refers to the grouping of individual items into economical shipping quantities. Piggyback service (B) refers to the loading of truck trailers onto railroad cars for transportation and is incorrect. Diversion in transit (D) is also incorrect. This refers to the redirection of carloads already in transit. Birdyback service (E) refers to loading trucks or trailers onto airplanes for faster transport to their place of destination. This answer is also incorrect.

67. **(D)** This question relates to how economic needs guide most consumer behavior. Economic needs are concerned with making the best use of a consumer's time and money. This may include the lowest price, convenience and/or quality for the best value. Economic needs include economy of purchase or use (A), which is not the best answer; efficiency in operation or use (B), which is not the most correct answer and improvement of earnings (C), which is not the correct answer. Choice (E) omits improvement of earnings, which makes this an incorrect answer also.

68.　**(E)**　When striving to satisfy basic human needs such as accomplishment, fun, relaxation, and others as stated above, individuals would find themselves in both the self-esteem needs level and the love and belongingness needs level of the hierarchy. Physiological needs (A) are needs for food, drink, rest, and sex. Safety needs (B) are needs for protection or well-being. Self-actualization (C) is also incorrect. This needs level refers to people who strive for total fulfillment of their maximum capabilities, and is only reached by a small portion of the population. Love and belongingness (D) is a good answer, however it is not the best choice.

69.　**(E)**　Selective retention, selective perception, and selective exposure all comprise the selective processes. Selective retention (A) means that we remember only what we want to remember, and is true, but is not the most correct response. Selective perception (B) refers to the fact that we screen out ideas, or modify those ideas and messages that conflict with what we have already learned and with our beliefs, and is true, but not the most correct response. Selective exposure (C) means that our eyes and minds seek out and notice only what interests us, we selectively expose ourselves to our environment, however it is not the most correct answer. Selective response (D) is fictitious. A response, however is an effort to satisfy a need. This is an incorrect answer.

70.　**(C)**　A response is an attempt to satisfy a drive. A drive is a very strong stimulus, conscious or unconscious, that encourages a person to act. Cues (A) are "things" that individuals choose to respond to, such as advertising. Learned behavior (B) is a change in an individual's thought process, and is incorrect. Attitudes and beliefs (D) are an individual's point of view or opinion. Because there is a correct choice, all of the above (E) is incorrect.

71.　**(E)**　Both life-style analyses and an analysis of a person's day-to-day living are referred to as psychographics. (A) is a true statement, but is not the best answer. (B) is totally made up and therefore incorrect. This is not a definition of a psychographic. (C) is true, but not the best choice. (D) refers to geographics, or locations of consumers.

72.　**(C)**　A reference group may influence one's purchase behavior because people make comparisons between themselves and others. Reference groups are the social, economic, or professional groups an individual uses to evaluate their opinions or beliefs. A social class (A) is a group of people who have approximately equal social position as viewed by society. (B) is not relevant to the question at hand and is incorrect. (D) may be a status symbol, but this has no bearing on the question, so it is incorrect. An opinion leader (E) may be part of a reference group, but this refers to an individual rather than a group.

73. **(E)** All of the above statements reflect personal selling and are true. Personal selling is part of the promotional mix of marketing. In order to make it more effective, there should be a desire to combine aspects of advertising and sales promotion (A), although this is not the most correct response. Personal selling is the most flexible (B) of all of the promotion variables, however, this is not the most correct response. (C) is true, however, not the most correct response. Personal selling is expensive (D), especially per contact, and that is one of the reasons it should be combined with the other promotional mix variables. This, however, is not the most correct response.

74. **(B)** The AIDA model includes the four basic promotional jobs of attention, interest, desire, and action. Getting attention is necessary to make consumers aware of a company's offerings. The marketer must then hold the interest of the potential customer. Arousing desire in the consumer affects the adoption process in a positive way, perhaps building preference. Action may gain a trial for the product or service. This may lead to future purchase decisions. The other answers (A), (C), (D), and (E) are simply not the correct steps in the process, and are thus incorrect.

75. **(E)** Two of the above characteristics are particular to innovators. They are the first to adopt and they are eager to try new ideas and are willing to take risks. Additionally they tend to be young and well-educated, and have lots of mobility with many contacts outside their local social group and community. (A) is incorrect because innovators only make up about 3-5% of the adopting public. (B) is true but is not the most correct response. Likewise (C) is true, but is not the most correct response to the question. (D) is not correct. Although the innovators are the first to adopt new products, they do not consist of the majority of adopters, rather they consist of the minority of the consumers who are likely to adopt a new product.

76. **(B)** Early adopters are well respected by their peers, and are opinion leaders. They tend to be younger and more creative than the late adopters. (A) is incorrect, the opposite is true, they are respected by their peers. (C) is also incorrect. Early adopters tend to be young, not old. (D) is

incorrect. Early adopters are not conservative, but are more creative than the late adopters. (E) is incorrect, as early adopters represent only about 10-15% of the adopting public. Unlike innovators, early adopters have fewer contacts outside their own social groups or communities.

77. **(E)** Marketers know the importance of personal conversations and recommendations by opinion leaders. If opinion leaders reject products, the products themselves may never become successful. (A) is true, but is not the most correct answer. Opinion leaders do have the greatest amount of contact with salespeople, so marketers use this information to their advantage. (B) is also true, but is not the most correct response. Opinion leaders are important for the success of a product. Opinion leaders spread word-of-mouth information and advice to other consumers (C), but this is not the best response. If an opinion leader goes to a movie and thinks the movie is dull, she or he may tell their social network, thus reducing the number of people who will attend the show. Because of this, (D) might have a negative influence on sales, but again, this is not the best response.

78. **(D)** The early majority have all of the characteristics described above. (A) is incorrect. The late majority are cautious about new ideas. They are often older and more set in their ways. Laggards (B) prefer to do things the way they have been doing them over time. They are resistant to change. Nonadopters (C) are basically the same as laggards, and are suspicious of new ideas, thus this is an incorrect choice. Innovators (E) is an incorrect choice. Innovators are the first to adopt a product, and are eager to try new things.

79. **(C)** Pushing means using a normal promotional effort such as personal selling or sales promotions to help sell the whole marketing mix to possible members of the channel of distribution. This approach utilizes channel members in "pushing" the product down the distribution chain, or channel, to the final consumer. Pulling helps to stimulate sales and demand for a company's products or services by having the consumer ask for the product, thus increasing the chance that a channel member will want to carry the product. It is common to utilize both pushing and pulling strategies at the same time. Answers (A), (B), (D), and (E) are incorrect.

80. **(B)** Primary demand is building demand for an entire product category (i.e., coffee) rather than a specific brand (i.e., Maxwell House). (A) is incorrect because final demand does not exist. Secondary demand

(C) is also incorrect for the same reason. Tertiary demand (D) is another fictitious term and is incorrect. Selective demand (E) is creating demand for a specific brand rather than an entire product category, and does not fit as an answer for this particular question.

81. **(B)** Pricing to achieve maximization of profits does not always lead to higher prices. Demand and supply may bring high prices if the competition cannot offer a good substitute product. (A) is incorrect. High prices are not always charged in order to develop profit maximization. (C) and (D) are incorrect because the price of competition is usually developed based upon the elasticity of price for a given product or market. (E) is not the correct choice, because one of the above is true.

82. **(C)** Larger sales volumes do not necessarily lead to higher profits for a company. (A) and (B) may be objectives but are too vague, and are incorrect in reference to sales-oriented objectives. (D) is incorrect. It would be a correct answer if it read "...usually easier to measure a firm's market share..." rather than "...never easier...". (E) is incorrect because all of the above are not true.

83. **(A)** With the introduction of every new product, there is a group of consumers willing to pay premium prices to try it. This provides an opportunity to launch the product at higher prices before competition forces the prices down. The skimming policy attempts to "skim the cream" off of the top of the market, thus recouping research and development costs early on prior to reducing the price for the rest of the market. Flexible pricing (B) refers to offering different prices to different customers, and is incorrect. One-price policies (C) are policies that offer products to the customers for the same price. Penetration pricing (D) refers to offering the product to the market with an initial low price, and is the opposite of skimming. Odd/even pricing (E) is a form of psychological pricing, setting prices with odd or even endings depending on consumer perception, and is an incorrect response.

84. **(C)** Trade discounts, also known as functional discounts, are given for various activities performed by the channel member for the producer. Quantity discounts (A) are given to encourage volume purchases. Cash discounts (B) are given to encourage buyers to pay their bills early. Cumulative quantity discounts (D) are give to encourage volume purchases like quantity discounts, but allow the purchaser to buy products at different times until they have accumulated enough in purchases to

qualify for a volume discount. Seasonal discounts (E) are given to encourage buyers to purchase products early, and out-of-season, to free up space for the manufacturer, among other reasons. It is not the correct choice.

85.   **(E)**   This billing method is utilized by producers to encourage the early payment of invoices. It helps to increase cash flow for the manufacturer or producer. Most buyers take advantage of these types of terms because it allows a substantial savings on the purchase. (A), (B), (C), and (D) are different terms allowing for different discounts. They may not even make sense, and are thus incorrect choices.

86.   **(C)**   The Robinson-Patman Act makes illegal selling the same products to different buyers at different prices, therefore (C) is the correct choice. The Wheeler Lea Amendment (A) bans unfair or deceptive acts in commerce. The Unfair Trade Practice Acts (B) puts a lower limit on prices. The Magnuson-Moss Act (D) is a law requiring that producers provide a clearly written warranty for consumer products. The Lanham Act (E) prohibits a company from misrepresenting another companies' products.

87.   **(C)**   The Sherman Act covers price fixing, therefore (C) is the correct answer. The Robinson-Patman Act (A) makes illegal selling the same products to different buyers at different prices. The Wheeler Lea Amendment (B) bans unfair or deceptive acts in commerce. The Unfair Trade Practice Acts (D) put a lower limit on prices. The Lanham Act (E) prohibits a company from misrepresenting another companies' products.

88.   **(E)**   The U.S. Bureau of the Census defines wholesaling as concerned with activities of those persons or establishments which sell to retailers and other merchants (A), and/or to industrial (B), institutional(C), and commercial users (D). Therefore, (E) is the correct answer.

89.   **(D)**   The activity wholesalers would not perform is to create product designs. Wholesalers' activities include regrouping goods (A) to provide the quantity and assortment customers want at the lowest cost, carrying stocks (B) to carry inventory so their customers do not have to store large amounts of products, delivery of goods (C) to provide prompt delivery at low cost, anticipation of needs (E) to forecast customers' demands and buy accordingly.

90.   **(E)**   Wholesalers can store inventory (A) to reduce a producer's need to carry large stocks, thus cutting the producer's warehousing ex-

penses, supply capital (B) to reduce a producer's need for working capital by buying the producer's output and carrying it in inventory until it is sold, reduce credit risk (C) by selling to customers the wholesaler knows and taking the loss if these customers do not pay, provide market information (D) as an informed buyer and seller closer to the market, the wholesaler reduces the producer's need for market research. All of the above (E) is the correct answer.

91. **(E)** Merchant wholesalers own (take title to) the products they sell. Cash-and-carry wholesalers (A) operate as service wholesalers, except that the customer must pay cash. Rack jobbers (B) specialize in nonfood products sold through grocery stores and supermarkets, often displayed on wire racks owned by the rack jobber. Producers' cooperatives (C) operate almost as full-service wholesalers with the profits going to the cooperative's customer members. Mail-order wholesalers (D) sell out of a catalog that may be distributed widely to smaller industrial customers or retailers who might not be called on by other middlemen.

92. **(D)** Service wholesalers can be broken down into general merchandise wholesalers (A), single-line (general-line) wholesalers (B), or specialty wholesalers (C). The correct answer is (D).

93. **(B)** General merchandise wholesalers originally developed to serve the early retailers such as general stores, which carry a wide variety of non-perishable items. Single-line wholesalers (A) carry a narrower line of merchandise than general merchandise wholesalers. Specialty wholesalers (C) carry an even more narrow range of products and offer more information and services that other types of service wholesalers. Rack jobbers (D) specialize in nonfood products sold through grocery stores and supermarkets, often displayed on wire racks owned by the rack jobber. Limited-function wholesalers (E) provide only limited wholesaling functions.

94. **(B)** Specialty wholesalers carry a very narrow range of products and offer more information and services than other types of service wholesalers. Limited-function wholesalers (A) provide only limited wholesaling functions. Single-line wholesalers (C) carry a narrower line of merchandise than general merchandise wholesalers. General merchandise wholesalers (D) carry a wide variety of non-perishable items. Drop shippers own the products they sell, but they do not handle, stock, or deliver them.

95. **(E)** Cash-and-carry wholesalers will only accept cash (B). Some retailers, such as small auto repair shops, are too small to be served profitably by a service wholesaler, so the cash and carry wholesalers cater to these types of businesses on a cash basis (A). A truck wholesaler delivers products that they stock in their own trucks (C). Drop shippers take title to the products they sell, but do not handle, stock, or deliver them (D).

96. **(C)** Brokers bring buyers and sellers together; Sylvia Garcia is a broker. Selling agents (A) are responsible for the marketing job for producers. A selling agent may handle the entire output of one or more producers. Commission merchants (B) handle products shipped to them by sellers, complete the sale, and send the money, minus their commission, to each seller. Manufacturers' agents sell similar products for several non-competing producers, for a commission on what is sold. Rack jobbers specialize in nonfood products sold through grocery stores and supermarkets, often displayed on wire racks owned by the rack jobber.

97. **(B)** For certain products such as livestock, fur, tobacco, and used cars, demand and supply conditions change very fast. Auction companies bring buyers and sellers together. Sales finance companies (A) finance inventories. Field warehousers (C) are firms that segregate some of a company's finished products on the company's own property and issue warehouse receipts that can be used to borrow money. Brokers (D) bring buyers and sellers together. Factors (E) are wholesalers of credit. They buy accounts receivable, which provides their customers with working capital.

98. **(C)** Bathroom tissue is a product which is purchased on a frequent and routinized basis. These types of products are called staples. An impulse product (A) is unplanned and bought quickly such as those candy bars you buy right before you leave a store. A heterogeneous product (B) involves extensive problem-solving and often the consumer needs help in making a decision. An emergency product (D) is purchased when the need is great and there are time pressures. A specialty product (E) is one that the consumer will make a special effort to find because of the limited distribution of the product.

99. **(B)** Annie prefers Guess jeans but may choose another brand if it has a lower price and similar quality. This is called brand preference. In brand recognition (A) you may not intend to purchase the product but you recognize the brand name. If Annie refused to buy any other jeans but

Guess jeans, she would show brand insistence (C). Brand nonrecognition (D) is when the final consumers do not recognize a brand. Because (B) is the correct answer, (E) could not be correct.

100. **(E)**   Kenmore is a family brand (brand name for several products) of Sears, so (E) is the correct choice. Dealer brands (A) such as Ace Hardware are created by middlemen. Manufacturer brands (B) are created by manufacturers and include brands such as Whirlpool, Ford, and IBM. A licensed brand (C) is a well-known brand that sellers pay to use, such as Walt Disney. An individual brand name (D) separates brand names for each product.

PRACTICE
TEST 3

CLEP PRINCIPLES OF MARKETING
Test 3

(Answer sheets appear in the back of this book.)

Section 1

TIME: 45 Minutes
50 Questions

DIRECTIONS: Each of the questions or incomplete statements below is followed by five possible answers or completions. Select the best choice in each case and fill in the corresponding oval on the answer sheet.

---

1. Johanna wants to start a new dance studio and needs to calculate the cost and selling price she should charge for lessons. Her accountant told her that the markup percent ON COST should be 15%, and that the amount of markup should be $17.00. What should her cost and selling price be?

   (A) cost = $100; selling price = $90

   (B) cost = $113.33; selling price = $130.33

   (C) cost = $113.33; selling price = $150

   (D) cost = $100; selling price = $19.55

   (E) cost = $13; selling price = $30

2. What is the markup percent based on cost, where the cost is $500, and the markup is $250?

   (A) 50%

   (B) 100%

   (C) 10%

   (D) 33.3%

(E)   The selling price is needed to calculate the answer.

3.   If there is a markup on a retail selling price of $95 where the selling price is $3,400, what is the percent markup on selling price?

(A)   100%   (D)   3.95%

(B)   2.7%   (E)   2.8%

(C)   2.9%

4.   Calculate the cost, at retail, of a product that sells for $400, and has a markup percent, at retail, of 40%.

(A) $160   (D) $440

(B) $240   (E) $500

(C) $286

5.   If the regular selling price of a product at Johnson Industries is $500, and the owner, Bit Johnson, decides he wants to mark the product down to $480, what is the dollar amount markdown?

(A) $480

(B) $200

(C) $75

(D) $20

(E)   There is no real markdown because the cost of the product is unknown.

6.   If Marianne wants to calculate the percent markdown of a product that she is selling for $100, with a markdown dollar amount of $37, what percentage figure would she come up with?

(A)   37%   (D)   15%

(B)   3.7%   (E)   17%

(C)   12%

7.   Which of the following formulas should you use if you want to calculate "maintained markup"?

(A)   Markup = Retail Selling Price – Cost

(B) Maintained Markup % = Initial Markup % – (Retail Reduction % (100% – Initial Markup %))

(C) Maintained Markup % = Initial Markup % – Retail Reduction %

(D) Retail Selling Price = Maintained Markup % – Cost

(E) Initial Markup % =

$$\frac{\text{Maintained Markup\% + Retail Reduction\%}}{100\ \%\ (\text{Net Sale}) + \text{Retail Reduction\%}}$$

8. An invoice states terms of 2/10 net 30, where the invoice amount is $100. What is the cash discount for someone paying the invoice in 25 days?

(A) $2

(B) $4

(C) $6

(D) $1

(E) There is no cash discount.

9. Major Mark's buying office just purchased some leather belts for $32 each. They want a 35% markup at retail on the belts. What retail price should they charge in order to get that markup?

(A) This cannot be calculated from the information given.

(B) $50

(C) $49.23

(D) $53.85

(E) $43.20

10. Baby's Notion and Lotion shop requires a minimum markup of 50% at retail on a new line of lotions. If Baby feels that the line of lotions should retail for $20 per lotion, which of the following is the maximum amount she should pay for each lotion she buys?

(A) $12

(B) $14

(C) $15

(D) $16.80

(E) None of the above.

11. A toy manufacturer needs to store inventory. It would most likely use which of the following?

    (A) Private warehouses

    (B) Public warehouses

    (C) Distribution centers

    (D) Containerization

    (E) They do not need storage, they ship when they manufacture the product.

12. Which of the following would be the worst choice when transporting a bulky product, such as coal?

    (A) Water

    (B) Rail

    (C) Air

    (D) Truck

    (E) All of the above would be equal choices.

13. Pillsbury has one manufacturing plant for each of their products. Which of the following would they utilize in order to get a mixture of their products to individual stores?

    (A) Distribution centers   (D) Freight forwarders

    (B) Public warehouses   (E) Air distribution

    (C) Private warehouses

14. The Horilla Company recently changed its operation to intermesh transporting functions with other marketing functions rather than handling it as an afterthought. By doing this Horilla could focus on minimizing costs for a given level of service. What approach did Horilla Company change to?

    (A) Total cost approach   (D) Logistics

    (B) Variable cost approach   (E) Quality first concept

    (C) Physical distribution concept

15. For which of the following consumer goods would an individual most likely compare price, quality, and/or style?

    (A) Convenience goods   (D) Industrial goods

    (B) Shopping goods   (E) Unsought goods

    (C) Specialty goods

16. Which of the following consumer goods are infrequently purchased, and require extensive decision-making time?

    (A) Convenience goods   (D) Consumer goods

    (B) Shopping goods   (E) Unsought goods

    (C) Specialty goods

17. Which of the following stages in the new product development process involves the firm estimating how many units must be sold in order to cover the cost of production?

    (A) Idea generation   (D) Test marketing

    (B) Screening and evaluation (E) Development and testing

    (C) Business analysis

18. Which of the following stages in the new product process includes manufacturing, laboratory, and consumer tests?

    (A) New product strategy development

    (B) Idea generation

    (C) Screening and evaluation

    (D) Test marketing

    (E) Development and testing

19. The failure of a new product is usually attributable to all of the following except which one?

    (A) Too small a target market

    (B) Bad timing

    (C) Poor execution of the marketing mix

(D) Existence and quality of "protocol"

(E) All of the above.

20. From a consumer's viewpoint, what kind of innovation would an improved electric blanket be?

(A) Innovation

(B) Continuous innovation

(C) Dynamically continuous innovation

(D) Discontinuous innovation

(E) None of the above.

21. Environmental scanning is an important step in planning a market opportunity analysis. In relation to international marketing, which of the following environments deals with nationalism (putting a country's interests before everything else)?

(A) Economic   (D) Legal

(B) Technological   (E) Natural environmental

(C) Political

22. Which of the following is not part of the marketing mix?

(A) Product   (D) Promotion

(B) Price   (E) Channels of distribution

(C) Planning

23. Which of the following steps are included in both marketing research and scientific research studies?

(A) Problem definition

(B) Evaluation of alternative actions

(C) Recommendations for "correct actions"

(D) Findings

(E) All of the above.

24. When designing a research study, the researcher must make sure that the research study actually measures what it is supposed to measure. This concept is called

    (A) reliability.   (D) observation.

    (B) validity.   (E) sampling statistics.

    (C) communication.

25. Which of the following acts were enacted to reduce, or stop, the lessening of competition in the United States?

    (A) Killem Off Act   (D) Clayton Act

    (B) Sherman Act   (E) None of the above.

    (C) Magnuson-Moss Act

26. Reciprocity means

    (A) buy from me and I'll buy from you.

    (B) buy from me or I'll ruin your product's name.

    (C) buy from me and I'll give you free samples.

    (D) I'll buy from you no matter who you buy from.

    (E) None of the above.

27. Which of the following conditions are favorable to successful branding?

    (A) The dependability and availability of the product are limited.

    (B) The demand for the general product class is small.

    (C) There are not economies of scale.

    (D) The demand is strong enough so that the market price can be high enough to make the branding effort profitable.

    (E) All of the above are favorable conditions for successful branding.

28. SIC stands for

    (A) Single industry code.

    (B) Several innovative classes.

(C) Standard industrial classification.

(D) Sub-industrial codes.

(E) Standard industry code.

29. The United States Government market is a large market in and of itself. The U.S. spends billions every year on products and services. Some marketers choose to ignore this market, why?

(A) Afraid of not being paid

(B) Too much competition

(C) Not enough competition

(D) Too much red tape (bureaucracy)

(E) (B) and (C) only are correct.

30. Sellers usually approach organizational customers directly. They do this through sales representatives. The use of representatives helps to

(A) personally pressure a customer to buy from you.

(B) adjust the marketing mix for each individual customer.

(C) size up the customer to decide if you want to call on them again.

(D) see the look in their eyes as you talk about the product.

(E) None of the above.

31. Which of the following is not a step in the five-step marketing research process?

(A) Problem definition   (D) Writing the proposal

(B) Solving the problem   (E) Analyzing the situation

(C) Interpreting the data

32. The accuracy of quantitative data is effected by

(A) the response rate.   (D) All of the above.

(B) the sample size.   (E) None of the above.

(C) the sampling procedure.

33. Which of the following is true about a Market Information System (MIS)?

    (A) MIS is a way of continually gathering and analyzing data to provide marketing managers with information they need to make decisions.

    (B) MIS is very expensive and only large firms can develop an effective system.

    (C) The information obtained from the MIS is all the information a manager needs to know for decision-making.

    (D) MIS should only be used when all other avenues for research have been explored.

    (E) MIS should not be used in marketing.

34. Most small companies

    (A) usually do not have separate marketing research departments.

    (B) may use outside research specialists.

    (C) can afford a reliable marketing information system.

    (D) depend on sales people or managers to conduct what research they do.

    (E) All of the above.

35. Income that is left after paying for the family's necessities and that is used for "luxuries" is called

    (A) discretionary income.

    (B) disposable income.

    (C) net profit.

    (D) gross profit.

    (E) there is no such definition or word.

36. Which of the following factors of income effect spending patterns?

    (A) Geographic location of a customer's family

    (B) Geographic boundaries

    (C) Marital status, age, and the age of the children of a family

(D) (A) and (C) only.

(E) All of the above.

37. Which of the following describes the typical buying behavior of the senior citizen?

(A) They feel affluent and free. They buy basic household goods, and are more interested in recreation, cars, and clothes.

(B) They feel financially well off. The house may be paid for, thus they may move into an apartment or travel, and they're not interested in new products.

(C) There is a big drop in income, which means they may keep their home but cut back on most purchases except medical care and other health-related items.

(D) Their income is still strong but they are likely to sell their home and continue with their current lifestyle.

(E) None of the above are true.

38. An important family life-cycle category to sell to, and an attractive market for many products and services because of the unusually high income period for the workers in the demographic segment, may be

(A) empty nesters.

(B) senior citizens.

(C) divorced people.

(D) single/unmarried people.

(E)   young marrieds with children.

39. The predominately growing population in the job market, which boosts economic growth, is changing the United State's economy and is creating new opportunities for marketers. Which of the following would best describe this category?

(A) College graduates

(B) Minorities

(C) Married women with paying jobs

(D) Children

(E) High school graduates

40. Why is it often desirable for a marketing manager to combine personal selling with advertising, public relations, direct marketing, and sales promotion?

    (A) To provide immediate feedback

    (B) To provide flexibility

    (C) To save on personal selling expense

    (D) To help salespeople adapt to their environments

    (E) To provide message interpretation

41. Which of the following promotional methods may best be described as mass selling?

    (A) Personal selling and sales promotion

    (B) Advertising and publicity

    (C) Encoding and decoding

    (D) Personal selling and public relations

    (E) Product and promotion

42. Numerous individuals are involved in the management of the promotion mix. Sales promotion managers would most likely manage which of the following?

    (A) Salespeople

    (B) The company's mass selling effort

    (C) The company's sales promotion effort filling in gaps between personal selling and mass selling

    (D) The effective promotion blend fitting this blend to the various departments and personalities involved in promotion, and coordinating these efforts

    (E) Public relations

43. Sales promotion expenditures are growing and are aimed toward which of the following group(s)?

    (A) Final consumers or users

    (B) Middlemen, or intermediaries

(C)   Employees

(D)   Mature markets

(E)   All of the above.

44.   Whenever the product involves a physical good, the place variable of the marketing mix requires physical distribution. Another name for physical distribution is

(A)   place utility.

(D)   transportation.

(B)   diversion in transit.

(E)   conveyance.

(C)   logistics.

45.   Transporting is the marketing function of moving goods. Transportation provides which of the following utilities?

(A)   Time utility

(B)   Possession utility

(C)   Place utility

(D)   Only (A) and (C)

(E)   All of the above utilities are provided by transportation.

46.   The total cost approach of physical distribution includes which of the following?

(A)   Evaluating each physical distribution system

(B)   Cost accounting

(C)   Inventory carrying costs

(D)   All of the above.

(E)   None of the above.

47.   Which social class group is matched correctly with their approximate size for those social classes in the United States?

(A)   Upper-class—32%

(B)   Upper-middle class—38%

(C)   Lower-middle class—1.5%

(D) Upper-lower (or "working") class—12.5%

(E) Lower-lower class—16%

48. Which of the following is NOT included in the five-step problem-solving process utilized by consumers when purchasing products and services?

(A) Awareness of a problem

(B) Information gathering and recall

(C) Alternative solution evaluation

(D) Solution selection

(E) Purchase decision sharing among friends and family

49. A music lover wanting a higher-quality sound from a CD player is most apt to use which of the following levels of problem solving?

(A) Limited problem-solving

(B) Routinized response behavior

(C) Extensive problem-solving

(D) Psychological variable problem-solving

(E) Social influences

50. When a consumer experiences cognitive dissonance, this means

(A) without confirmation, the adopter may buy something else next time he makes a purchase.

(B) the consumer's doubts may lead to tension.

(C) the customer is experiencing uncertainty about the correctness of his purchase decision.

(D) the consumer may seek additional information to confirm his purchase decision.

(E) All of the above may happen.

Section 2

TIME: 45 Minutes
50 Questions

DIRECTIONS: Each of the questions or incomplete statements below is followed by five possible answers or completions. Select the best choice in each case and fill in the corresponding oval on the answer sheet.

---

51. Communicating information between the seller and the potential buyer, or others in the channel, to influence attitudes and behavior is known as

    (A) marketing.

    (B) promotion.

    (C) pricing.

    (D) channels of distribution.

    (E) All of the above.

52. Which type of allowance is used for new items, slower-moving items, or higher-margin items?

    (A) Trade-in allowance

    (B) Prize-money allowance

    (C) Advertising allowance

    (D) Stocking allowance

    (E) Weekly allowance

53. What is the term used that means the seller pays the cost of loading the products onto some transportation vehicle, then at the point of loading title passes to the buyer who usually also assumes responsibility for damage en route and pays the freight costs?

    (A) Freight absorption pricing

    (B) Zone pricing

    (C) F.O.B. pricing

    (D) Uniformed delivered pricing

    (E) Loading cost pricing

54. Which of the following terms refers to products that are bought often and routinely, without much thought?

(A) Impulse products   (D) Services

(B) Emergency products   (E) Durable goods

(C) Staples

55. Which of the following are products used to produce other products?

(A) Emergency goods   (D) Convenience products

(B) Consumer products   (E) Specialty goods

(C) Industrial products

56. The use of a name, term, symbol, design, or a combination thereof that may or may not be registered is called

(A) a trademark.   (D) a service mark.

(B) a brand.   (E) brand recognition.

(C) a brand name.

57. Which of the following are (is) used by a company to help separate brand names for each of the company's products, when the products are of varying quality or type?

(A) Licensed brands   (D) Individual brands

(B) Dealer brands   (E) Licensed-dealer brands

(C) Manufacturer brands

58. Packaging involves

(A) promotion.   (D) containment.

(B) product identification.   (E) All of the above.

(C) protection.

59. The marketing environment does not include which of the following?

(A) Objectives and resources of the firm

(B) Economic and technological environments

(C) Political and legal environments

(D) Cultural and social environments

(E) Employment environments

60. Which of the following are important when considering what objectives a firm sets for themselves?

    (A) To engage in specific activities that will perform a socially and economically useful function

    (B) To develop an organization to carry on the business and implement its strategies

    (C) To earn the highest possible profits

    (D) All of the above are true.

    (E) Only (A) and (B) are true.

61. Which of the following would NOT be a marketing objective?

    (A) Product objectives

    (B) Channels of distribution objectives

    (C) Employee training objectives

    (D) Promotion objectives

    (E) Price objectives

62. A marketing manager must compete for customers with competitors who are offering very similar types of products, and where there are just a few sellers in the industry. This environmental situation would best be described as

    (A) an oligopoly.   (D) industry leadership.

    (B) head-on competition.   (E) a monopoly.

    (C) democracy.

63. Which of the following would be examples of economic environments that are not monitored by a marketing manager in a large corporation?

    (A) Consumer's income levels

    (B) Interest rates

    (C) Rates of inflation

    (D) Competitor's advertising budgets

    (E) Exchange rates

64. Which of the following are (is) common mistakes a marketing manager could make when introducing a new product?

   (A) Incorrectly estimating how long it will take for potential competitors to enter the market

   (B) Failing to consider that there will be competition

   (C) Discounting how aggressive the competition may be

   (D) Ignoring competitors' strengths and weaknesses

   (E) All of the above are mistakes that could be made.

65. Which of the following acts deals with deceptive advertising, selling practices, and deceptive pricing?

   (A) The Sherman Act

   (B) The Clayton Act

   (C) The Federal Trade Commission Act

   (D) The Magnuson-Moss Act

   (E) The Antimerger Act

66. Businesses and business managers are subject to which of the following for violation of Federal Antimonopoly Law?

   (A) Criminal actions

   (B) Local actions

   (C) Civil actions

   (D) Criminal and civil actions

   (E) None of the above.

67. Which of the following would make up the cultural and social environment that have an effect on consumer's buying behaviors?

   (A) Languages people speak

   (B) Religious beliefs

   (C) Consumer's views on marriage and family

   (D) All of the above.

   (E) (B) and (C) only.

68. When assessing a market situation utilizing the GE Strategic Planning Grid, which of the following is (are) not considered when looking at business strengths?

    (A) How long a company has been in business

    (B) If the firm has people with the right talents for implementation

    (C) Whether the plan is consistent with the firm's profit objectives

    (D) Whether the plan is consistent with the firm's image

    (E) Whether the plan could establish a profitable market share given its technical capability, costs, and size

69. A multi-product firm is most likely to use which type of strategic planning approach when considering alternative products?

    (A) Total profit approach   (D) Portfolio management

    (B) ROI approach   (E) All of the above.

    (C) GE Planning Grid approach

70. When developing a final price for a product, the marketing manager needs to know several things about product cost. Which of the following costs, in relation to accounting costs, is most related to product output?

    (A) Break-even point   (D) Total variable cost

    (B) Average cost   (E) Total fixed cost

    (C) Total cost

71. Which of the following best describes "value in use" pricing?

    (A) The price the customers expect to pay for many of the products they purchase

    (B) Setting some very low prices in order to get customers into retail stores

    (C) Setting very low prices to attract customers, with the intent to sell more expensive products once the customers are in the store

    (D) Setting prices that will capture some of what the customers will save by substituting the firm's product for one that is currently being used by the customer

(E) None of the above define "value in use" pricing.

72. Which of the following is not part of a target return strategy when it deals with pricing?

   (A) It is a variation of the average-cost method, since the desired target return is added into the total cost.

   (B) This approach has the same weaknesses as other average-cost pricing methods.

   (C) If the quantity actually sold is less than the quantity used to set the price, then the company does not earn its target return even though the target return seems to be part of the price structure.

   (D) Adding a target return to the cost of a product is outdated.

   (E) All of the above are part of target return strategies.

73. Regional Wal-Mart stores are selling a specific shirt for $19.99 because the store managers believe that customers react better to these types of prices. This type of pricing may be categorized as

   (A) bait pricing.   (D) price leveling.

   (B) odd-even pricing.   (E) price discrimination.

   (C) prestige pricing.

74. A shaver is priced very low. The blades that are sold for the shaver have a higher price, and a larger profit margin. The idea is to increase the profits for the blades. What is this type of pricing called?

   (A) Prestige pricing

   (B) Product-bundle pricing

   (C) Complementary product pricing

   (D) Full-line pricing

   (E) Demand backward pricing

75. Bit Johnson sells four units of his famous BJ733 barbecue grill system, resulting in a total revenue of $420.00. His total revenue for five units is $460.00. The price on the four units is $105.00 per unit and the price for the five units (per unit) is $92.00. What is the marginal revenue for the fifth unit?

(A) $13.00   (D) $52.00

(B) $40.00   (E) $26.00

(C) –$40.00

76. Marianne Johnson Cookies has a total cost for producing delicious macaroon cookies of $102,000. The quantity produced is 90,000 units with a total fixed cost of $30,000. Estimate the average cost.

(A) $3.40

(B) $3.00

(C) $1.13

(D) $1.18

(E) Cannot be estimated from the information given.

77. Which of the following best describes the conditions found in the market maturity stage of the product life cycle?

(A) Consumers view the products in the market as homogenous.

(B) Industry profits begin to rise.

(C) Promotional advertising is unnecessary.

(D) Industry sales are at their lowest point.

(E) New firms can only enter the market during this phase.

78. Which stage of the product life cycle would have the lowest industry profits, where a firm entering may experience profit losses?

(A) Market introduction

(B) Market growth

(C) Market maturity

(D) Sales decline

(E) Sales and profits decline, then rise

79. Alarid Incorporated wants to know how their new product idea will fit the needs of the consumers. The best way to accomplish this would be by which of the following?

(A) Concept testing

(B)   Manufacturing the product to see if anybody buys it

(C)   Produce only the ideas that have a large return on investment (ROI)

(D)   Test market the product in a few selected cities

(E)   Introduce the product using a roll-out strategy

80.   Alison goes to McDonald's and places an order for a burger and fries. The person who is receiving that order for McDonald's is called

(A)   an order getter.

(D)   a technical representative.

(B)   an order taker.

(E)   a food hasher.

(C)   a sales supporter.

81.   A company that has sales representatives working on some of the same accounts is utilizing which of the following?

(A)   Technical reps

(D)   Missionary selling

(B)   Supporting salespeople

(E)   Order taking

(C)   Team selling

82.   Ninfa is walking down an aisle in a supermarket. Noticing a display of cookies, she suddenly has a craving for them. The cookies are an example of what type of good?

(A)   A staple

(D)   A specialty product

(B)   A shopping good

(E)   An unsought good

(C)   An impulse good

83.   Brian and Frank sell many different varieties of products. All of the products that Brian and Frank offer to their consumers are called

(A)   product assortment.

(B)   product line.

(C)   individually branded products.

(D)   product variety.

(E)   product life cycle.

84. Ken and Sally's baby, Jennifer, has begun to cry. Ken goes to Jennifer's room to see why, and finds that Jennifer needs a diaper change. Ken asks Sally to bring a disposable diaper to him so that he can change the baby. While looking, Sally discovers there are no diapers and that she or Ken must immediately go to the store to purchase this item. The diaper is a good example of what type of good?

   (A) Emergency good

   (B) Specialty good

   (C) Unsought good

   (D) Impulse good

   (E) Shopping good

85. Jan Winfield will only buy Levi jeans. If one store does not have her size, she will go to another store to purchase them. This is an example of which of the following?

   (A) Brand preference

   (B) Brand recognition

   (C) Brand nonrecognition

   (D) Brand insistence

   (E) Brand rejection

86. A clothing company decides to purchase a manufacturer of cosmetics. The clothing company has no experience in cosmetics. This strategy would be referred to as

   (A) product development.

   (B) market penetration.

   (C) market development.

   (D) diversification.

   (E) a balancing strategy.

87. Which of the following sales promotion techniques are generally NOT aimed at middlemen, or intermediaries?

   (A) Trade shows

   (B) Push money

   (C) Aisle displays

   (D) Catalogs

   (E) All of the above are traditionally aimed at middlemen or intermediaries.

88. A write-up in the local paper's "Dining Out" column includes information about your restaurant. This best represents what type of promotion?

    (A) Sales promotion
    (B) Publicity
    (C) Personal selling
    (D) Advertising
    (E) Merchandising

89. Which of the following products would most likely utilize intensive distribution?

    (A) Shopping products
    (B) Specialty products
    (C) Unsought products
    (D) Convenience products
    (E) All of the above mentioned products should utilize intensive distribution.

90. A selective distribution policy might be used to avoid selling to wholesalers and/or retailers for a number of reasons. Which of the following reason(s) could be given for following a selective strategy?

    (A) Retailers/wholesalers have a poor credit rating.
    (B) The intermediaries have a reputation for making too many returns or requests for service calls.
    (C) The middlemen place orders that are too small to justify making calls or providing service.
    (D) The intermediaries are not in a position to do a satisfactory job.
    (E) All of the above are good reasons.

91. There are four types of regrouping activities associated with physical distribution management. Of these four, which one involves separating products into grades and/or quality that may be desired by the different target markets?

    (A) Assorting
    (B) Bulk breaking
    (C) Accumulating
    (D) Sorting
    (E) All of the above are true.

92. Suzanne Marie is a salesperson who utilizes a prepared and memorized presentation of the product she sells every time she goes out on sales calls. This approach to selling is better known as

    (A) cold calling.

    (B) a sales presentation.

    (C) a canned sales approach.

    (D) consultative selling.

    (E) the selling formula approach.

93. An organized way of continually gathering and analyzing data to provide marketing managers with the most up-to-date information they need to make decisions is called

    (A) decision support systems (DSS).

    (B) marketing models.

    (C) marketing research.

    (D) marketing information systems (MIS).

    (E) consumer panels.

94. A poorly written and worded question that has different meanings to different respondents, when used in a marketing research setting, is said to have poor

    (A) validity.   (D) confidence interval.

    (B) accuracy.   (E) sample.

    (C) reliability.

95. What type of research seeks to find in-depth, open-ended responses?

    (A) Quantitative   (D) Experimental

    (B) Marketing   (E) Qualitative

    (C) Chi square

96. Tuttie Babe Bikes, a manufacturer of mountain, ten speed, and other bikes, wants to divide its entire market into different groups. One group is for those who exercise, another for those who need trans-

portation, and so on. They want to develop a different marketing mix for each of these groups. This process of dividing consumers into different groups with similar needs is called

(A) positioning.

(D) combining.

(B) market.

(E) marketing.

(C) segmenting.

97. The Butzie Company wants to expand its geographical area. Butzie wants to open stores on the West Coast, as well as operate the ones they currently have in the Grand Rapids, Michigan, area. What type of opportunity is Butzie pursuing?

(A) Market development

(D) Product development

(B) Market penetration

(E) Market segmentation

(C) Diversification

98. Poudre Pie Burgers started a new promotion for its stores. They have a "Burger-of-the-Month." The burger is a new brand that consumers have not seen before and it is only offered for a particular month. This is an example of what type of marketing opportunity, or strategy?

(A) Diversification

(B) Product development

(C) Market development

(D) Market penetration

(E) Standardization and grading

99. The difference between the quantity of products that is economically feasible to create for a manufacturer or producer, and the quantity of products desired by the final users of that product is called

(A) discrepancy of quantity.

(D) accumulating.

(B) discrepancy of assortment.

(E) advertising.

(C) regrouping.

100. Vertical marketing channel-systems, in which the whole channel focuses on the same target market at the end of the channel, could best be described as which of the following?

    (A) A corporate channel system

    (B) An administered channel system

    (C) A contractual channel system

    (D) It could be described by both (A) and (B).

    (E) It could be described by (A), (B), or (C).

CLEP PRINCIPLES OF MARKETING
TEST 3

ANSWER KEY

Section 1

1.	(B)	14.	(C)	27.	(D)	39.	(C)
2.	(A)	15.	(B)	28.	(C)	40.	(C)
3.	(E)	16.	(C)	29.	(D)	41.	(B)
4.	(B)	17.	(C)	30.	(B)	42.	(C)
5.	(D)	18.	(E)	31.	(D)	43.	(E)
6.	(A)	19.	(D)	32.	(D)	44.	(C)
7.	(B)	20.	(C)	33.	(A)	45.	(D)
8.	(E)	21.	(C)	34.	(E)	46.	(D)
9.	(C)	22.	(C)	35.	(A)	47.	(E)
10.	(E)	23.	(E)	36.	(E)	48.	(E)
11.	(B)	24.	(B)	37.	(C)	49.	(C)
12.	(C)	25.	(D)	38.	(A)	50.	(E)
13.	(A)	26.	(A)				

Section 2

51.	(B)	64.	(E)	77.	(A)	89.	(D)
52.	(B)	65.	(C)	78.	(A)	90.	(E)
53.	(C)	66.	(D)	79.	(A)	91.	(D)
54.	(C)	67.	(D)	80.	(B)	92.	(C)
55.	(C)	68.	(A)	81.	(C)	93.	(D)
56.	(B)	69.	(D)	82.	(C)	94.	(A)
57.	(D)	70.	(D)	83.	(A)	95.	(E)
58.	(E)	71.	(D)	84.	(A)	96.	(C)
59.	(E)	72.	(D)	85.	(D)	97.	(A)
60.	(D)	73.	(B)	86.	(C)	98.	(B)
61.	(C)	74.	(C)	87.	(C)	99.	(A)
62.	(A)	75.	(B)	88.	(B)	100.	(E)
63.	(D)	76.	(C)				

DETAILED EXPLANATIONS OF ANSWERS

TEST 3

Section 1

1. **(B)** This is a difficult question, however the answer can be calculated as C = $113.33, while the SP = $130.33. The formula to calculate cost and selling price is as follows: Markup % on Cost × Cost = Amount of Markup. Thus, .15 × Cost = $17. Since $17/.15 = $113.33, this is the cost. Because this is the cost (A), (C), (D), and (E) cannot be correct. SP = Cost + Markup, so SP = $113.33 + .15($113.33) or SP = $113.33 + $17, which equals SP = $130.33.

2. **(A)** To find markup percent on cost, the amount of markup is divided by the cost. (B), (C), and (D) are incorrect because $250/$500 = 50%. (E) is an incorrect choice because the answer can be calculated from the information given. Remember, the calculations are based upon cost, not retail selling price.

3. **(E)** The markup percent would be 2.8 percent. The markup on retail selling price is calculated by dividing the amount of markup by the selling price, thus (A), (B), (C), and (D) are incorrect choices. $95/$3,400 = 2.79% rounded to 2.8%.

4. **(B)** Because Retail Selling Price(SP) = Cost(C) + Markup(M), C = SP – M. (A) is the amount of markup (.40 × $400 = $160) and is therefore not the cost. (C), (D), and (E) are incorrect because C = $400 – $160 (.4 × 400), or $240. Additionally, if the retail price is $400, the cost cannot be more than that, which (D) at $440 and (E) at $500 are. Remember, this calculation is performed on the retail selling price, not the cost.

5. **(D)** To calculate markdown, the new selling price is subtracted from the original, or regular price. (A), (B), and (C) are incorrect because

$500 - $480 = $20. Additionally, a markdown of $480 would make the selling price of the product $20. A markdown of $200 would make the selling price $300, and a markdown of $75 would make the selling price $425. (E) is incorrect because there is a real markdown, and it can be calculated from the information given.

6.   **(A)**   In order to calculate markdown percentages, the amount of markdown is divided by the new selling price of the product, therefore (B), (C), (D), and (E) are all incorrect because 37/100 = 37%. If Marianne wanted to calculate the percentage markdown from the original selling price of the product, she would use the original selling price as the denominator instead of the new selling price. Since the original selling price is not given in the problem, this calculation cannot be performed.

7.   **(B)**   In order to determine what percentage you should use for the maintained markup, you need to subtract the retail reduction percentage times 100% minus the initial markup percent. (A) is incorrect for maintained markup, although it is a way to calculate markup price. (C) is an incorrect formula for maintained markup percent. (D) is also incorrect for determining maintained markup percent. (E) is incorrect although it gives the correct formula for determining the initial markup percent.

8.   **(E)**   The term 2/10 net 30 means that if the invoice is paid within ten days, the buyer is afforded a 2% discount. In this case, the invoice was paid after the ten-day period offering the discount, thus there is no discount. (A) is incorrect, although it would be correct if the buyer were to pay the invoice within the allotted ten-day period. (B), (C), and (D) are incorrect even if the invoice were paid within the ten-day period. The invoice must be paid within the 30-day period as 2/10 net 30 means that there is a 2% discount if paid within ten days, but the net (or balance) due must be paid within thirty days.

9.   **(C)**   Major Mark's Buying Office must sell the belts for $49.23 in order to achieve their desired markup. (A) is incorrect because the information is adequate to determine the sales price. (B) is incorrect because 35% = Retail Sales Price − $32/SP. Thus, .35(Sales Price) = Sales Price − $32, and .65(Sales Price) = $32, so the Selling Price would have to be $49.23. (D) and (E) are also incorrect calculations of the sales price based upon a 35% markup and a $32 cost.

10.   **(E)**   If Baby is retailing her lotions at $20 per lotion, and needs to

achieve a 50% markup at retail, she cannot pay over $10 for each bottle of lotion that she purchases. (A), (B), (C), and (D) have costs that are too high for Baby to achieve her desired markup. Remember that Sales Price = Cost + Markup (SP = C + M). Therefore, $20 (Baby's Retail Price) = C + 50%($20). So, $20 = C + 10, and therefore the C = $10. The maximum Baby can pay for each of the bottles of lotion is $10. Of course, less would provide for a greater markup.

11.   **(B)**   Public warehouses are independent storing facilities that are used by companies with a large range of fluctuation between busy seasons (for example, Christmas for the toy manufacturer) and slow seasons. Private warehouses (A) would be inefficient for companies who would only use it a few months out of the year, such as a toy manufacturer. Distribution centers (C) are utilized in redistributing products. They do not specialize in storage. (D) containerization refers to the regrouping activity of putting items into economical shipping quantities, and is not the correct answer. (E) is incorrect because the toy manufacturer is more than likely going to need storage facilities.

12.   **(C)**   Air would be the worst choice, and is the correct answer. Because of the high cost of air transportation, heavy items, such as coal, cost too much to ship via this mode of transportation. Water (A) would be a feasible choice for heavy, bulky items if this mode is available. Water would also be the least expensive. Rail (B) and truck (D) would be acceptable ways to transport coal, although rail would be the least expensive of the two, and probably the better choice. All of the above (E) are not acceptable methods of transportation, and this answer is not a good choice.

13.   **(A)**   Pillsbury needs a distribution center to get their desired mix of products to each of their individual customers. A public warehouse (B), or a private warehouse (C) refer only to the ownership of the warehouse (i.e., a private warehouse is owned by the company while public warehouses have independent owners), and would not help to redistribute Pillsbury's products. Freight forwarders (D), while they do combine shipments, do that function for different firms or companies, not for the same company. Air distribution (E), although a potential mode of transportation, is a poor answer because it has nothing to do with product mixture.

14.   **(C)**   The essence of the physical distribution concept is to consider transporting along with all of the other marketing considerations, and strive for the lowest cost for a level of service. While the total cost ap-

proach (A) may seem like the correct answer, it refers to picking the best transportation in relation to cost. It does not stress the integration of transporting in the decision-making process. The variable cost approach (B) is not a correct answer. All costs must be looked at when deciding on a transportation mode. Additionally, when integrating all of the functions, this approach would not be considered. Logistics (D) is simply another name for transportation and is incorrect. The quality first concept (E) is a fictitious term and doesn't apply here.

15. **(B)** Of the choices given, shopping goods are items that the consumer would take the time to compare price, quality, and/or style when making a decision to purchase. Convenience goods are items that the consumer needs and purchases frequently, but with a minimum of shopping effort; price would not be that important so (A) is not correct. Specialty goods are items that the consumer would make a special effort to search out and buy, and again, a higher price may not be a deterrent to purchase, therefore (C) is incorrect. Industrial goods are products used in the production of other products for final consumption and are not consumer goods, therefore (D) is not the best choice. (E) is incorrect because unsought goods are goods that the consumer does not know about or initially want.

16. **(C)** Specialty goods are products that a consumer will make a special effort to search out and buy. Specialty goods are usually expensive and the unique brand and/or status is stressed by the seller. (A) is incorrect. Convenience goods are frequently purchased and require little shopping time and effort. Shopping goods are also infrequently purchased, but require comparisons among several alternatives, so (B) is not the best choice. Consumer goods (D) is incorrect. Consumer goods includes ALL goods purchased by the ultimate consumer. (E) is incorrect because unsought goods are products the consumer initially does not want, or may not know about.

17. **(C)** The firm would make a business project for a break-even point in units during the business analysis phase. Idea generation (A) is incorrect. This is the process of developing a useful pool of ideas to turn into products. Screening and evaluation (B) is also incorrect. This involves internal and external evaluations of the new product ideas allowing the elimination of those ideas that don't appear to be profitable or feasible. Test marketing (D) involves exposing the new product to realistic purchase conditions in order to test the marketing mix variables, as well as

repurchase rates. Development and testing (E) involves turning an idea into a prototype and testing this prototype for numerous things such as safety and packaging.

18.   **(E)**   This involves turning the product idea into a prototype, and testing for packaging, product safety, and other problems to make sure the product is feasible to manufacture. The new product strategy development phase (A) is incorrect. This phase is concerned with an overall strategy, or fit, for a new product. The firm is trying to define the role the new product should play in the overall product mix. (B) is incorrect. Idea generation involves developing a pool of ideas as candidates for the new product. Screening and evaluation (C) is also incorrect. This phase involves utilizing internal and external evaluations to eliminate ideas that don't "fit" for the firm, or that aren't reasonable and feasible. The test marketing phase (D) is also incorrect. In this phase the product is actually tested under controlled market conditions.

19.   **(D)**   The biggest difference between successful and unsuccessful products is a well-defined target market statement, or "protocol." A protocol identifies customers' needs to be satisfied and includes a statement of wants and preferences. If a protocol exists, chances are that a product will succeed, not fail. Too small of a target market (A) may make a new product fail. Bad timing (B) is also a cause for product failure. Introducing a product too early or too late can mean doom for the product, thus this answer is incorrect. All of the marketing mix variables must be controlled and executed as planned; poor execution will almost always spell failure for a product, thus (C) is incorrect. Since there is a correct answer, All of the above (E) is incorrect.

20.   **(C)**   An improved electric blanket would be considered a dynamically continuous innovation. Radically new behavior is not required by the consumer to use an electric blanket, although a slight change in behavior is required. An innovation would simply be a new product or concept on the market, so (A) is incorrect. With continuous innovation, no new behaviors are required so (B) would not be the best choice. Discontinuous innovation involves making the consumer establish entirely new consumption patterns. A significant amount of time must be spent by the seller educating the consumer so (D) is not correct. Since there is a correct answer, (E) is incorrect.

21.   **(C)**   The political environment of a country deals with how the

people feel about their country and government. They may express their feelings with actions. (A) is incorrect because the economic environment would concentrate more on the GDP, imports, exports, etc. (B) is also incorrect. The technological environment would deal more with now equipped and skilled the country is when dealing with technological advances. The legal environment (D) deals with the country's law and legal/judicial systems. The natural environment (E) would also be incorrect, because the concern here would be the physical environment.

22.   **(C)**   Planning, although a necessary function of marketing, is not a part of the marketing mix. The development of a successful marketing strategy depends on the effective combination of those elements that make up what is called the marketing mix. These elements include channels of distribution (place); product; price and integrated marketing communications (promotion). (A) is part of the marketing mix and deals with the development of products including packaging, branding, and labeling. (B) is part of the marketing mix and deals with selecting the best, or most correct, price for a product so that it will be profitable. Promotion (D) is a marketing mix variable that deals with the development of integrated marketing communications. Promotion provides communication via personal selling, advertising, and sales promotion (along with other methods). Channels of distribution (E) is an important marketing mix variable and is the method used to get the product to the final consumer, or end user.

23.   **(E)**   When designing either a marketing research study or scientific study the researcher must understand what problem (A) needs to be solved. Additionally, the researcher must develop alternatives in order to have a choice of options of what to do, so (B) is not the best choice. The researcher must also make a best decision, or a most correct choice, from given alternatives, so (C) is not the best choice. (D) is incorrect because findings should be stated and communicated to the users of the data.

24.   **(B)**   Validity means that the study actually measures what it purports to measure. Reliability (A) means that the research instrument measures the same thing over and over. Communication (C) deals with a method of gathering data and reporting the findings. Observation (D) is a type of research. Finally, sampling statistics (E) refer to the means used to generalize a sample to a population.

25.   **(D)**   The Clayton Act's entire focus is to increase competition. (A) is incorrect; there is no such act. The focus of the Sherman Act (B) is

to reduce monopolies resulting in restraint of trade. The Magnuson Moss Act (C) was enacted primarily to deal with unreasonable practices in product warranties. (E) is incorrect because one of the above is true.

26. **(A)** "You scratch my back and I'll scratch yours" is known as reciprocity. (B) is incorrect, and is basically a threat. (C) is incorrect and may be bribery. (D) is not the best answer, and may not be too smart. (E) is incorrect because one of the answers is correct.

27. **(D)** The demand of a product should be strong enough to make the branding effort possible. If there is no dependability and availability of a product (A), favorable branding will not occur. The demand for the general product (B) should be large, not small, for favorable branding conditions. Economies of scale (C) should be present for favorable branding to occur. Because (D) is the correct choice, (E) cannot be correct.

28. **(C)** A standard industrial classification allows potential businesses, and buyers to select, by a code or classification, businesses who may be potential suppliers or customers. Answers (A), (B), (D), and (E) are fictitious definitions.

29. **(D)** Some marketers ignore the government market because they feel that the government red tape is more trouble than the business is worth. (A) is incorrect. The government does pay, although sometimes the payments are a little late in coming. (B) is incorrect, there is a lot of competition, however this is a big market. Not enough competition (C) is incorrect; the government market has plenty of competition. (E) is incorrect because there is a correct choice, and because it would be impossible to have too much and not enough competition.

30 **(B)** By utilizing sales representatives, the seller gets more of a chance to adjust the marketing mix variables for each individual customer. Duress is not legal, therefore (A) is incorrect. (C) is incorrect. You never know who's worth selling to. The least likely customer may turn out to be a large account months later. (D) is incorrect. Although it's good to see the look in the customer's eyes, you still must have the autonomy to adjust the marketing mix, thus increasing your chance of a sale. (E) is an incorrect choice, because marketing mix adjustment is the correct answer.

31. **(D)** Writing the proposal is not part of the five-step process. The proposal includes what steps should be undertaken to complete the re-

search and solve the problem, but is not part of the process in and of itself. (A) is part of the five-step process, thus it is incorrect. (B) is also incorrect as problem solution is an integral part of the process. (C) is incorrect; the process must include data interpretation. (E) is also part of the five-step marketing research process, and is thus, incorrect.

32. **(D)**   All of the above are required in order to have accurate, reliable, and valid research results. (A) is required for data accuracy, but is not the best answer and is incorrect. (B) and (C) are also required to give data accuracy, but are not the best choices. Since all of the above are required, none of the above (E) is incorrect.

33. **(A)**   MIS is a way of continually gathering and analyzing data that can be used for decision-making. (B) is incorrect. With the development of low-cost micro-computers, small as well as large firms can access powerful MIS systems. (C) is not the best choice because marketing managers must use marketing research to supplement data that have become available through MIS. (D) is incorrect. Other avenues of research should be explored, but not at the expense of MIS. Marketers should have an effective MIS implemented for better marketing results, thus (E) is incorrect.

34. **(E)**   Most small companies usually don't have separate marketing research departments (A); the cost is too high. Although (A) is true it is not the best answer. (B) is true but not the best answer, even though small firms do use outside specialists. Small companies can afford a reliable MIS (C), but this too, is not the best answer. There is a dependence on managers and salespeople to conduct research at smaller firms (D), but this is not the best answer. All of the choices are true.

35. **(A)**   Discretionary income is what is left over for a family to spend on luxury-type items after taxes and necessities. Disposable income (B) is income used to pay for necessities, after taxes. Net profit (C) is money a company has earned from operations during a specified time period, and is incorrect. Gross profit (D) is the money used to pay for the expenses of running a business. (E) is incorrect because there is a term associated with this definition.

36. **(E)**   Geographic locations (A) of a customer's family may effect how often, and when, the customers spend money for specific products, but the answer is not the most correct. Geographic boundaries (B) have a limited effect on where a consumer may shop, but is not the best answer.

Marital status, age, and the ages of a family's children (C) effect what type of expenditures a family may make but is not the most correct answer. (D) is incorrect, although (A) and (C) are true.

37.　**(C)**　The typical senior citizen sees a dramatic drop in their income. They may keep their home, but all expenditures, except medical and medical-related purchases, are cut back. (A) is incorrect. This would most likely describe a single, unmarried consumer. (B) is incorrect. This definition would most likely fit an empty-nester (older couples with no children living at home, yet the head-of-the-household still in the workforce). (D) is incorrect and would probably best describe a sole survivor who is still working. (E) is incorrect, because one of the above is true.

38.　**(A)**　The children have left the house, thus these people are able to spend their money in other ways. Additionally, they tend to have higher incomes which can be spent on themselves. Their homes are paid-off, or almost paid off, and their expenses are low. Senior citizens (B) have lower incomes and tend to have additional expenditures on health care. Many divorced individuals (C) actually find themselves in a financial bind, and their expenditures are limited to necessities. Single/unmarrieds (D) will not start off with a high income. Young marrieds with children (E) will find most of their money going to the children and child-related expenditures.

39.　**(C)**　Married women with paying jobs represent approximately 60% of the wives in the U.S. In the 1950s, only about 24% were working outside the home. This is generating new income and creating new opportunities for marketers. It is interesting to note that those working women earn approximately 65% of their male counterparts. College graduates (A) have not really changed the U.S. economy that much, or given new opportunities to marketers. Minorities (B) also have not given the marketer that many new opportunities, or boosted economic growth the way married women with paying jobs have. This portion of the population should be monitored however, as it continues to grow. Children (D) are not a predominate growing population because of declining birthrates, even though they are beginning to make up a larger market. High school graduate populations (E) is incorrect. This group is not increasing, and has not really boosted economic growth nor created too many new opportunities for marketers. This group, however, should be monitored for changing purchase behaviors such as high technology.

40. **(C)** Although salespeople are included in most marketing mixes, personal selling has the disadvantage of being very expensive per contact. Therefore it is desirable to include other methods of promotion with personal selling. (A) is incorrect. Personal selling provides the most immediate feedback of all promotional activities. (B) is incorrect. Flexibility is really a benefit of personal selling. (D) is also incorrect. These other promotional activities do not really help the salesperson adapt to any environment. Finally (E) is incorrect. Personal selling is actually the best way to provide for interpretation of messages.

41. **(B)** Advertising and publicity are methods of communicating with large numbers of people at the same time and can be referred to as mass selling. (A) is incorrect because personal selling is face-to-face with one person or a small group of people. (C) describes two steps of the communication process, and is incorrect. Personal selling and public relations (D) are incorrect. Public relations, one could argue, may be mass selling, however, as stated above, personal selling is not. Product and promotion (E) are two variables of the marketing mix, and are not promotional methods, thus the answer is incorrect.

42. **(C)** Sales promotion managers manage the company's sales promotion activities, filling the gap between personal selling and mass selling. (A) is incorrect because sales managers manage salespeople. (B) is incorrect. Advertising managers generally manage the advertising functions, while public relations directors manage the publicity function. (D) is not the best choice. Marketing managers would best be left to manage this function. Public relations (E) are a function of mass selling, and would most likely be managed by a public relations director. This answer is not the most correct choice.

43. **(E)** Sales promotion activities should be aimed at final consumers, intermediaries, employees, and mature markets in order to be effective. Final consumers (A) is true, but not the most correct choice. Firms utilize sales promotions aimed at final consumers to increase demand, or to speed up the time of purchase. (B) is true but not the most correct choice. If the firm wants to stress price-related matters, then sales promotions aimed toward intermediaries may be effective. (C) is true but also not the best choice. Emphasis on getting new customers, introducing new products or selling an entire company line of products would be instances where sales promotions should be used for employees. Finally, (D) is true but not the most correct choice. Mature markets utilize heavy sales promotions where competition for customers and attention from middlemen is required.

44. **(C)** Logistics is another common term used for physical distribution. Place requires distribution decisions and the correct channel of distribution is critical for product success. Place utility (A) is achieved through physical distribution. However, physical distribution also provides time utility and makes possession or ownership utility possible. Diversion in transit (B) allows redirection of goods already in transit. (D) is not correct. Transportation is just one of the variables, or activities, associated with physical distribution. Conveyance (E) is a synonym for transportation and is incorrect.

45. **(D)** Transportation provides for both time and place utility. Transportation adds value to a marketing strategy, but adds this value at a cost. If the cost is less than the value added to the product, the transportation mode should be utilized. (A) is true but not the best answer. Time utility is created by transporting product, but so is place utility. (B) is incorrect. Possession utility is helped by transportation, but transportation alone does not create possession utility. (C) is true but is not the most correct choice. Place utility is provided for by transportation, but, as stated above, transportation also provides time utility. All of the above are not true, so (E) is an incorrect answer.

46. **(D)** In developing total cost for a physical distribution system (PDS), the distribution manager must take into account each PDS, its cost accounting system, and inventory carrying costs. (A) is incorrect by itself because the total cost approach includes more than just PDS evaluation. (B) is also incorrect by itself, but must be taken into account when utilizing the total cost approach. The underlying concept of unit cost directly relates to the cost accounting function. (C) is true but also an incorrect choice. When developing a total cost approach, the physical distribution manager must make sure that carrying costs are not excluded or ignored. None of the above (E) is incorrect.

47. **(E)** The lower-lower class makes up approximately 16% of the American population. The relative size of the other groups is as follows: (A) is incorrect and should be 1.5%; (B) is also incorrect and should be 12.5%; (C) is incorrect and should be 32%; and (D) is also incorrect, and should be 38%. These figures are important for marketers, especially in the product development areas, so they can develop effective products and marketing plans for given markets.

48. **(E)** Purchase decision sharing is not part of the five-step

problem-solving process. Although many consumers share decisions, this step should be called purchase evaluation. (A) is part of the problem-solving process and is therefore incorrect. (B) is also not the best answer, although information gathering and/or recall is part of the process. Development of alternative solutions (C) is essential to the process, and is therefore also incorrect. Solution selection (D) is incorrect, although it too, is part of the problem-solving process.

49. **(C)** This person is seeking an infrequently purchased, expensive, potentially high-risk product and would most likely utilize extensive problem-solving. Limited problem-solving (A) would be used by a consumer when they regularly select a particular means of personal needs satisfaction, such as buying a recently issued CD. (B) is incorrect. Routinized response would be used for a low involvement, regularly purchased product such as sugar, salt, or a favorite brand of beer. Psychological variables (D) include motivation, perception, etc., and are not related to this particular question. Social influences (E) include family, social class, reference groups, et. al., and are not relevant to this level of problem-solving.

50. **(E)** Without confirmation the adopter may buy something else the next time he makes a purchase (A). Additionally, he may not comment positively about the product to others. Doubts about a purchase lead to tension, which cause cognitive dissonance. This answer is not the best choice, although it is accurate. (B) is also an incorrect choice, although the information is true. Tension *is* caused by purchase doubts. (C) is incorrect, again when, as with the other choices, considered in light of choice (E). When a customer experiences uncertainty about a purchase, this is known as cognitive dissonance. (D) the consumer may seek additional information about the product in order to confirm that the purchase was the correct decision; the statement is true, but, even so, does not by itself constitute the best answer.

Section 2

51. **(B)** The communication of information between buyer and seller to influence an outcome behavior is known as promotion. Marketing (A) provides direction to make sure the right products are produced and delivered to customers. It includes the entire marketing mix of price, place, promotion, and channels of distribution, and is thus incorrect. Pricing (C)

is also incorrect and is one of the marketing mix variables that deals with the economic aspect of setting a final price for the product. Channels of distribution (D) are concerned with getting the product to the consumer.

52.   **(B)**   Prize money, also referred to as PMs or push money allowances is used to help stimulate sales of products in the above categories. (A) is incorrect, and would probably be utilized with larger type items such as cars or certain types of machinery. Using a trade-in allowance, the seller can reduce the cost of an expensive item without reducing the list cost. (C) is incorrect. Advertising allowances are given to channel members to encourage them to promote the supplier's product locally. (D) is also incorrect. A stocking, or slotting allowance is given, mostly to retailers, to get them to give the producer or supplier additional, or more ideal, shelf space. A weekly allowance (E) is given to one's children for work they may perform around the house, and is an incorrect choice.

53.   **(C)**   (A) means absorbing freight costs so that a firm's delivered price meets the nearest competitors, and is incorrect. (B) refers to making an average freight charge to all buyers within specific geographic areas and is incorrect. (D) is also incorrect and refers to making an average freight charge to all buyers. (E) is a nonsense answer and is incorrect.

54.   **(C)**   Staples are purchased often. They are sold in convenient places like food stores, discount stores, and vending machines. (A) is incorrect, because impulse items are unplanned purchases, and are not routinely purchased. Emergency products (B) are purchased immediately when needed. Customers do not shop around for emergency goods, and they are not purchased routinely or often, thus the answer is incorrect. Services (D) may fall under any of the stated categories, so this is not the most correct answer. Durable goods (E) are long-lasting products and are purchased with a lot of thought, since they tend to be expensive, thus this answer is incorrect.

55.   **(C)**   Industrial products are bought and sold and are used in the building or manufacturing of other products to be sold. Emergency goods (A) are consumer products that the consumer needs immediately, and is not the correct answer. Consumer products (B) are sold to the final consumer and are not used to manufacture or produce other products. Convenience products (D) are consumer products that are purchased without much time and effort by final consumers. This is the incorrect answer. Finally, specialty goods are products meant for the final consumer, and are

goods that the consumer will spend time and effort on to purchase, thus (E) is incorrect.

56. **(B)** Brands include all of the aforementioned, and may or may not be legally registered. A trademark includes only those words, symbols, or marks that are legally registered for use by a company, thus (A) is incorrect. A brand name (C) is the pronounceable part of the brand. It is a word, letter, or group of words and letters, and is not the most correct choice. A servicemark (D) must be legally registered just like a trademark. A servicemark provides protection for a service rather than a product, and is not the most correct answer. Brand recognition (E) simply means that the customers recognize or have heard of the brand, and is incorrect.

57. **(D)** Individual branding is used to accomplish the above purpose of separating brands. It is used to help avoid consumer confusion of the products offered for sale by a company or business unit. Licensed brands (A) are well-known brand that resellers generally pay a fee to offer for sale to consumers. Dealer brands (B) are brands that are owned or created by intermediaries. Manufacturer's brands (D) are brands owned and/or created by manufacturers or producers. Finally, licensed-dealer brands (E) is incorrect. These brands would be owned by a dealer and licensed to other dealers.

58. **(E)** Packaging involves product identification, differentiation, utility creation, protection, containment, and promotion, thus all of the above are correct. (A), (B), (C), and (D) are all true of packaging, however, they would not be the correct choice.

59. **(E)** The employment environment is one of the variables that make up the economic environment for an organization or company. It is not included as a primary marketing environment in and of itself. The marketing manager must plan an appropriate marketing mix based on the objectives and resources of the firm (A), so this is not the most correct choice. The economic and technological environments (B) and their effects on the company MUST be closely monitored, thus this is incorrect. (C) is incorrect because the marketing manager must be aware of the political and legal environments surrounding the products and company to assure compliance with the law. And finally, (D) is incorrect because cultural and social environments must be continually assessed to make sure the marketing manager understands how the consumers are viewing the firm's offerings.

60.   **(D)**   When setting objectives, a firm seeks to engage in specific activities that will perform a socially and economically useful function. The firm also seeks to implement effective strategies and to earn a profit.

61.   **(C)**   Employee training objectives fit under human resource or organizational design objectives. It is the marketing manager's job to help a company decide which products best fit the company's mission and goals, thus (A) is true, but incorrect. (B) is an incorrect choice because it is a marketing function to decide which channels of distribution are the best fit for the company. Promotion (D) is also a marketing function, and thus is incorrect. Price (E) is also an incorrect choice. The marketing manager, especially in retail management, must decide on pricing objectives and policies in order to make the product marketable.

62.   **(A)**   According to a traditional economic point of view, most products move toward oligopolistic competition or pure competition as they move through the product life cycle. The above situation best describes a situation with relatively few sellers. (B) is not the most correct answer, although it may refer to the above situation. The competition may be head-on, or it may not be. (C) is also incorrect. Democracy refers to a governmental environment. (D) is also incorrect. Industry leadership is a descriptive phrase for the company which has top sales, or market share, in a particular industry or field. (E) is incorrect. A monopoly would best be defined as little, or no competition, with one company dominating an industry.

63.   **(D)**   Competitor's advertising budgets would probably be monitored as part of the competitive environment, not the economic environment. This process would most likely be carried out by the advertising manager, and not the marketing manager. Consumer's income levels (A) would be monitored in an economic environmental analysis. If consumer's income levels drop, there could be an effect on spending patterns, and thus sales, so the answer is incorrect. Interest rates (B) should also be monitored. Interest rates effect the total price borrowers must pay for products, so the interest rates effect when and if a consumer will make a purchase. Rates of inflation (C) must be considered by a marketing manager because prices of products might have to be raised in order to cover the rising costs. Exchange rates (E) are important to monitor in an economic environment, especially if the company is involved in any aspects of international trade.

64. **(E)** All of the above are common mistakes that are made by marketing managers when introducing products. (A) is true but not the most correct answer. A marketing manager must count on competition, and must have a strategy that deals with the competition when they enter the market. Likewise for (B), it is true but not the most correct response. Many companies look to copy successful existing products. (C) is true, but also incorrect. Competitors are quick to respond to good, profit-generating ideas, and will take whatever action is necessary to gain market share. (D) is also not the most correct response. The competition's strengths and weaknesses must be measured. This will allow the marketing manager an edge when competing for consumer business.

65. **(C)** The Federal Trade Commission (FTC) Act is legislation aimed at dealing with unfair methods of competition. The Sherman Act (A) is primarily concerned with restraint of trade and monopoly creation, and is incorrect. The Clayton Act (B) is legislation dealing with policies businesses have that may, or intend to, lessen competition, so it is incorrect. The Magnuson-Moss Act (D) is primarily concerned with product warranties. The Antimerger Act (E) seeks to reduce the lessening of competition, and is incorrect.

66. **(D)** Businesses and managers are subject to both criminal prosecution as well as civil actions for violation of Federal Antimonopoly laws. (A) is not the most correct choice, although businesses and business managers are subject to criminal laws. (B) is not the best choice. Marketers must be aware of the local laws as they relate to various regulations affecting their business. Marketers are subject to civil actions (C), however this is not the most correct, or best, response. (E) is totally incorrect.

67. **(D)** The language people speak is part of the site-specific culture, and has an effect on how buyers behave (A). Although this answer is true, it is not the most correct. Additionally, religious beliefs (B) held by individuals will influence a consumer's behavior and effect the way consumers respond to promotions and specific products. Although true, this is not the most correct answer. Views on marriage and the family (C) will effect a consumer's choice of products and will have an impact on selective exposure and retention, but this is not the most correct response. (E) is not correct.

68. **(A)** The General Electric Planning Grid helps managers make three-part judgments (high, medium, or low) about business strengths and

industry attractiveness of proposed or existing product market plans. How long a company has been in business is not a primary factor when utilizing the GE Grid to assess business strengths. (B) is a factor. If the company doesn't have the people with talents such as technical knowledge, marketing skills, etc., the weakness hinders the probability of success for the plan. (C) is a factor. If the product does not fit into the overall profit objectives, then it may not be a good fit for the company. (D) is also a factor utilized in business strength analysis. A firm works hard and spends a lot of time and money developing a particular image. Any product development or introduction assessment utilizing the GE Grid would have to pay heed to the firm's image, and not introduce a product that may conflict with such an image. (E) is also a factor. The firm must consider its abilities and size, as well as the cost of the proposed plan to introduce a product. If a situation arises that is not profitable, or if there are not enough resources and/or capabilities available to the firm to create a positive and profitable market share situation, the market opportunity should not be used.

69. **(D)**   Portfolio management treats alternative products as though they were stock investments, and helps to force the marketing manager to look at them more objectively and to make comparisons to determine which of the product opportunities should be pursued. The total profit approach (A) is certainly a possible consideration; however, since this is a multi-product firm, it needs to make comparisons among different products, and make decisions on the viability of different products, thus, (A) is not the most correct response. (B) is not the best choice. Although ROI is a possible evaluation tool, it is not the best tool to use when comparisons between multiple product opportunities are available. The GE Planning Grid (C) evaluates opportunity based on business strengths and industrial attractiveness, but does not compare alternative product opportunities, and is not the best choice. (E) is simply not the best answer.

70. **(D)**   Total variable costs are costs such as expenses for parts and wages and are directly related to the output of the product. The break-even point (A) has a relationship with product output, but not directly, and is not the most correct choice. Average costs (B) are calculated by dividing the total cost by the related quantities, and has a relation to product output, but not as directly as variable costs. Total cost (C) includes not only variable costs, but also fixed costs, and is not the best response. Total fixed costs (E) is not the best response because fixed costs have a "fixed" total cost no matter how many of the products are produced. The fixed costs are incurred even when there is no output.

71. **(D)** Value in use pricing refers to setting prices with the intent of substituting a firm's product for one that is currently being used. (A) is not the best choice. The correct word for the description in (A) would be reference pricing. (B) refers to leader pricing, and is an incorrect choice. By offering low prices on some popular items, retailers can get buyers into their stores where they hope, in addition to the lower priced products, the customers will make additional purchases of higher markup products. (C) is called bait pricing, or bait-and-switch pricing, and is incorrect. There are regulations making bait-and-switch pricing illegal in many situations, so the retailer must be careful about what they offer, and how it is offered. (E) is incorrect because the definition of value in use pricing is given in answer (D).

72. **(D)** This method has actually become very popular in recent years, and is not outdated. Target return pricing is a variation of the average-cost method since the desired target return is added into the total cost. (A) is incorrect. This approach to pricing has all of the weaknesses as other average-cost pricing methods (B), thus the answer is incorrect. (C) is a good example of how target return pricing may not work, thus is also not the most correct response. (E) is incorrect because (D) is simply not a correct assumption of target return pricing.

73. **(B)** In executing odd-even pricing, the marketer makes sure that the final prices end in certain numbers that are either odd or even depending on what the consumers think they should be. Customers expect to pay even pricing for certain products, and odd prices for other types of products. At a grocery store for example, over eighty percent of the products probably end with an odd number, such as $.99. (A) is incorrect. Bait pricing is setting very low prices to get customers into the retail store. Prestige pricing (C) is setting a higher price to suggest high product quality or status. This is a type of psychological pricing and is not the most correct response. Price leveling (D) is setting a strategy as to what overall pricing structure you want for your organization. For example should one sell at market price, above market price, or below market price? Wal-Mart, in the example, probably sells at a below market price level. Thus the answer is incorrect. Price discrimination (E) refers to adopting a pricing strategy that sets different prices for different customers. This answer is incorrect.

74. **(C)** In complementary product pricing, certain products are priced as a group to ensure sales of a complementary product that may

have a higher markup percentage, and/or that may have higher stock turn-over rates. Prestige pricing (A) is setting a rather high price to suggest high product quality, or status to the buyer, and is incorrect. Product-bundle pricing (B) is setting one price for a specific set of products, and is incorrect. Full-line pricing (D) is incorrect. In full-line pricing, the mar-keter sets the price for an entire, or full, line of products. Demand back-ward pricing (E) is setting an acceptable price for the final consumer (one in which the consumer is willing to pay) and working backward to the producer to see what they can charge. This type of pricing looks to the consumer, or market, to set the price. The answer is incorrect.

75. **(B)** Marginal revenue for this problem is calculated by subtracting the $420.00 total revenue for four units from the $460.00 total revenue for the five units. This is the formula used to calculate marginal revenue. The price per unit given for this problem is simply not needed and not taken into account when making calculations for marginal revenue. When this calcula-tion is performed there is a marginal revenue figure of $40.00 (A), (C), (D), and (E) are not the correct answer, and are miscalculations or guesses.

76. **(C)** The average cost is calculated by dividing the total cost of $102,000 by the related quantity produced of 90,000. The most correct response would be $1.13 (although one may have calculated $1.13333333). Depending on rounding, the best, and only, choices would be $1.13 or $1.14. (A), (B), and (D) are incorrect calculations and are incorrect choices. Total fixed costs have already been taken into account with the total cost figure and are not added back in to the formula, thus this figure is not needed. (E) is incorrect because there is plenty of infor-mation given to make the calculations.

77. **(A)** The question focuses on the understanding of the product life cycle and its maturity stage. In market maturity products vary only slightly from that of the competition. Because of this a lot of product differentiation is minute, and the focus may be on low prices. In addition competitors may have copied marketing variables from the industry leader. (B) is incorrect. Industry profits begin to decline in this phase because of the numbers of competitors who have entered the market. Promotional advertising is necessary during this phase, so that companies can point out their product differences, thus (C) is incorrect. (D) is incor-rect. Industry sales are not at their lowest, conversely, they are at their highest. (E) is also incorrect. A firm can enter the market during any phase of the product life cycle.

78. **(A)** During the market introduction phase, a new idea is being brought to the market. Consumers are not looking for the product, so firms must invest heavily in promotion to begin to secure sales for their products. (B) is incorrect. During growth, profits for the industry actually are rising, and then peak. Maturity (C) is also incorrect. Although the profits decrease during this stage, they are not at their lowest. (D) is also incorrect. In the sales decline stage profits will eventually become zero, but this is not the lowest of the four stages. In introduction, there may be negative profits. (E) is not one of the four stages of the product life cycle and is incorrect.

79. **(A)** The question focuses on the new product development process, and one's understanding of that process. The best way for a company to determine if a new product idea will be successful is through concept testing. Concept testing uses market research techniques to get feedback on the size of the market, consumer enthusiasm and acceptance, profitability, and costs. It focuses on product ideas not actual products. (B) is incorrect. Placing all product into the market before any type of research is conducted spells doom for the product. Additionally it can be expensive. If there is no need for the product, or there is no profit potential, there is no sense in introducing it. (C) is also incorrect. Although companies find ideas with a high ROI attractive, this alone does not determine if there is a want or even a need for the product. Test marketing (D) is a good idea, but without a product to test market it can't be done. Remember, the company is testing an idea, not a product, thus this answer is incorrect. Roll-out (E) also assumes that there is a product, and is incorrect. A roll-out strategy may be a good idea once the product has gone through the product development process and has been screened and tested.

80. **(B)** Order takers are salespeople who sell to the regular, or the typical customers. Most sales transactions are completed through the order takers. The order takers are not concerned with generating new business. Order getters (A) are concerned with the generation of new business, thus the answer is incorrect. Their job is primarily looking for customers and new business development. A sales supporter (C) is a type of missionary salesperson. The supporters assist with the sales transactions. They may be technical representatives or missionary sales staff who try and generate goodwill. This answer is incorrect. A technical representative (D) is not concerned with generating sales, rather, with assisting the order takers and getters. This is a type of sales supporting, not order taking, and is incorrect. (E) is also incorrect. This is not a type of salesperson at all.

81. **(C)**   Team selling has different sales representatives working together on the same account. It may utilize some of the other types of sales people stated above. (A) is incorrect. Technical specialists may be part of a teamselling situation, however their main job is to provide technical assistance to the order-oriented sales people. (B) is also incorrect. These types of salespeople also support the order-oriented staff, but do not try to generate orders themselves. They may be part of the team selling situation, or they may not. (D) is incorrect. Missionary salespeople are a type of supporting salespeople. They generally work for producers calling on intermediaries and their customers to offer support, or to increase goodwill. (E) is also incorrect. Order takers are those individuals who sell to the regular, or typical customer. They also may be part of the teamselling situation.

82. **(C)**   Ninfa didn't plan on buying the cookies, but when she saw them she had a craving to eat those cookies. The cookies were an unplanned purchase, but were purchased because of a strong sudden need, thus the cookies are impulse goods. (A) is incorrect because a staple good is one that is purchased often and without much thought. Milk and bread are good examples of staples. Shopping goods (B) are products that are sought after. They take time and energy to find, but are worth that effort, thus shopping goods is not the most correct response. (D) is incorrect. Specialty goods are products that the person will spend a large amount of time seeking out. Additionally, a lot of effort goes into finding and purchasing specialty goods. (E) is also incorrect. An unsought good is a product that a customer would not want, or perhaps doesn't even know about. Ninfa had seen or heard about the cookies, so they are not unsought goods.

83. **(A)**   A product assortment is all of the individual products offered for sale to consumers. (B) is incorrect, because a product line is a set of individual products that are closely related by type of product, style, price, or some other characteristic. For example, if Brian and Frank sold shampoos, then all of their shampoo offerings would be a product line. (C) is incorrect. The individually-branded product is a single product, not a group of products. A single bottle of Frank's Brand shampoo may be an example of an individually branded product. (D) is incorrect because product variety is not a marketing term. It may be a term in consumer language that would refer to a retailer's mix of products. (E) is incorrect. A product life cycle is a concept used to measure where a product is in reference to an entire industry.

84. **(A)**   Ken and Sally must put a diaper on the baby or suffer the consequences. (B) is incorrect because it would take Ken too long, and too much effort to find a particular type of diaper, and the product is needed now. (C) is also incorrect. An unsought good is a product that the consumer may not know exists, or doesn't want. Ken and Sally both know that diapers exist, and they want one immediately. (D) is incorrect. Ken and Sally need the diaper to assist in their task. They did not have a sudden craving based on seeing a display or product, they went to the store with the purchase in mind. (E) is also incorrect because the only reason for the trip to the store is the diaper purchase. They will not take their time and shop around, spending time and effort in the process.

85. **(D)**   Jan will buy only Levi jeans, and refuses to substitute another product for them. She is willing to shop around until she finds the Levis that fit. Brand preference (A) is incorrect. Jan doesn't prefer Levis, she will only buy Levis. With brand preference, Jan would buy Levis over a competing brand, however would be willing to settle for another brand if Levis weren't available. (B) is incorrect. Brand recognition refers to the fact that the customer remembers, or recognizes the brand or brand name. This doesn't include always buying, or even usually buying the product. In fact with brand recognition the consumer may have never tried the product or brand. (C) refers to the consumer not recognizing the brand, and is incorrect. If the customer doesn't remember the brand, they are not going to insist on purchasing it. Brand rejection (E) is incorrect. With brand rejection, the consumer will not purchase a particular brand for some reason, which usually deals with the brand's image.

86. **(C)**   When a company diversifies, they move into an entirely new line of business. (A) is incorrect. Product development is used to create a new or improved product, and to sell it in the current market situation. Market penetration (B) is also incorrect. In market penetration the company would use a more aggressive marketing mix to try and take additional market share, or increase sales of their current product in their current market. (D) refers to the attempt, or strategy, of selling present products in new markets, thus market development is incorrect. (E) is also incorrect. If the company employs a balancing strategy they are trying to sell current products, in current markets, without any additional funding for, or changes in, the marketing mix.

87. **(C)**   Aisle displays are generally aimed at the final consumer or user of the good, and are frequently seen in retail stores, especially grocery

stores. Trade shows (A) are aimed toward the intermediaries and try to solicit orders for particular types of products. Push money (B), is given to intermediaries in order to encourage them to pay particular attention to a manufacturer's product or product line. This is an incorrect response. Catalogs (D) are sent to intermediaries to give additional product information, such as discounts, price, technical data, etc.; this is an incorrect answer. Final consumers may also utilize catalogs. (E) is incorrect, because all of the above are not traditional methods of promoting to intermediaries or middlemen.

88.　**(B)**　Publicity is an unpaid form of nonpersonal communication. Sales promotion (A) refers to those activities that support advertising and personal selling. Point-of-purchase displays, contests, and sweepstakes would be examples of sales promotion, however, a write-up in a local column is not a type of sales promotion, thus this response is incorrect. (C) is incorrect. Personal selling is one-on-one (or a few-on-a-few), direct, personal communication. It doesn't use mass media, but is personal. Advertising (D) is paid-for communication that deals with a "mass" audience. Publicity is unpaid, and thus advertising is incorrect. Merchandising (E) is either in-store, or used to sell intermediaries. It generally does not utilize a mass media, and it is paid for, thus the answer is not the most correct.

89.　**(D)**　This question asks which products generally utilize an intensive distribution strategy. Since consumers do not want to spend a great deal of time and effort looking for convenience products, the manufacturer, producer, or service provider should strive to get this class of product distributed virtually everywhere they can, making sure it is convenient for the consumer to get to. Shopping goods (A) offer the consumer either price or quality. Consumers are willing to search out shopping goods and spend some time and effort in the purchase. This product would not, generally, utilize intensive distribution. Specialty products (B), likewise, are products the consumer is willing to drive greater distances to find. The consumer is willing to exert energy and time looking for this type of product, so intensive distribution would not be used, and this is an incorrect choice. Unsought goods (C) are products that the customer is uninterested in. Generally, a customer will not purchase unsought goods because of lack or knowledge or need. This is an incorrect choice. Finally, (E) is also incorrect. All of the above would most certainly not traditionally utilize intensive distribution.

90. **(E)** The question deals with the establishment of a selective distribution policy that is used to avoid sales to certain intermediaries. All of the reasons stated above are excellent reasons to utilize this type of distribution. (A) is true but not the most correct response. Poor credit translates to inefficient use of cash for the producer or manufacturer, and perhaps a poor cash flow. Too many returns (B) cause additional expenses for the producer in terms of human and capital resources. If there is only one intermediary making these returns, the problem is probably with the channel member, and not the products themselves. In order to create economies of scale, the producers need to produce in large enough amounts to make cost of the product competitive with other products on the market. Sales in very small amounts cost the manufacturer (C). If there are numerous small accounts, the manufacturer may want to consider utilizing distributors for their products. Thus (C) is true, but not the most correct response. (D) is also true, but not the most correct response. If the intermediary channel member cannot help with product sales in a satisfactory (or better) manner, than the manufacturer may want to avoid doing business with them.

91. **(D)** There are four types of regrouping activities: assorting, bulk breaking, accumulating, and sorting. Sorting involves placing products into special categories by quality and or grades, to help satisfy the targeted markets. Assorting (A) involves putting together a variety of products to give the target market(s) the assortment they want and need. Bulk breaking (B) involves the division of larger quantities into smaller ones during the channel of distribution. As the product gets closer and closer to the final user, more bulk breaking occurs. This answer is incorrect. Accumulating (C) involves collecting products from many small manufacturers or producers so that a shipment of these products can be offered or sold to other members of the channel. (E) is incorrect because sorting is the name of the process used to separate products based upon grade or quality (or both) for the targeted markets.

92. **(C)** Any prepared sales presentation, where the salesperson doesn't vary from the "script" is called a canned, or prepared, approach. Cold calling (A) is the process of calling on customers without an appointment. They may or may not have a need for the product. The prospective buyer does not contact the company (or create a "lead") in cold calling. A sales presentation (B) would include all of the approaches taken in selling. Quite simply, a sales presentation is an attempt at making a sale. Consultative selling (D) is where the potential customer is asked (or consulted) about their needs and wants in a product. The presentation is modified

each time a call is made depending on the potential customer's needs. A close is not attempted in consultative selling until the customer's needs are determined. The selling formula approach (E) is not the most correct response. In sales formula selling, the salesperson begins with a prepared presentation, or outline, and then takes the potential buyer through a series of logical steps (based upon the outline) in an attempt to close the sale.

93. **(D)**   All of the choices can possibly be incorporated into an MIS, however, an MIS is the name given for the process. (A) is incorrect because a decision support system is a computer program allowing the marketing manager ease in getting and using the information contained in an MIS. (B) is incorrect. A marketing model is part of the decision support system (or DSS). A marketing model is basically an analysis of the relationship between the various marketing variables. Marketing research is an application of the scientific method of analysis, and is used for information gathering just like an MIS, however it is problem specific, not ongoing, thus (C) is incorrect. A consumer panel (E) is a method of gathering data. It can be an ongoing continuous process, however, the information is usually problem specific or exploratory. Consumer panels are not comprehensive systems, but rather tools to gain the information needed for the MIS, thus (E) is incorrect.

94. **(A)**   Validity is the extent that a research instrument (such as a questionnaire) measures what it purports, or is intended, to measure. If the question has a different meaning to different people, it is invalid. (B) is incorrect. Accuracy refers to the extent that collected data are error free. A poorly worded question may not have an impact on accuracy. Reliability (C) is incorrect. Reliability refers to the fact that the questionnaire, or research instrument, measures the same thing over and over. Thus every time the instrument is used it measures the same thing. The research can be reliable, however it still may not be valid. In other words it is measuring the incorrect thing over and over. (D) is incorrect. Confidence intervals have to do with sampling accuracy. A confidence interval is the range on either side of an estimate that would likely contain the true population values. (E) samples, have nothing to do with question wording, and are thus incorrect. Samples are small portions of a population under study that should reflect the overall population.

95. **(E)**   By definition, qualitative research seeks to find in-depth, open-ended responses to questions posed. This type of research tries to elicit thoughts respondents may have about a particular topic without giv-

ing too many guidelines. Quantitative research (A) seeks structured responses that can be summarized and generalized to populations, thus this response is incorrect. Marketing research (B) includes both quantitative and qualitative data, and is too broad a category. Chi square (C) is also incorrect. This is a statistical technique used to help summarize quantitative data. Experimental (D) is also incorrect. In an experimental setting the researcher would generally use quantitative data.

96.   **(C)**   This is the process of clustering people, current or potential consumers, into groups or segments with like needs or wants. (A) is incorrect. Positioning defines how consumers view brands in a market. (B) is not the most correct response. A market refers to the entire population who may have a need for a product. No thought is given to breaking the market down into smaller homogenous groups or segments. (D) is also incorrect. Combiners take the smaller segments, and combine them into larger subgroups. And finally, marketing (E) is the entire process of getting a product or service from the producer to the final consumer, and thus is not the best response.

97.   **(A)**   If a company sells their current products in new markets, this is referred to as market development. (B) is incorrect. Market penetration involves selling the present products in the current markets. (C) is also incorrect. Diversification would mean that Butzie is moving into an entirely new line of products (or product) and offering these products in an entirely new market. Product development (D) involves selling new products in current markets, and is incorrect. Market segmentation (E) is the process of dividing up the targeted market into smaller homogenous groups of consumers who will purchase in the same manner. This answer is also incorrect.

98.   **(B)**   Poudre Pie wants to offer a new or improved product into her present market, and thus is pursuing product development. (A) is incorrect. Poudre would have to move into an entirely new market, with an entirely new product, if she wanted to pursue diversification. (C) is incorrect. Market development refers to the expanding of the current market, while offering the products sold at present. (D) is also incorrect. If Poudre were to pursue market penetration she would attempt to increase sales of her current products in her current market by being more aggressive with her marketing mix. Standardization and grading (E) is the process where products are standardized and/or graded according to size, quality, style, or some other characteristic. This answer is not the most correct.

99. **(A)** A producer wishes to take advantage of economies of scale when producing a product. In other words as the number produced increases, the cost per unit (not total costs) goes down. Thus it is economically advantageous to produce in greater numbers. Consumers don't want to consume in large numbers, they have a need for smaller amounts of product for consumption. This difference is referred to as a discrepancy of quantity. (B) is incorrect. Discrepancy of assortment is the difference in the types of products produced by a manufacturer and needed or wanted, by consumers. Regrouping (C) refers to adjusting the quantities and/or assortments of products handled at each level of the channel of distribution, so it is incorrect. Accumulating (D) involves the collection of products from smaller producers, thus is incorrect. Advertising (E) involves communicating, in a non-personal atmosphere, via some type of medium, with large numbers of consumers or potential consumers.

100. **(E)** Vertical marketing channels of distribution can be a corporate channel (A) where the corporation owns the entire channel of distribution. However this is not the best response. It can be an administered channel (B) where the channel members informally agree on which services the channel members will perform, however this is not the most correct response. A vertical channel system could also be contractual (C) where the members agree, by contract, to cooperate with each other, and also which functions should be provided by each of the members. This however, is not the most correct response. (D) is true, both corporate channels and administered channels could provide or develop a vertical channel system, however, so could a system under contract, which (D) leaves out, thus this is not the best response.

ANSWER SHEETS

CLEP PRINCIPLES OF MARKETING– TEST 1

SECTION 1

1. Ⓐ Ⓑ Ⓒ Ⓓ Ⓔ
2. Ⓐ Ⓑ Ⓒ Ⓓ Ⓔ
3. Ⓐ Ⓑ Ⓒ Ⓓ Ⓔ
4. Ⓐ Ⓑ Ⓒ Ⓓ Ⓔ
5. Ⓐ Ⓑ Ⓒ Ⓓ Ⓔ
6. Ⓐ Ⓑ Ⓒ Ⓓ Ⓔ
7. Ⓐ Ⓑ Ⓒ Ⓓ Ⓔ
8. Ⓐ Ⓑ Ⓒ Ⓓ Ⓔ
9. Ⓐ Ⓑ Ⓒ Ⓓ Ⓔ
10. Ⓐ Ⓑ Ⓒ Ⓓ Ⓔ
11. Ⓐ Ⓑ Ⓒ Ⓓ Ⓔ
12. Ⓐ Ⓑ Ⓒ Ⓓ Ⓔ
13. Ⓐ Ⓑ Ⓒ Ⓓ Ⓔ
14. Ⓐ Ⓑ Ⓒ Ⓓ Ⓔ
15. Ⓐ Ⓑ Ⓒ Ⓓ Ⓔ
16. Ⓐ Ⓑ Ⓒ Ⓓ Ⓔ
17. Ⓐ Ⓑ Ⓒ Ⓓ Ⓔ
18. Ⓐ Ⓑ Ⓒ Ⓓ Ⓔ
19. Ⓐ Ⓑ Ⓒ Ⓓ Ⓔ
20. Ⓐ Ⓑ Ⓒ Ⓓ Ⓔ
21. Ⓐ Ⓑ Ⓒ Ⓓ Ⓔ
22. Ⓐ Ⓑ Ⓒ Ⓓ Ⓔ
23. Ⓐ Ⓑ Ⓒ Ⓓ Ⓔ
24. Ⓐ Ⓑ Ⓒ Ⓓ Ⓔ
25. Ⓐ Ⓑ Ⓒ Ⓓ Ⓔ
26. Ⓐ Ⓑ Ⓒ Ⓓ Ⓔ
27. Ⓐ Ⓑ Ⓒ Ⓓ Ⓔ
28. Ⓐ Ⓑ Ⓒ Ⓓ Ⓔ
29. Ⓐ Ⓑ Ⓒ Ⓓ Ⓔ
30. Ⓐ Ⓑ Ⓒ Ⓓ Ⓔ
31. Ⓐ Ⓑ Ⓒ Ⓓ Ⓔ
32. Ⓐ Ⓑ Ⓒ Ⓓ Ⓔ
33. Ⓐ Ⓑ Ⓒ Ⓓ Ⓔ
34. Ⓐ Ⓑ Ⓒ Ⓓ Ⓔ
35. Ⓐ Ⓑ Ⓒ Ⓓ Ⓔ
36. Ⓐ Ⓑ Ⓒ Ⓓ Ⓔ
37. Ⓐ Ⓑ Ⓒ Ⓓ Ⓔ
38. Ⓐ Ⓑ Ⓒ Ⓓ Ⓔ
39. Ⓐ Ⓑ Ⓒ Ⓓ Ⓔ
40. Ⓐ Ⓑ Ⓒ Ⓓ Ⓔ
41. Ⓐ Ⓑ Ⓒ Ⓓ Ⓔ
42. Ⓐ Ⓑ Ⓒ Ⓓ Ⓔ
43. Ⓐ Ⓑ Ⓒ Ⓓ Ⓔ
44. Ⓐ Ⓑ Ⓒ Ⓓ Ⓔ
45. Ⓐ Ⓑ Ⓒ Ⓓ Ⓔ
46. Ⓐ Ⓑ Ⓒ Ⓓ Ⓔ
47. Ⓐ Ⓑ Ⓒ Ⓓ Ⓔ
48. Ⓐ Ⓑ Ⓒ Ⓓ Ⓔ
49. Ⓐ Ⓑ Ⓒ Ⓓ Ⓔ
50. Ⓐ Ⓑ Ⓒ Ⓓ Ⓔ

SECTION 2

51.	Ⓐ Ⓑ Ⓒ Ⓓ Ⓔ		76.	Ⓐ Ⓑ Ⓒ Ⓓ Ⓔ	
52.	Ⓐ Ⓑ Ⓒ Ⓓ Ⓔ		77.	Ⓐ Ⓑ Ⓒ Ⓓ Ⓔ	
53.	Ⓐ Ⓑ Ⓒ Ⓓ Ⓔ		78.	Ⓐ Ⓑ Ⓒ Ⓓ Ⓔ	
54.	Ⓐ Ⓑ Ⓒ Ⓓ Ⓔ		79.	Ⓐ Ⓑ Ⓒ Ⓓ Ⓔ	
55.	Ⓐ Ⓑ Ⓒ Ⓓ Ⓔ		80.	Ⓐ Ⓑ Ⓒ Ⓓ Ⓔ	
56.	Ⓐ Ⓑ Ⓒ Ⓓ Ⓔ		81.	Ⓐ Ⓑ Ⓒ Ⓓ Ⓔ	
57.	Ⓐ Ⓑ Ⓒ Ⓓ Ⓔ		82.	Ⓐ Ⓑ Ⓒ Ⓓ Ⓔ	
58.	Ⓐ Ⓑ Ⓒ Ⓓ Ⓔ		83.	Ⓐ Ⓑ Ⓒ Ⓓ Ⓔ	
59.	Ⓐ Ⓑ Ⓒ Ⓓ Ⓔ		84.	Ⓐ Ⓑ Ⓒ Ⓓ Ⓔ	
60.	Ⓐ Ⓑ Ⓒ Ⓓ Ⓔ		85.	Ⓐ Ⓑ Ⓒ Ⓓ Ⓔ	
61.	Ⓐ Ⓑ Ⓒ Ⓓ Ⓔ		86.	Ⓐ Ⓑ Ⓒ Ⓓ Ⓔ	
62.	Ⓐ Ⓑ Ⓒ Ⓓ Ⓔ		87.	Ⓐ Ⓑ Ⓒ Ⓓ Ⓔ	
63.	Ⓐ Ⓑ Ⓒ Ⓓ Ⓔ		88.	Ⓐ Ⓑ Ⓒ Ⓓ Ⓔ	
64.	Ⓐ Ⓑ Ⓒ Ⓓ Ⓔ		89.	Ⓐ Ⓑ Ⓒ Ⓓ Ⓔ	
65.	Ⓐ Ⓑ Ⓒ Ⓓ Ⓔ		90.	Ⓐ Ⓑ Ⓒ Ⓓ Ⓔ	
66.	Ⓐ Ⓑ Ⓒ Ⓓ Ⓔ		91.	Ⓐ Ⓑ Ⓒ Ⓓ Ⓔ	
67.	Ⓐ Ⓑ Ⓒ Ⓓ Ⓔ		92.	Ⓐ Ⓑ Ⓒ Ⓓ Ⓔ	
68.	Ⓐ Ⓑ Ⓒ Ⓓ Ⓔ		93.	Ⓐ Ⓑ Ⓒ Ⓓ Ⓔ	
69.	Ⓐ Ⓑ Ⓒ Ⓓ Ⓔ		94.	Ⓐ Ⓑ Ⓒ Ⓓ Ⓔ	
70.	Ⓐ Ⓑ Ⓒ Ⓓ Ⓔ		95.	Ⓐ Ⓑ Ⓒ Ⓓ Ⓔ	
71.	Ⓐ Ⓑ Ⓒ Ⓓ Ⓔ		96.	Ⓐ Ⓑ Ⓒ Ⓓ Ⓔ	
72.	Ⓐ Ⓑ Ⓒ Ⓓ Ⓔ		97.	Ⓐ Ⓑ Ⓒ Ⓓ Ⓔ	
73.	Ⓐ Ⓑ Ⓒ Ⓓ Ⓔ		98.	Ⓐ Ⓑ Ⓒ Ⓓ Ⓔ	
74.	Ⓐ Ⓑ Ⓒ Ⓓ Ⓔ		99.	Ⓐ Ⓑ Ⓒ Ⓓ Ⓔ	
75.	Ⓐ Ⓑ Ⓒ Ⓓ Ⓔ		100.	Ⓐ Ⓑ Ⓒ Ⓓ Ⓔ	

CLEP PRINCIPLES OF MARKETING– TEST 2

SECTION 1

1.	Ⓐ Ⓑ Ⓒ Ⓓ Ⓔ					26.	Ⓐ Ⓑ Ⓒ Ⓓ Ⓔ				
2.	Ⓐ Ⓑ Ⓒ Ⓓ Ⓔ					27.	Ⓐ Ⓑ Ⓒ Ⓓ Ⓔ				
3.	Ⓐ Ⓑ Ⓒ Ⓓ Ⓔ					28.	Ⓐ Ⓑ Ⓒ Ⓓ Ⓔ				
4.	Ⓐ Ⓑ Ⓒ Ⓓ Ⓔ					29.	Ⓐ Ⓑ Ⓒ Ⓓ Ⓔ				
5.	Ⓐ Ⓑ Ⓒ Ⓓ Ⓔ					30.	Ⓐ Ⓑ Ⓒ Ⓓ Ⓔ				
6.	Ⓐ Ⓑ Ⓒ Ⓓ Ⓔ					31.	Ⓐ Ⓑ Ⓒ Ⓓ Ⓔ				
7.	Ⓐ Ⓑ Ⓒ Ⓓ Ⓔ					32.	Ⓐ Ⓑ Ⓒ Ⓓ Ⓔ				
8.	Ⓐ Ⓑ Ⓒ Ⓓ Ⓔ					33.	Ⓐ Ⓑ Ⓒ Ⓓ Ⓔ				
9.	Ⓐ Ⓑ Ⓒ Ⓓ Ⓔ					34.	Ⓐ Ⓑ Ⓒ Ⓓ Ⓔ				
10.	Ⓐ Ⓑ Ⓒ Ⓓ Ⓔ					35.	Ⓐ Ⓑ Ⓒ Ⓓ Ⓔ				
11.	Ⓐ Ⓑ Ⓒ Ⓓ Ⓔ					36.	Ⓐ Ⓑ Ⓒ Ⓓ Ⓔ				
12.	Ⓐ Ⓑ Ⓒ Ⓓ Ⓔ					37.	Ⓐ Ⓑ Ⓒ Ⓓ Ⓔ				
13.	Ⓐ Ⓑ Ⓒ Ⓓ Ⓔ					38.	Ⓐ Ⓑ Ⓒ Ⓓ Ⓔ				
14.	Ⓐ Ⓑ Ⓒ Ⓓ Ⓔ					39.	Ⓐ Ⓑ Ⓒ Ⓓ Ⓔ				
15.	Ⓐ Ⓑ Ⓒ Ⓓ Ⓔ					40.	Ⓐ Ⓑ Ⓒ Ⓓ Ⓔ				
16.	Ⓐ Ⓑ Ⓒ Ⓓ Ⓔ					41.	Ⓐ Ⓑ Ⓒ Ⓓ Ⓔ				
17.	Ⓐ Ⓑ Ⓒ Ⓓ Ⓔ					42.	Ⓐ Ⓑ Ⓒ Ⓓ Ⓔ				
18.	Ⓐ Ⓑ Ⓒ Ⓓ Ⓔ					43.	Ⓐ Ⓑ Ⓒ Ⓓ Ⓔ				
19.	Ⓐ Ⓑ Ⓒ Ⓓ Ⓔ					44.	Ⓐ Ⓑ Ⓒ Ⓓ Ⓔ				
20.	Ⓐ Ⓑ Ⓒ Ⓓ Ⓔ					45.	Ⓐ Ⓑ Ⓒ Ⓓ Ⓔ				
21.	Ⓐ Ⓑ Ⓒ Ⓓ Ⓔ					46.	Ⓐ Ⓑ Ⓒ Ⓓ Ⓔ				
22.	Ⓐ Ⓑ Ⓒ Ⓓ Ⓔ					47.	Ⓐ Ⓑ Ⓒ Ⓓ Ⓔ				
23.	Ⓐ Ⓑ Ⓒ Ⓓ Ⓔ					48.	Ⓐ Ⓑ Ⓒ Ⓓ Ⓔ				
24.	Ⓐ Ⓑ Ⓒ Ⓓ Ⓔ					49.	Ⓐ Ⓑ Ⓒ Ⓓ Ⓔ				
25.	Ⓐ Ⓑ Ⓒ Ⓓ Ⓔ					50.	Ⓐ Ⓑ Ⓒ Ⓓ Ⓔ				

SECTION 2

51. Ⓐ Ⓑ Ⓒ Ⓓ Ⓔ
52. Ⓐ Ⓑ Ⓒ Ⓓ Ⓔ
53. Ⓐ Ⓑ Ⓒ Ⓓ Ⓔ
54. Ⓐ Ⓑ Ⓒ Ⓓ Ⓔ
55. Ⓐ Ⓑ Ⓒ Ⓓ Ⓔ
56. Ⓐ Ⓑ Ⓒ Ⓓ Ⓔ
57. Ⓐ Ⓑ Ⓒ Ⓓ Ⓔ
58. Ⓐ Ⓑ Ⓒ Ⓓ Ⓔ
59. Ⓐ Ⓑ Ⓒ Ⓓ Ⓔ
60. Ⓐ Ⓑ Ⓒ Ⓓ Ⓔ
61. Ⓐ Ⓑ Ⓒ Ⓓ Ⓔ
62. Ⓐ Ⓑ Ⓒ Ⓓ Ⓔ
63. Ⓐ Ⓑ Ⓒ Ⓓ Ⓔ
64. Ⓐ Ⓑ Ⓒ Ⓓ Ⓔ
65. Ⓐ Ⓑ Ⓒ Ⓓ Ⓔ
66. Ⓐ Ⓑ Ⓒ Ⓓ Ⓔ
67. Ⓐ Ⓑ Ⓒ Ⓓ Ⓔ
68. Ⓐ Ⓑ Ⓒ Ⓓ Ⓔ
69. Ⓐ Ⓑ Ⓒ Ⓓ Ⓔ
70. Ⓐ Ⓑ Ⓒ Ⓓ Ⓔ
71. Ⓐ Ⓑ Ⓒ Ⓓ Ⓔ
72. Ⓐ Ⓑ Ⓒ Ⓓ Ⓔ
73. Ⓐ Ⓑ Ⓒ Ⓓ Ⓔ
74. Ⓐ Ⓑ Ⓒ Ⓓ Ⓔ
75. Ⓐ Ⓑ Ⓒ Ⓓ Ⓔ

76. Ⓐ Ⓑ Ⓒ Ⓓ Ⓔ
77. Ⓐ Ⓑ Ⓒ Ⓓ Ⓔ
78. Ⓐ Ⓑ Ⓒ Ⓓ Ⓔ
79. Ⓐ Ⓑ Ⓒ Ⓓ Ⓔ
80. Ⓐ Ⓑ Ⓒ Ⓓ Ⓔ
81. Ⓐ Ⓑ Ⓒ Ⓓ Ⓔ
82. Ⓐ Ⓑ Ⓒ Ⓓ Ⓔ
83. Ⓐ Ⓑ Ⓒ Ⓓ Ⓔ
84. Ⓐ Ⓑ Ⓒ Ⓓ Ⓔ
85. Ⓐ Ⓑ Ⓒ Ⓓ Ⓔ
86. Ⓐ Ⓑ Ⓒ Ⓓ Ⓔ
87. Ⓐ Ⓑ Ⓒ Ⓓ Ⓔ
88. Ⓐ Ⓑ Ⓒ Ⓓ Ⓔ
89. Ⓐ Ⓑ Ⓒ Ⓓ Ⓔ
90. Ⓐ Ⓑ Ⓒ Ⓓ Ⓔ
91. Ⓐ Ⓑ Ⓒ Ⓓ Ⓔ
92. Ⓐ Ⓑ Ⓒ Ⓓ Ⓔ
93. Ⓐ Ⓑ Ⓒ Ⓓ Ⓔ
94. Ⓐ Ⓑ Ⓒ Ⓓ Ⓔ
95. Ⓐ Ⓑ Ⓒ Ⓓ Ⓔ
96. Ⓐ Ⓑ Ⓒ Ⓓ Ⓔ
97. Ⓐ Ⓑ Ⓒ Ⓓ Ⓔ
98. Ⓐ Ⓑ Ⓒ Ⓓ Ⓔ
99. Ⓐ Ⓑ Ⓒ Ⓓ Ⓔ
100. Ⓐ Ⓑ Ⓒ Ⓓ Ⓔ

CLEP PRINCIPLES OF MARKETING– TEST 3

SECTION 1

1. (A) (B) (C) (D) (E)		26. (A) (B) (C) (D) (E)	
2. (A) (B) (C) (D) (E)		27. (A) (B) (C) (D) (E)	
3. (A) (B) (C) (D) (E)		28. (A) (B) (C) (D) (E)	
4. (A) (B) (C) (D) (E)		29. (A) (B) (C) (D) (E)	
5. (A) (B) (C) (D) (E)		30. (A) (B) (C) (D) (E)	
6. (A) (B) (C) (D) (E)		31. (A) (B) (C) (D) (E)	
7. (A) (B) (C) (D) (E)		32. (A) (B) (C) (D) (E)	
8. (A) (B) (C) (D) (E)		33. (A) (B) (C) (D) (E)	
9. (A) (B) (C) (D) (E)		34. (A) (B) (C) (D) (E)	
10. (A) (B) (C) (D) (E)		35. (A) (B) (C) (D) (E)	
11. (A) (B) (C) (D) (E)		36. (A) (B) (C) (D) (E)	
12. (A) (B) (C) (D) (E)		37. (A) (B) (C) (D) (E)	
13. (A) (B) (C) (D) (E)		38. (A) (B) (C) (D) (E)	
14. (A) (B) (C) (D) (E)		39. (A) (B) (C) (D) (E)	
15. (A) (B) (C) (D) (E)		40. (A) (B) (C) (D) (E)	
16. (A) (B) (C) (D) (E)		41. (A) (B) (C) (D) (E)	
17. (A) (B) (C) (D) (E)		42. (A) (B) (C) (D) (E)	
18. (A) (B) (C) (D) (E)		43. (A) (B) (C) (D) (E)	
19. (A) (B) (C) (D) (E)		44. (A) (B) (C) (D) (E)	
20. (A) (B) (C) (D) (E)		45. (A) (B) (C) (D) (E)	
21. (A) (B) (C) (D) (E)		46. (A) (B) (C) (D) (E)	
22. (A) (B) (C) (D) (E)		47. (A) (B) (C) (D) (E)	
23. (A) (B) (C) (D) (E)		48. (A) (B) (C) (D) (E)	
24. (A) (B) (C) (D) (E)		49. (A) (B) (C) (D) (E)	
25. (A) (B) (C) (D) (E)		50. (A) (B) (C) (D) (E)	

SECTION 2

51. Ⓐ Ⓑ Ⓒ Ⓓ Ⓔ
52. Ⓐ Ⓑ Ⓒ Ⓓ Ⓔ
53. Ⓐ Ⓑ Ⓒ Ⓓ Ⓔ
54. Ⓐ Ⓑ Ⓒ Ⓓ Ⓔ
55. Ⓐ Ⓑ Ⓒ Ⓓ Ⓔ
56. Ⓐ Ⓑ Ⓒ Ⓓ Ⓔ
57. Ⓐ Ⓑ Ⓒ Ⓓ Ⓔ
58. Ⓐ Ⓑ Ⓒ Ⓓ Ⓔ
59. Ⓐ Ⓑ Ⓒ Ⓓ Ⓔ
60. Ⓐ Ⓑ Ⓒ Ⓓ Ⓔ
61. Ⓐ Ⓑ Ⓒ Ⓓ Ⓔ
62. Ⓐ Ⓑ Ⓒ Ⓓ Ⓔ
63. Ⓐ Ⓑ Ⓒ Ⓓ Ⓔ
64. Ⓐ Ⓑ Ⓒ Ⓓ Ⓔ
65. Ⓐ Ⓑ Ⓒ Ⓓ Ⓔ
66. Ⓐ Ⓑ Ⓒ Ⓓ Ⓔ
67. Ⓐ Ⓑ Ⓒ Ⓓ Ⓔ
68. Ⓐ Ⓑ Ⓒ Ⓓ Ⓔ
69. Ⓐ Ⓑ Ⓒ Ⓓ Ⓔ
70. Ⓐ Ⓑ Ⓒ Ⓓ Ⓔ
71. Ⓐ Ⓑ Ⓒ Ⓓ Ⓔ
72. Ⓐ Ⓑ Ⓒ Ⓓ Ⓔ
73. Ⓐ Ⓑ Ⓒ Ⓓ Ⓔ
74. Ⓐ Ⓑ Ⓒ Ⓓ Ⓔ
75. Ⓐ Ⓑ Ⓒ Ⓓ Ⓔ

76. Ⓐ Ⓑ Ⓒ Ⓓ Ⓔ
77. Ⓐ Ⓑ Ⓒ Ⓓ Ⓔ
78. Ⓐ Ⓑ Ⓒ Ⓓ Ⓔ
79. Ⓐ Ⓑ Ⓒ Ⓓ Ⓔ
80. Ⓐ Ⓑ Ⓒ Ⓓ Ⓔ
81. Ⓐ Ⓑ Ⓒ Ⓓ Ⓔ
82. Ⓐ Ⓑ Ⓒ Ⓓ Ⓔ
83. Ⓐ Ⓑ Ⓒ Ⓓ Ⓔ
84. Ⓐ Ⓑ Ⓒ Ⓓ Ⓔ
85. Ⓐ Ⓑ Ⓒ Ⓓ Ⓔ
86. Ⓐ Ⓑ Ⓒ Ⓓ Ⓔ
87. Ⓐ Ⓑ Ⓒ Ⓓ Ⓔ
88. Ⓐ Ⓑ Ⓒ Ⓓ Ⓔ
89. Ⓐ Ⓑ Ⓒ Ⓓ Ⓔ
90. Ⓐ Ⓑ Ⓒ Ⓓ Ⓔ
91. Ⓐ Ⓑ Ⓒ Ⓓ Ⓔ
92. Ⓐ Ⓑ Ⓒ Ⓓ Ⓔ
93. Ⓐ Ⓑ Ⓒ Ⓓ Ⓔ
94. Ⓐ Ⓑ Ⓒ Ⓓ Ⓔ
95. Ⓐ Ⓑ Ⓒ Ⓓ Ⓔ
96. Ⓐ Ⓑ Ⓒ Ⓓ Ⓔ
97. Ⓐ Ⓑ Ⓒ Ⓓ Ⓔ
98. Ⓐ Ⓑ Ⓒ Ⓓ Ⓔ
99. Ⓐ Ⓑ Ⓒ Ⓓ Ⓔ
100. Ⓐ Ⓑ Ⓒ Ⓓ Ⓔ

ADDITIONAL ANSWER SHEETS

CLEP PRINCIPLES OF MARKETING– TEST __

SECTION 1

1.	Ⓐ Ⓑ Ⓒ Ⓓ Ⓔ					26.	Ⓐ Ⓑ Ⓒ Ⓓ Ⓔ			
2.	Ⓐ Ⓑ Ⓒ Ⓓ Ⓔ					27.	Ⓐ Ⓑ Ⓒ Ⓓ Ⓔ			
3.	Ⓐ Ⓑ Ⓒ Ⓓ Ⓔ					28.	Ⓐ Ⓑ Ⓒ Ⓓ Ⓔ			
4.	Ⓐ Ⓑ Ⓒ Ⓓ Ⓔ					29.	Ⓐ Ⓑ Ⓒ Ⓓ Ⓔ			
5.	Ⓐ Ⓑ Ⓒ Ⓓ Ⓔ					30.	Ⓐ Ⓑ Ⓒ Ⓓ Ⓔ			
6.	Ⓐ Ⓑ Ⓒ Ⓓ Ⓔ					31.	Ⓐ Ⓑ Ⓒ Ⓓ Ⓔ			
7.	Ⓐ Ⓑ Ⓒ Ⓓ Ⓔ					32.	Ⓐ Ⓑ Ⓒ Ⓓ Ⓔ			
8.	Ⓐ Ⓑ Ⓒ Ⓓ Ⓔ					33.	Ⓐ Ⓑ Ⓒ Ⓓ Ⓔ			
9.	Ⓐ Ⓑ Ⓒ Ⓓ Ⓔ					34.	Ⓐ Ⓑ Ⓒ Ⓓ Ⓔ			
10.	Ⓐ Ⓑ Ⓒ Ⓓ Ⓔ					35.	Ⓐ Ⓑ Ⓒ Ⓓ Ⓔ			
11.	Ⓐ Ⓑ Ⓒ Ⓓ Ⓔ					36.	Ⓐ Ⓑ Ⓒ Ⓓ Ⓔ			
12.	Ⓐ Ⓑ Ⓒ Ⓓ Ⓔ					37.	Ⓐ Ⓑ Ⓒ Ⓓ Ⓔ			
13.	Ⓐ Ⓑ Ⓒ Ⓓ Ⓔ					38.	Ⓐ Ⓑ Ⓒ Ⓓ Ⓔ			
14.	Ⓐ Ⓑ Ⓒ Ⓓ Ⓔ					39.	Ⓐ Ⓑ Ⓒ Ⓓ Ⓔ			
15.	Ⓐ Ⓑ Ⓒ Ⓓ Ⓔ					40.	Ⓐ Ⓑ Ⓒ Ⓓ Ⓔ			
16.	Ⓐ Ⓑ Ⓒ Ⓓ Ⓔ					41.	Ⓐ Ⓑ Ⓒ Ⓓ Ⓔ			
17.	Ⓐ Ⓑ Ⓒ Ⓓ Ⓔ					42.	Ⓐ Ⓑ Ⓒ Ⓓ Ⓔ			
18.	Ⓐ Ⓑ Ⓒ Ⓓ Ⓔ					43.	Ⓐ Ⓑ Ⓒ Ⓓ Ⓔ			
19.	Ⓐ Ⓑ Ⓒ Ⓓ Ⓔ					44.	Ⓐ Ⓑ Ⓒ Ⓓ Ⓔ			
20.	Ⓐ Ⓑ Ⓒ Ⓓ Ⓔ					45.	Ⓐ Ⓑ Ⓒ Ⓓ Ⓔ			
21.	Ⓐ Ⓑ Ⓒ Ⓓ Ⓔ					46.	Ⓐ Ⓑ Ⓒ Ⓓ Ⓔ			
22.	Ⓐ Ⓑ Ⓒ Ⓓ Ⓔ					47.	Ⓐ Ⓑ Ⓒ Ⓓ Ⓔ			
23.	Ⓐ Ⓑ Ⓒ Ⓓ Ⓔ					48.	Ⓐ Ⓑ Ⓒ Ⓓ Ⓔ			
24.	Ⓐ Ⓑ Ⓒ Ⓓ Ⓔ					49.	Ⓐ Ⓑ Ⓒ Ⓓ Ⓔ			
25.	Ⓐ Ⓑ Ⓒ Ⓓ Ⓔ					50.	Ⓐ Ⓑ Ⓒ Ⓓ Ⓔ			

SECTION 2

51.	Ⓐ Ⓑ Ⓒ Ⓓ Ⓔ					76.	Ⓐ Ⓑ Ⓒ Ⓓ Ⓔ			
52.	Ⓐ Ⓑ Ⓒ Ⓓ Ⓔ					77.	Ⓐ Ⓑ Ⓒ Ⓓ Ⓔ			
53.	Ⓐ Ⓑ Ⓒ Ⓓ Ⓔ					78.	Ⓐ Ⓑ Ⓒ Ⓓ Ⓔ			
54.	Ⓐ Ⓑ Ⓒ Ⓓ Ⓔ					79.	Ⓐ Ⓑ Ⓒ Ⓓ Ⓔ			
55.	Ⓐ Ⓑ Ⓒ Ⓓ Ⓔ					80.	Ⓐ Ⓑ Ⓒ Ⓓ Ⓔ			
56.	Ⓐ Ⓑ Ⓒ Ⓓ Ⓔ					81.	Ⓐ Ⓑ Ⓒ Ⓓ Ⓔ			
57.	Ⓐ Ⓑ Ⓒ Ⓓ Ⓔ					82.	Ⓐ Ⓑ Ⓒ Ⓓ Ⓔ			
58.	Ⓐ Ⓑ Ⓒ Ⓓ Ⓔ					83.	Ⓐ Ⓑ Ⓒ Ⓓ Ⓔ			
59.	Ⓐ Ⓑ Ⓒ Ⓓ Ⓔ					84.	Ⓐ Ⓑ Ⓒ Ⓓ Ⓔ			
60.	Ⓐ Ⓑ Ⓒ Ⓓ Ⓔ					85.	Ⓐ Ⓑ Ⓒ Ⓓ Ⓔ			
61.	Ⓐ Ⓑ Ⓒ Ⓓ Ⓔ					86.	Ⓐ Ⓑ Ⓒ Ⓓ Ⓔ			
62.	Ⓐ Ⓑ Ⓒ Ⓓ Ⓔ					87.	Ⓐ Ⓑ Ⓒ Ⓓ Ⓔ			
63.	Ⓐ Ⓑ Ⓒ Ⓓ Ⓔ					88.	Ⓐ Ⓑ Ⓒ Ⓓ Ⓔ			
64.	Ⓐ Ⓑ Ⓒ Ⓓ Ⓔ					89.	Ⓐ Ⓑ Ⓒ Ⓓ Ⓔ			
65.	Ⓐ Ⓑ Ⓒ Ⓓ Ⓔ					90.	Ⓐ Ⓑ Ⓒ Ⓓ Ⓔ			
66.	Ⓐ Ⓑ Ⓒ Ⓓ Ⓔ					91.	Ⓐ Ⓑ Ⓒ Ⓓ Ⓔ			
67.	Ⓐ Ⓑ Ⓒ Ⓓ Ⓔ					92.	Ⓐ Ⓑ Ⓒ Ⓓ Ⓔ			
68.	Ⓐ Ⓑ Ⓒ Ⓓ Ⓔ					93.	Ⓐ Ⓑ Ⓒ Ⓓ Ⓔ			
69.	Ⓐ Ⓑ Ⓒ Ⓓ Ⓔ					94.	Ⓐ Ⓑ Ⓒ Ⓓ Ⓔ			
70.	Ⓐ Ⓑ Ⓒ Ⓓ Ⓔ					95.	Ⓐ Ⓑ Ⓒ Ⓓ Ⓔ			
71.	Ⓐ Ⓑ Ⓒ Ⓓ Ⓔ					96.	Ⓐ Ⓑ Ⓒ Ⓓ Ⓔ			
72.	Ⓐ Ⓑ Ⓒ Ⓓ Ⓔ					97.	Ⓐ Ⓑ Ⓒ Ⓓ Ⓔ			
73.	Ⓐ Ⓑ Ⓒ Ⓓ Ⓔ					98.	Ⓐ Ⓑ Ⓒ Ⓓ Ⓔ			
74.	Ⓐ Ⓑ Ⓒ Ⓓ Ⓔ					99.	Ⓐ Ⓑ Ⓒ Ⓓ Ⓔ			
75.	Ⓐ Ⓑ Ⓒ Ⓓ Ⓔ					100.	Ⓐ Ⓑ Ⓒ Ⓓ Ⓔ			

CLEP PRINCIPLES OF MARKETING– TEST __

SECTION 1

1.	Ⓐ Ⓑ Ⓒ Ⓓ Ⓔ	26.	Ⓐ Ⓑ Ⓒ Ⓓ Ⓔ
2.	Ⓐ Ⓑ Ⓒ Ⓓ Ⓔ	27.	Ⓐ Ⓑ Ⓒ Ⓓ Ⓔ
3.	Ⓐ Ⓑ Ⓒ Ⓓ Ⓔ	28.	Ⓐ Ⓑ Ⓒ Ⓓ Ⓔ
4.	Ⓐ Ⓑ Ⓒ Ⓓ Ⓔ	29.	Ⓐ Ⓑ Ⓒ Ⓓ Ⓔ
5.	Ⓐ Ⓑ Ⓒ Ⓓ Ⓔ	30.	Ⓐ Ⓑ Ⓒ Ⓓ Ⓔ
6.	Ⓐ Ⓑ Ⓒ Ⓓ Ⓔ	31.	Ⓐ Ⓑ Ⓒ Ⓓ Ⓔ
7.	Ⓐ Ⓑ Ⓒ Ⓓ Ⓔ	32.	Ⓐ Ⓑ Ⓒ Ⓓ Ⓔ
8.	Ⓐ Ⓑ Ⓒ Ⓓ Ⓔ	33.	Ⓐ Ⓑ Ⓒ Ⓓ Ⓔ
9.	Ⓐ Ⓑ Ⓒ Ⓓ Ⓔ	34.	Ⓐ Ⓑ Ⓒ Ⓓ Ⓔ
10.	Ⓐ Ⓑ Ⓒ Ⓓ Ⓔ	35.	Ⓐ Ⓑ Ⓒ Ⓓ Ⓔ
11.	Ⓐ Ⓑ Ⓒ Ⓓ Ⓔ	36.	Ⓐ Ⓑ Ⓒ Ⓓ Ⓔ
12.	Ⓐ Ⓑ Ⓒ Ⓓ Ⓔ	37.	Ⓐ Ⓑ Ⓒ Ⓓ Ⓔ
13.	Ⓐ Ⓑ Ⓒ Ⓓ Ⓔ	38.	Ⓐ Ⓑ Ⓒ Ⓓ Ⓔ
14.	Ⓐ Ⓑ Ⓒ Ⓓ Ⓔ	39.	Ⓐ Ⓑ Ⓒ Ⓓ Ⓔ
15.	Ⓐ Ⓑ Ⓒ Ⓓ Ⓔ	40.	Ⓐ Ⓑ Ⓒ Ⓓ Ⓔ
16.	Ⓐ Ⓑ Ⓒ Ⓓ Ⓔ	41.	Ⓐ Ⓑ Ⓒ Ⓓ Ⓔ
17.	Ⓐ Ⓑ Ⓒ Ⓓ Ⓔ	42.	Ⓐ Ⓑ Ⓒ Ⓓ Ⓔ
18.	Ⓐ Ⓑ Ⓒ Ⓓ Ⓔ	43.	Ⓐ Ⓑ Ⓒ Ⓓ Ⓔ
19.	Ⓐ Ⓑ Ⓒ Ⓓ Ⓔ	44.	Ⓐ Ⓑ Ⓒ Ⓓ Ⓔ
20.	Ⓐ Ⓑ Ⓒ Ⓓ Ⓔ	45.	Ⓐ Ⓑ Ⓒ Ⓓ Ⓔ
21.	Ⓐ Ⓑ Ⓒ Ⓓ Ⓔ	46.	Ⓐ Ⓑ Ⓒ Ⓓ Ⓔ
22.	Ⓐ Ⓑ Ⓒ Ⓓ Ⓔ	47.	Ⓐ Ⓑ Ⓒ Ⓓ Ⓔ
23.	Ⓐ Ⓑ Ⓒ Ⓓ Ⓔ	48.	Ⓐ Ⓑ Ⓒ Ⓓ Ⓔ
24.	Ⓐ Ⓑ Ⓒ Ⓓ Ⓔ	49.	Ⓐ Ⓑ Ⓒ Ⓓ Ⓔ
25.	Ⓐ Ⓑ Ⓒ Ⓓ Ⓔ	50.	Ⓐ Ⓑ Ⓒ Ⓓ Ⓔ

SECTION 2

51. (A) (B) (C) (D) (E)
52. (A) (B) (C) (D) (E)
53. (A) (B) (C) (D) (E)
54. (A) (B) (C) (D) (E)
55. (A) (B) (C) (D) (E)
56. (A) (B) (C) (D) (E)
57. (A) (B) (C) (D) (E)
58. (A) (B) (C) (D) (E)
59. (A) (B) (C) (D) (E)
60. (A) (B) (C) (D) (E)
61. (A) (B) (C) (D) (E)
62. (A) (B) (C) (D) (E)
63. (A) (B) (C) (D) (E)
64. (A) (B) (C) (D) (E)
65. (A) (B) (C) (D) (E)
66. (A) (B) (C) (D) (E)
67. (A) (B) (C) (D) (E)
68. (A) (B) (C) (D) (E)
69. (A) (B) (C) (D) (E)
70. (A) (B) (C) (D) (E)
71. (A) (B) (C) (D) (E)
72. (A) (B) (C) (D) (E)
73. (A) (B) (C) (D) (E)
74. (A) (B) (C) (D) (E)
75. (A) (B) (C) (D) (E)

76. (A) (B) (C) (D) (E)
77. (A) (B) (C) (D) (E)
78. (A) (B) (C) (D) (E)
79. (A) (B) (C) (D) (E)
80. (A) (B) (C) (D) (E)
81. (A) (B) (C) (D) (E)
82. (A) (B) (C) (D) (E)
83. (A) (B) (C) (D) (E)
84. (A) (B) (C) (D) (E)
85. (A) (B) (C) (D) (E)
86. (A) (B) (C) (D) (E)
87. (A) (B) (C) (D) (E)
88. (A) (B) (C) (D) (E)
89. (A) (B) (C) (D) (E)
90. (A) (B) (C) (D) (E)
91. (A) (B) (C) (D) (E)
92. (A) (B) (C) (D) (E)
93. (A) (B) (C) (D) (E)
94. (A) (B) (C) (D) (E)
95. (A) (B) (C) (D) (E)
96. (A) (B) (C) (D) (E)
97. (A) (B) (C) (D) (E)
98. (A) (B) (C) (D) (E)
99. (A) (B) (C) (D) (E)
100. (A) (B) (C) (D) (E)

CLEP PRINCIPLES OF MARKETING– TEST __

SECTION 1

1.	Ⓐ	Ⓑ	Ⓒ	Ⓓ	Ⓔ	26.	Ⓐ	Ⓑ	Ⓒ	Ⓓ	Ⓔ
2.	Ⓐ	Ⓑ	Ⓒ	Ⓓ	Ⓔ	27.	Ⓐ	Ⓑ	Ⓒ	Ⓓ	Ⓔ
3.	Ⓐ	Ⓑ	Ⓒ	Ⓓ	Ⓔ	28.	Ⓐ	Ⓑ	Ⓒ	Ⓓ	Ⓔ
4.	Ⓐ	Ⓑ	Ⓒ	Ⓓ	Ⓔ	29.	Ⓐ	Ⓑ	Ⓒ	Ⓓ	Ⓔ
5.	Ⓐ	Ⓑ	Ⓒ	Ⓓ	Ⓔ	30.	Ⓐ	Ⓑ	Ⓒ	Ⓓ	Ⓔ
6.	Ⓐ	Ⓑ	Ⓒ	Ⓓ	Ⓔ	31.	Ⓐ	Ⓑ	Ⓒ	Ⓓ	Ⓔ
7.	Ⓐ	Ⓑ	Ⓒ	Ⓓ	Ⓔ	32.	Ⓐ	Ⓑ	Ⓒ	Ⓓ	Ⓔ
8.	Ⓐ	Ⓑ	Ⓒ	Ⓓ	Ⓔ	33.	Ⓐ	Ⓑ	Ⓒ	Ⓓ	Ⓔ
9.	Ⓐ	Ⓑ	Ⓒ	Ⓓ	Ⓔ	34.	Ⓐ	Ⓑ	Ⓒ	Ⓓ	Ⓔ
10.	Ⓐ	Ⓑ	Ⓒ	Ⓓ	Ⓔ	35.	Ⓐ	Ⓑ	Ⓒ	Ⓓ	Ⓔ
11.	Ⓐ	Ⓑ	Ⓒ	Ⓓ	Ⓔ	36.	Ⓐ	Ⓑ	Ⓒ	Ⓓ	Ⓔ
12.	Ⓐ	Ⓑ	Ⓒ	Ⓓ	Ⓔ	37.	Ⓐ	Ⓑ	Ⓒ	Ⓓ	Ⓔ
13.	Ⓐ	Ⓑ	Ⓒ	Ⓓ	Ⓔ	38.	Ⓐ	Ⓑ	Ⓒ	Ⓓ	Ⓔ
14.	Ⓐ	Ⓑ	Ⓒ	Ⓓ	Ⓔ	39.	Ⓐ	Ⓑ	Ⓒ	Ⓓ	Ⓔ
15.	Ⓐ	Ⓑ	Ⓒ	Ⓓ	Ⓔ	40.	Ⓐ	Ⓑ	Ⓒ	Ⓓ	Ⓔ
16.	Ⓐ	Ⓑ	Ⓒ	Ⓓ	Ⓔ	41.	Ⓐ	Ⓑ	Ⓒ	Ⓓ	Ⓔ
17.	Ⓐ	Ⓑ	Ⓒ	Ⓓ	Ⓔ	42.	Ⓐ	Ⓑ	Ⓒ	Ⓓ	Ⓔ
18.	Ⓐ	Ⓑ	Ⓒ	Ⓓ	Ⓔ	43.	Ⓐ	Ⓑ	Ⓒ	Ⓓ	Ⓔ
19.	Ⓐ	Ⓑ	Ⓒ	Ⓓ	Ⓔ	44.	Ⓐ	Ⓑ	Ⓒ	Ⓓ	Ⓔ
20.	Ⓐ	Ⓑ	Ⓒ	Ⓓ	Ⓔ	45.	Ⓐ	Ⓑ	Ⓒ	Ⓓ	Ⓔ
21.	Ⓐ	Ⓑ	Ⓒ	Ⓓ	Ⓔ	46.	Ⓐ	Ⓑ	Ⓒ	Ⓓ	Ⓔ
22.	Ⓐ	Ⓑ	Ⓒ	Ⓓ	Ⓔ	47.	Ⓐ	Ⓑ	Ⓒ	Ⓓ	Ⓔ
23.	Ⓐ	Ⓑ	Ⓒ	Ⓓ	Ⓔ	48.	Ⓐ	Ⓑ	Ⓒ	Ⓓ	Ⓔ
24.	Ⓐ	Ⓑ	Ⓒ	Ⓓ	Ⓔ	49.	Ⓐ	Ⓑ	Ⓒ	Ⓓ	Ⓔ
25.	Ⓐ	Ⓑ	Ⓒ	Ⓓ	Ⓔ	50.	Ⓐ	Ⓑ	Ⓒ	Ⓓ	Ⓔ

SECTION 2

51.	Ⓐ	Ⓑ	Ⓒ	Ⓓ	Ⓔ	76.	Ⓐ	Ⓑ	Ⓒ	Ⓓ	Ⓔ
52.	Ⓐ	Ⓑ	Ⓒ	Ⓓ	Ⓔ	77.	Ⓐ	Ⓑ	Ⓒ	Ⓓ	Ⓔ
53.	Ⓐ	Ⓑ	Ⓒ	Ⓓ	Ⓔ	78.	Ⓐ	Ⓑ	Ⓒ	Ⓓ	Ⓔ
54.	Ⓐ	Ⓑ	Ⓒ	Ⓓ	Ⓔ	79.	Ⓐ	Ⓑ	Ⓒ	Ⓓ	Ⓔ
55.	Ⓐ	Ⓑ	Ⓒ	Ⓓ	Ⓔ	80.	Ⓐ	Ⓑ	Ⓒ	Ⓓ	Ⓔ
56.	Ⓐ	Ⓑ	Ⓒ	Ⓓ	Ⓔ	81.	Ⓐ	Ⓑ	Ⓒ	Ⓓ	Ⓔ
57.	Ⓐ	Ⓑ	Ⓒ	Ⓓ	Ⓔ	82.	Ⓐ	Ⓑ	Ⓒ	Ⓓ	Ⓔ
58.	Ⓐ	Ⓑ	Ⓒ	Ⓓ	Ⓔ	83.	Ⓐ	Ⓑ	Ⓒ	Ⓓ	Ⓔ
59.	Ⓐ	Ⓑ	Ⓒ	Ⓓ	Ⓔ	84.	Ⓐ	Ⓑ	Ⓒ	Ⓓ	Ⓔ
60.	Ⓐ	Ⓑ	Ⓒ	Ⓓ	Ⓔ	85.	Ⓐ	Ⓑ	Ⓒ	Ⓓ	Ⓔ
61.	Ⓐ	Ⓑ	Ⓒ	Ⓓ	Ⓔ	86.	Ⓐ	Ⓑ	Ⓒ	Ⓓ	Ⓔ
62.	Ⓐ	Ⓑ	Ⓒ	Ⓓ	Ⓔ	87.	Ⓐ	Ⓑ	Ⓒ	Ⓓ	Ⓔ
63.	Ⓐ	Ⓑ	Ⓒ	Ⓓ	Ⓔ	88.	Ⓐ	Ⓑ	Ⓒ	Ⓓ	Ⓔ
64.	Ⓐ	Ⓑ	Ⓒ	Ⓓ	Ⓔ	89.	Ⓐ	Ⓑ	Ⓒ	Ⓓ	Ⓔ
65.	Ⓐ	Ⓑ	Ⓒ	Ⓓ	Ⓔ	90.	Ⓐ	Ⓑ	Ⓒ	Ⓓ	Ⓔ
66.	Ⓐ	Ⓑ	Ⓒ	Ⓓ	Ⓔ	91.	Ⓐ	Ⓑ	Ⓒ	Ⓓ	Ⓔ
67.	Ⓐ	Ⓑ	Ⓒ	Ⓓ	Ⓔ	92.	Ⓐ	Ⓑ	Ⓒ	Ⓓ	Ⓔ
68.	Ⓐ	Ⓑ	Ⓒ	Ⓓ	Ⓔ	93.	Ⓐ	Ⓑ	Ⓒ	Ⓓ	Ⓔ
69.	Ⓐ	Ⓑ	Ⓒ	Ⓓ	Ⓔ	94.	Ⓐ	Ⓑ	Ⓒ	Ⓓ	Ⓔ
70.	Ⓐ	Ⓑ	Ⓒ	Ⓓ	Ⓔ	95.	Ⓐ	Ⓑ	Ⓒ	Ⓓ	Ⓔ
71.	Ⓐ	Ⓑ	Ⓒ	Ⓓ	Ⓔ	96.	Ⓐ	Ⓑ	Ⓒ	Ⓓ	Ⓔ
72.	Ⓐ	Ⓑ	Ⓒ	Ⓓ	Ⓔ	97.	Ⓐ	Ⓑ	Ⓒ	Ⓓ	Ⓔ
73.	Ⓐ	Ⓑ	Ⓒ	Ⓓ	Ⓔ	98.	Ⓐ	Ⓑ	Ⓒ	Ⓓ	Ⓔ
74.	Ⓐ	Ⓑ	Ⓒ	Ⓓ	Ⓔ	99.	Ⓐ	Ⓑ	Ⓒ	Ⓓ	Ⓔ
75.	Ⓐ	Ⓑ	Ⓒ	Ⓓ	Ⓔ	100.	Ⓐ	Ⓑ	Ⓒ	Ⓓ	Ⓔ

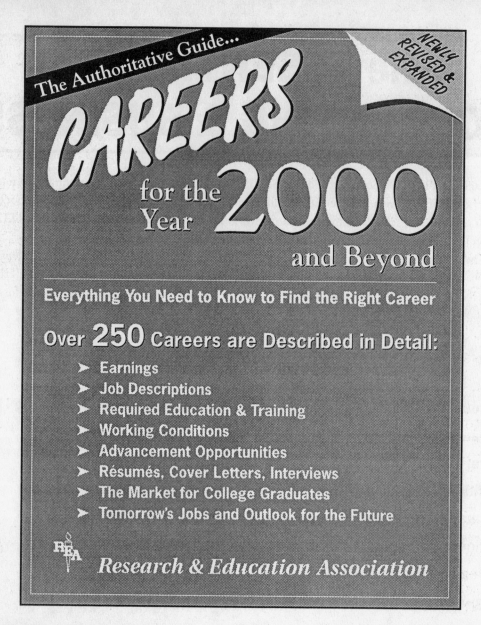

REA's **Problem Solvers**

The "PROBLEM SOLVERS" are comprehensive supplemental textbooks designed to save time in finding solutions to problems. Each "PROBLEM SOLVER" is the first of its kind ever produced in its field. It is the product of a massive effort to illustrate almost any imaginable problem in exceptional depth, detail, and clarity. Each problem is worked out in detail with a step-by-step solution, and the problems are arranged in order of complexity from elementary to advanced. Each book is fully indexed for locating problems rapidly.

ACCOUNTING
ADVANCED CALCULUS
ALGEBRA & TRIGONOMETRY
AUTOMATIC CONTROL
   SYSTEMS/ROBOTICS
BIOLOGY
BUSINESS, ACCOUNTING, & FINANCE
CALCULUS
CHEMISTRY
COMPLEX VARIABLES
COMPUTER SCIENCE
DIFFERENTIAL EQUATIONS
ECONOMICS
ELECTRICAL MACHINES
ELECTRIC CIRCUITS
ELECTROMAGNETICS
ELECTRONIC COMMUNICATIONS
ELECTRONICS
FINITE & DISCRETE MATH
FLUID MECHANICS/DYNAMICS
GENETICS
GEOMETRY

HEAT TRANSFER
LINEAR ALGEBRA
MACHINE DESIGN
MATHEMATICS for ENGINEERS
MECHANICS
NUMERICAL ANALYSIS
OPERATIONS RESEARCH
OPTICS
ORGANIC CHEMISTRY
PHYSICAL CHEMISTRY
PHYSICS
PRE-CALCULUS
PROBABILITY
PSYCHOLOGY
STATISTICS
STRENGTH OF MATERIALS &
   MECHANICS OF SOLIDS
TECHNICAL DESIGN GRAPHICS
THERMODYNAMICS
TOPOLOGY
TRANSPORT PHENOMENA
VECTOR ANALYSIS

*If you would like more information about any of these books,
complete the coupon below and return it to us or visit your local bookstore.*

RESEARCH & EDUCATION ASSOCIATION
61 Ethel Road W. • Piscataway, New Jersey 08854
Phone: (732) 819-8880

Please send me more information about your Problem Solver books

Name _____

Address _____

City _____ State _____ Zip _____